TOKYO NOIR

IN AND OUT OF JAPAN'S UNDERWORLD

JAKE ADELSTEIN

SCRIB

Melbourne | London | M

Scribe Publications
18–20 Edward St, Brunswick, Victoria 3056, Australia
2 John St, Clerkenwell, London, WC1N 2ES, United Kingdom
3754 Pleasant Ave, Suite 100, Minneapolis, Minnesota 55409, USA

Published by Scribe 2024
Reprinted 2024

Typeset in Fairfield LT by the publishers

Printed and bound in the UK by CPI Group (UK) Ltd, Croydon
CR0 4YY

Scribe is committed to the sustainable use of natural resources and
the use of paper products made responsibly from those resources.

978 1 761380 23 5 (Australian edition)
978 1 915590 89 3 (UK edition)
978 1 957363 91 2 (US edition)
978 1 761385 84 1 (ebook)

Catalogue records for this book are available from
the National Library of Australia and the British Library.

scribepublications.com.au
scribepublications.co.uk
scribepublications.com

TOKYO NOIR

Jake Adelstein has been an investigative journalist in Japan since 1993, reporting in both Japanese and English. From 2006 to 2007 he was the chief investigator for a US State Department–sponsored study of human trafficking in Japan. He has been writing for *The Daily Beast*, *The Japan Times*, and other publications since 2011, and was a special correspondent for *The Los Angeles Times*. Considered one of the foremost experts on organised crime in Japan, he works as a writer and consultant in Japan and the United States. He co-hosted and co-wrote the award-winning podcast about missing people in Nippon, *The Evaporated: gone with the gods* in 2023. He is the author of *Tokyo Vice: a western reporter on the police beat in Japan*, which is now a series on HBO Max, and also *The Last Yakuza: life and death in the Japanese underworld* (2023). He has appeared on CNN, NPR, the BBC, France 24, and other media outlets as a commentator on social issues in Japan, as well as its criminal justice system, politics, and nuclear industry giant, TEPCO.

CONTENTS

Part III
Reconstruction

Prologue

Conduct your victory like a funeral
When many people are being killed,
They should be mourned with heartfelt sorrow.
That is why a victory must be observed like a funeral.
—Lao Tzu, Chinese philosopher

October 28, 2008

Sometimes when you vanquish your enemy, you just feel like partying. I had picked the Westin Hotel Tokyo to meet my mentor, ex-prosecutor Toshiro Igari, for drinks. We had gathered to celebrate the demise of our mutual enemy, Tadamasa Goto, who had just been kicked out of the Yamaguchi-gumi on the 14th of that month. Goto was the Richard Branson of the yakuza—charismatic, filthy rich, once the largest shareholder of Japan Airlines, politically connected, and with 1,000 people in his organization. He was also a homicidal sociopath. In 2008 he had put out a contract on me and my family, which had resulted in all of us being put under police protection because I was trying to write something that didn't please him.

At the time, the Kobe-based Yamaguchi-gumi was the largest

of all criminal gangs in Japan, with nearly 80,000 members and a foothold in every industry in Japanese society. Goto had spearheaded their invasion of Tokyo turf and the gang wars that resulted. When he was kicked out, along with ten more top bosses very close to him, that was national news—not in yakuza fanzines, but the biggest newspapers in Japan gave it the kind of coverage reserved for the president of Sony being fired. It created a crisis in the organized crime world, the yakuza equivalent of "The Lehman Shock"—the so-called "Goto Shock."

I arrived early and waited in the lounge. I recognized Igari without even seeing his face; he had that sort of presence and the build of a yakuza boss in his black suit. There was something about his whole demeanor that reminded me of a bulldog, but a very smart bulldog.

I watched him arrive out of the corner of my eye as I read the tabloids. He found me quickly, and we headed to the restaurant to grab some dinner. He was wearing a bright white shirt under his dark, well-tailored suit, and no necktie. I was dressed in slacks and a gray shirt. I had come to sort of relish not wearing a suit anymore.

I was always impressed by him. It's not uncommon in Japan for prosecutors to go to work for dubious entities, especially the yakuza, when they retire. The phrase *yameken bengoshi* doesn't have good ring to it. It means "a lawyer who quit being a prosecutor," and communicates the general disdain held for former prosecutors who go into the private sector; it's almost a synonym for "shyster." Igari was one of the rare breed who chose honor over money, who chose to fight the yakuza after leaving law enforcement rather than go work for them. It was one of the many things I respected about him. Igari-san had become a legend in the law enforcement world, and was the author of several books on dealing with organized crime and preventing its incursion into the business world.

When we reached our seats, we exchanged the usual plea-santries, and he got right to the point.

"So, did you bring the stuff?"

"I did indeed," I said, passing him a manila envelope.

"I'll look at this later," he said. "I know myself—if I start reading this now, I won't be able to put it down, and then our food will get cold and my beer will get warm. So, first of all, congratulations. I'm sure that you are relieved to hear he's no longer a yakuza boss, but an ex-yakuza boss. And, frankly, he's such an asshole that I think all of Japan benefits."

Some cops had given me a rundown of what had happened, but Igari had sources that I definitely didn't have. I wanted to hear what he knew.

"The reports in the media have been lacking. Here's what I know. The reasons for his expulsion come down to a few things. He had been skipping board meetings, and when he invited a bunch of entertainers and actors to his birthday celebration while skipping another important meeting, it touched the nerves of the executives. The weekly magazine *Shukan Shincho* did a lavish article on the whole thing. Not good publicity."

I smiled. "Yeah, I didn't think it would be good publicity. I was disappointed to see they didn't actually have the balls to write his name."

Igari chortled. "Hah! Well, they wrote down the names of the famous people there. So there was that. And then, of course, your article on his liver transplant, and the book you contributed to—it stoked the fires of discontent. And so he was kicked out."

I nodded.

And then Igari said, just as he had written me in an email, "Your tenacity and your dedication to bringing him down paid off. You wrote the article that caused him to fall from grace, and that's impressive. That's an accomplishment. You did something that the police could never do."

I didn't know what to say to this. It still didn't quite seem real, but I felt I had accomplished something. After a long string of losses, it felt better to be on the winning side. I had written an article in the May 2008 edition of *The Washington Post* that exposed how Goto had made a deal with the FBI to get a visa to the U.S. How had he done it? He'd ratted out all his friends in the Yamaguchi-gumi, and provided some valuable intelligence to the authorities. In exchange, he had gotten a visa to the U.S. and picked up a new liver at UCLA, jumping ahead of more deserving, innocent people. In fact, three of his yakuza cronies had done the same—all at UCLA, perhaps without betraying their gangster brothers. He had screwed over the FBI as well, only delivering a fifth of what he promised before vanishing from the hospital after his surgery. He'd gotten his liver and gotten away; he must have made a deal with the devil, because no matter what he did, he almost always won. I thought a little about how much my victory had cost, and I ordered a Hibiki on the rocks. Japanese whisky was actually pretty good.

We were both in a fine mood. The Westin Hotel seemed the perfect place to celebrate: on another October night, seven years before, Igari had helped the hotel get rid of their most troublesome client and guest, Tadamasa Goto himself. This had once been Goto's second home. He had been banished from it, just as he he'd now been banished from his yakuza home.

The hotel was located in Ebisu Garden Place, which was once a hotspot in Tokyo. In 2001, it was the trendy place to be, located close to Ebisu Station, full of exciting new restaurants, a museum of photography, and an avant-garde cinema. The Westin was the high-end love hotel of the area, and had a glitzy status. The headquarters of Goto's gang were in the Shizuoka prefecture, but he was leading the Yamaguchi-gumi invasion of Tokyo, and came to the city often. Of course, he liked to stay in fancy hotels. He had become quite fond of the Westin, and would stay there for days on end. He would put down a deposit that was the yen equivalent of $10,000 every time he turned up; so, in terms of money, he was a great client for the hotel. The problem was that the longer he stayed, the more insolent and demanding he became. He and his cronies had a tendency to swindle the hotel staff, harass guests, and make the place a living hell for those staying or working there.

The hotel manager, who was nearing his retirement, decided that, as his final duty, he should get rid of this unwanted customer once and for all. And so, on a cold night in October, with much trepidation, he decided to pay a visit to Goto himself to ask him to leave. When he went to Goto's room, his men brought him face-to-face with the gremlin.

The manager did not mince words.

"Everyone here is aware that a famous yakuza boss is staying at this hotel, that being you. And, frankly, all the employees are frightened and uneasy, and this is an impediment to doing their job. I hesitate to ask, but could you do us the courtesy of checking out of the hotel?"

Goto was surprised at the request, but did not lose his temper. He asked to see the accommodation agreements for the hotel. (The agreement is the contract you sign when you register at a hotel in Japan.) While sitting in his desk chair, flanked by two bodyguards, he ran his fingers over the document, line by line, and fired back, "Where does it say here that yakuza aren't permitted to stay in this hotel? I don't see a word about it. Show me."

He threw the papers back at the hotel manager, who was at a loss for words.

Goto continued, "Is being a yakuza illegal? No, it is not. And yet you are asking me to leave. One of your best customers. And on what grounds?"

"On the grounds that you are disturbing the guests and the staff," the manager replied.

And so this went on. For minutes; for an hour; for three hours. And even the hotel manager refused to budge. Finally, he got on his hands and knees, crying, and pleading for Goto to leave. Goto, out of frustration or admiration, said to him, "You've got guts. I get it. Maybe I'll leave."

In the morning, Goto and his entourage took off. But they left one thing behind—their $10,000 deposit. This was a pain in the ass for the hotel, an albatross in a safe-deposit box. They didn't know where to send the money, and even if they did, might sending it back unilaterally be perceived as an insult to the yakuza? On the other hand, they didn't really want to invite the boss and his gang to come back to the hotel to collect the money. And so they decided to consult with a retired prosecutor, already well known for his ability to deal with yakuza and for his dislike of them. That man was Toshiro Igari, my mentor.

The bunch of documents I brought to Igari had come from one of Goto's underlings. They were the notes distributed at a meeting of the Goto-gumi upper echelon about changes in Japan's laws on organized crime. Of course, there was a former prosecutor who attended the meeting, now a lawyer for the mob, who explained the laws and its loopholes. You might wonder why one of Goto's own men would give me internal documents. The answer is simple: He hated his boss. I disliked him, too. I had many reasons. It was thanks to him that I was still under police protection and had had to hire an ex-yakuza as a bodyguard. I had been under protection since early 2008. There were nice things about that, but it was also expensive. Saigo, or Tsunami, as he was sometimes known, wouldn't drive anything less than a Mercedes-Benz, of course. The car ate gasoline like Takeru Kobayashi, the competitive eater, devours hot dogs. Saigo was a former Inagawa-kai yakuza boss, at one time having 150 men under his command. He'd been in the organization for twenty years before he was kicked out. He was not a fan of Goto, either.

"He's always been an arrogant, homicidal prick. If I ever saw him while driving you around, I'd run him over without flinching. I'd just claim I mistook the accelerator for the brake."

He earned his nickname Tsunami because, just like the natural phenomenon, he was an unpredictable storm of violent destruction that washed away everything in its path—if you pissed him off.

Goto's departure from the Yamaguchi-gumi had set off waves. A group of sympathizers, some big yakuza bosses, sent a protest letter to the executive branch of the Yamaguchi-gumi. When a copy of it leaked, the response of Kiyoshi Takayama, the underboss of the organization, was to permanently banish several of Goto's sympathizers, demote others, and temporarily banish several others. Igari explained that the Yamaguchi-gumi feared a yakuza civil war if Goto and his buddies weren't excised from the organization. The Yama-Ichi war a few years back had been a bloody debacle.

"What's next for Goto?" I asked Igari.

"If he's not careful, the Yamaguchi-gumi will decide he's a loose end and take him out. He's a simmering dumpster fire. The decision to remove him from the roster (*joseki*), rather than banish him, is a curious one. It does let him leave with some grace."

"Now that he's out of the yakuza, maybe he'll come check into the hotel again."

Igari laughed.

"I don't think so. A guy like that stays on the rosters as an organized crime member for at least five years. It'll be interesting to see what he does next."

I wanted to know a little bit more about his tangle with Tadamasa.

"So, I know that you had a run-in with him, but tell me the rest of the story."

And he proceeded to tell me.

The hotel had contacted him after they finally got rid of Goto and entourage, but hadn't figured out what to do with the deposit money that Goto had left behind. After a long back and forth between him and the cronies of the gangster, he drew up a legal agreement settling the bill and sent it to the offices of Goto.

Goto's personal secretary made a trip to his offices, and he handed over the deposit in cash. That would have been the end of the story, except that it inspired Igari—it made him think.

What if there had been something in the accommodation agreements that expressly forbade members of organized crime from staying at the hotel?

In fact and in theory, there were already restrictions on what organized crime members could do, and it was within the province of the hotel, or any establishment, to refuse service to criminal elements. The major crime groups had been designated as such under Japanese law, and their members were subject to restrictions. It was after much thinking on this incident that Igari came up with a simple but brilliant idea: the organized crime restriction clause. In Japanese, it was called *bōryokudan haijo joko*.

Igari enthusiastically explained it to me.

"I decided that we should use contract law and create an organized crime exclusionary clause that could be inserted into any contract or any agreement in Japan that would give people leverage when dealing with yakuza. As you and I both know, the laws here for dealing with these ruffians are weak and ineffective. That's when you limit the conversation to criminal law. But with contract law and civil law, we could certainly handicap the yakuza. And maybe, just maybe, we could create a foundation for not only keeping them out of hotels and golf courses, but also shunting them out of Japanese society."

He continued to explain with great enthusiasm.

"This hotel manager had a lot of courage, and I admire him. But you can't expect everyone to be a hero. So what if we took this case and learned from it?

If there had been a clause in the accommodation agreement that forbade yakuza from staying at the hotel, they could have kicked him out. It would have been easy and simple. If all businesses put in an organized crime exclusion clause in their contracts and trade agreements, they would have an easy out when there's trouble."

"How would that work?"

"Well, the staff would say, 'I'm sorry, but we can't do business with you because of this clause here, which says we don't and won't do business with anti-social forces. Please leave.' And that would be a valuable tool for dealing with these people on the ground level. That's what I thought."

I wasn't so sure.

"What exactly would the clause say?"

He pulled out his book that had been printed the previous November. The title: *Anti-Social Forces Will Eat Up Your Company*. It had a lovely garish green cover with a tiny yakuza boss in a rumpled gray suit and gray fedora holding a pistol in his hand, under Igari's name on the front flap. He flipped to the section of the clause that included an example.

I read it. It was a little obtuse.

"Igari-sensei, I'm still not sure how this would work in real life."

He laughed. He pulled another document out of his suitcase.

"This is a little simpler, Jake-san. It's a draft for a bank. I'm putting it together for a client—you might guess who they are."

"Citibank?"

He laughed.

"That would be telling."

This time, it was a lot clearer. I had never seen anything like it before when opening a bank account, but I had a feeling that it was going to be standard for any bank in the future.

Exclusion of Anti-Social Forces

The Customer represents, warrants and covenants to ensure that it, its parent, subsidiaries, related companies and those employees and shareholders with 50 percent of the voting rights (collectively, including the Customer, the "Related Parties") do not or shall not in the future fall under the following categories (collectively, the "Anti-Social Forces"):

(1) an organized crime group;

(2) a member of an organized crime group;

(3) a quasi-member of an organized crime group;

(4) a related company or association of an organized crime group;

(5) a corporate racketeer; or

(6) other equivalent groups of the above.

(Clause 19.1)

The Customer represents, warrants and covenants to ensure that the Related Parties themselves or through the use of third parties have never conducted or will not conduct in the future any of the following actions:

(1) a demand with violence;

(2) an unreasonable demand beyond the legal responsibility;

(3) use of intimidating words or actions in relation to transactions;

(4) an action to defame the reputation or interfere with the business of the Bank or any of its affiliates by spreading rumors, using fraudulent means or resorting to force; or

(5) other equivalent actions of the above.

(Clause 19.2)

Igari smiled, and gave me a copy.

"If a yakuza opens a bank account after signing this contract, he won't be able to protest if they close his account. If the bank suspects their customer is a yakuza, or a corporate account is for a yakuza front company, they can demand information to check it out. If the customer refuses to comply, they can shut down the account as well. He'll have to take the money and move it somewhere else."

"Well, what if he simply refuses to sign the agreement?"

"Then he can't get a bank account in the first place."

"What if they sign it, hiding their yakuza ties, and open a bank account anyway?"

Igari leaned back and folded his arms.

"That's what I hope for. In some cases, especially if the person signing it is a fully made member of a yakuza group, then he has committed fraud as soon as he's signed the agreement. Because, of course, they know that they're lying. Then it's not a civil case; it's a criminal case. In come the cops, and out goes the yakuza. He goes to jail; the account is closed."

"Wow."

That was good. I could see where this was going. If every institution in Japan put these clauses into contracts, in a few years many yakuza wouldn't be able to check into a hotel; they wouldn't even be able to open a bank account, rent a car, or buy a house.

Igari tapped his index finger on the table to make a point.

"The law," he said, tapping once, "is a medicine or a poison. It's all in how you apply it. If you want to fight the bad guys, you don't have to be a prosecutor. You just have to be a lawyer, and you just have to give a damn."

Yes, I knew what he meant.

"I almost went to law school."

"Ah, Jake, you wanted to be a lawyer? That's news to me. What happened?"

I had to think about that one for a second.

In 2005, I went back to Missouri with the intention of doing something completely different from being a reporter. My parents had agreed to subsidize me while I studied, and I prepared for the LSATs. All I remember from preparation is doing a lot of Venn diagrams, which are basically a lot of intersecting circles related to subject matters. I kind of hated them, and I kind of liked them. But that wasn't the reason I didn't go to law school. Even with my abysmal LSAT scores, I could've gone, thanks to some aggressive public relations on my part, and an interesting background. But I punted on the choice of starting a new life.

He asked me again.

"What happened? Am I hitting a sore spot there?"

I shrugged.

"I was accepted into a law school—a really good law school. But on the same day, I was offered a job coordinating a U.S. State Department–sponsored study of human trafficking in Japan. And without consulting anyone, I decided to take that job because it seemed more important to me. I figured there would always be law school, but human trafficking in Japan was an odious and terrible thing—and a huge source of money for the worst of the Yamaguchi-gumi and a gangster that we both really don't like."

He nodded several times.

"So … do you think you made the right decision? Do you regret not going—although you could still go? Do you think you would've led a better life if you had gone to law school?"

I tried to answer, but couldn't come up with the words.

He spread his hands, his fingers turned outward, and spoke like he was addressing a panel of judges.

"I think you made the right decision. You saw a chance to do something good, and you took it even at the expense of what could've been a cozy life. I have something I want you to think about."

He paused.

"Sometimes, I think we only encounter in life the injustices we are meant to correct. There's a greater purpose to things."

It was a surprisingly philosophical reflection from Igari.

"You could still go to law school. You did the right thing. You should never regret doing the right thing. How often do we have a chance to actually make a difference in the world? The world has many lawyers."

He was right, of course; there are no shortages of lawyers in this world, although there are perhaps not enough lawyers in Japan. But I was curious as to why he became a lawyer instead of riding out his career as a prosecutor.

I asked him point blank.

"It would be a long and boring story of how I ended up doing what I have done in my life so far. Another time."

He leaned forward. He told me was studying USA anti-mafia legislation and had a few questions. I promised to drop by his law office later in the week to discuss it with him.

The conversation eventually changed to a discussion of a company that had been in the news recently with possible ties to Goto.

"Well," I noted, "the company certainly looked clean. In fact, they had an ex-prosecutor on their board of directors. I was wondering if he might be a buddy of yours."

"Oh? That's news to me." Igari raised his eyebrows. "You know a lot about this company and the case," he said. "You've done your homework, Jake-san."

"Well," I paused, "I take a much deeper interest in things when I'm paid to look into them. Freelance journalism doesn't pay the bills."

Igari smiled.

"So you're doing 'due diligence' now?"

"Diligently. I have been for a while. Since 2006."

"Do you have a license?"

"Do I need one?"

He laughed, and asked to see my business card. I pulled it out.

"No, you don't need a license, but maybe you need a new job title."

He took a pen out of his pocket and scratched out the word *kisha*, "reporter," which I had attached to the end of my name, and wrote in the Japanese characters for *tantei,* aka "private detective."

Well, that was what I really was now. That was my gig.

I had to admit that it looked cool, in a goofy way.

Jake Adelstein, Private Eye.

PART I

UNUSUAL EVENTS AND THE LIMITING FAULT

CHAPTER ONE

Cowboys and yakuza

Japan has two governments—one is a functioning group of political factions that make up the public government. The other is a hidden government that gives directives to public institutions. That hidden government is mostly made up of the yakuza.

–TAKESHI KITANO, AWARD-WINNING FILM DIRECTOR

Early spring, 2007

Due diligence involves a lot of paperwork and sometimes more footwork than you could possibly imagine; hopefully you'll find the process of getting the job done as fascinating as I do. Real-world puzzle-solving is always going to interest me more than any novel, escape room, or video game. I do believe that the truth is out there; there is an answer if you ask the right questions.

It's probably why I loved becoming an investigative journalist and why I mostly liked my gig at the time.

I had some difficulty dealing with the fact I was no longer a reporter. I hadn't written an article in a year, almost two years. It felt strange to no longer be writing for a large audience, but instead to be writing reports that would only be read by one or two people. Maybe three at the most.

Before we had even ordered, the client handed me a new business card. In Japan, they are called *meishi*. Meishi are very important. You have to treat them like they have a soul. You can't write on them in front of the person giving you the business card, and even the way you handle the card says a lot about you and what you think of them.

My client was a foreigner, like myself. I didn't feel the need to give him any honorifics.

The business card he handed me wasn't his. This was the company he wanted me to investigate. It was printed on good Japanese paper, *washi*. The surface was rough, almost a little fuzzy, a sign of quality. It read in Japanese and English:

Nakatomi Holdings
Where Your Financial Future Is Made Today

The name seemed familiar and odd at the same time; Nakatomi isn't a common Japanese name. There was something amiss.

"We think this is a promising fund," said the client, "but we would still like a basic due diligence. You know, just run a few checks."

Due diligence, a fancy term for investigations into the reputation, risks, and legitimacy of a corporation or entity, was the work I was doing for the most part. I was getting a lot of investigation work; some of it paid well, and that was why I found myself eating way above my pay grade.

We were now at a table at the Oak Door in the Grand Hyatt Tokyo. The place was dimly lit, full of customers, and we had a table diagonally across from the coat check, tucked away in the far corner of the restaurant where no one could easily hear us. The nearest patrons sat three tables away. A chubby Japanese man wearing a good suit and gold-rimmed glasses was chortling away with a very tall blonde woman wearing a glittery black dress and sneakers. They were drinking champagne, the good stuff in the orange bottle. I'd guess they started the evening at the Heartland bar down the street, but that's probably not where they'd finish the night. The girl's laughter was raucous, and she threw back her head once and giggled. The Japanese man looked slightly red. They were clearly enjoying their evening.

I couldn't really say that on my end. The client, who I'd worked for before, was dressed in a navy blue suit, with a pinstriped white shirt and a slightly gaudy gold-plated Patek Philippe watch wound tight around his wrist. That was an achievement in itself because Patek Philippe goes to great lengths not to make ostentatious watches. He pushed his rectangular wireless eyeglasses slightly up until they were almost touching his eyelashes while he read the menu. He was extremely fastidious; his glasses always looked like he'd just polished them, spotless and shiny.

He was droning on, and I caught the words again, "basic due diligence." I cleared my throat.

"We don't do basic due diligence. If you want to know who you're getting into bed with, I can't tell you by just driving by their house. I have to go into the house, so to speak, rummage through their closets."

He nodded, "Yes, but we're almost certain we're on solid ground here. Almost everything checks out."

"Great. Then you don't need me. I'll just eat dinner now and have a drink."

The waiter floated over, and I ordered the Japanese steak

from the Miyazaki prefecture in what I thought was flawless Japanese, but the waiter replied to me in English.

"So you'll have the steak?"

"Yes," I replied in English and then asked him to cook it medium-rare and not to trim the fat, in Japanese.

The client, who, despite living several years in Japan still didn't speak a word of Japanese other than essential greetings, spoke up.

"I'll have the same thing," he said. He politely waved the waiter away. "Okay, why don't you go ahead and charge us the usual fee. That will be fine. But we need it quickly. In a week."

"That's a very short turnaround."

"It's one company. Just Nakatomi Holdings."

I'd heard that "just one company" line before.

"Let's not do the dance where you say, 'just one company,' which turns out to be a holding company for ten companies and then you want me to verify that none of the associated companies are unsavory or connected to anti-social forces. Because I'm not doing a ten-for-one, not in a week's time. Not for a flat fee."

He sipped his beer. I sipped my coffee.

Then it hit me: the company name. Nakatomi, as in the name of the fictional Nakatomi Plaza where the action movie *Die Hard* takes place. I imagine that's why they picked the name. I kept my thoughts to myself for the moment. He continued speaking.

"Just one company. Just Nakatomi Holdings. They've been around a long time. Since 1970."

I sighed.

"If it's a holding company, that means it probably has a number of companies that it oversees. And I want to be clear that I won't be able to look at every single company under the umbrella."

"It's more of an investors' union. An anonymous one."

I asked to see what he had for me. I was hoping he might have brought the company registration which would save me some time, but all he had for me was another business card, with a man's name on it in katakana, the foreign syllabary for scientific names and borrowed words. The firm's name and URL was on the card. I guess that was a start. Nakatomi was in Japanese; the Holdings part was represented phonetically in katakana. There was English on the other side.

It looked something like this:

中富ホールディングス

The complex characters, the kanji, are taken from Chinese, and have a Japanese pronunciation. In this case, Nakatomi. They could be read in other ways. Names in Japanese are a nightmare to figure out, even for Japanese people. The angular characters were katakana. Holdings in Japanese is pronounced like *hōrudinguzu*. There's a Japanese word that can be used that means the same thing, but there is a strange love for English-sounding Japanese in the business world here. It makes everything sound like a buzzword.

I accepted the case with some reservations.

"I have one question. Can you tell me, on background, what you want to do with this firm? Are they listed on the Japanese stock market? Are they planning to list? Are you going to partner with them? Anything that might give me some context or help me know what I should be looking for."

"No. But if there wasn't a suspicion that something wasn't quite kosher, we wouldn't come to you."

"Because I'm Jewish?"

He stared at me and said, "No, you being Jewish isn't really a part of why we're asking you. Do you know this firm?"

I decided to let my witty joke, which had already fallen flat, just quietly die, and shook my head. I realized that he didn't understand the origin of the word "kosher" and I didn't feel like explaining. I looked at the business card a little more closely.

The quality of a business card can also tell you a lot about a person or their firm in Japan. It's the gateway to knowledge.

The business card itself was not only printed on the finest Japanese paper; it was also slightly marbled with a pattern. It was an expensive card. The firm's office was located in Roppongi—but not in a particularly nice place. It was located in an old building about 200 meters from Tantra, the classy gentlemen's club that some might call a strip bar. Although Tantra, in terms of strip bars, was a kosher sort of place. They even had a beautiful statue of Tara, the Green Goddess, paying a sort of homage to the Tibetan Buddhist version of Tantric practice. The central idea of Tantra is that liberation from desire, especially sexual desire, can be accomplished from the desire itself. In other words, you can fuck your way out of being a sex addict if you meditate on it right and do it as a fully conscious and mystical act.

I didn't think most of the customers there were seeking spiritual enlightenment. It was a popular place for the investment bankers from Goldman Sachs to take their customers on the corporate expense account. Dodgy strip bars offered titties and beer; Tantra offered titties and champagne. Classy.

The client had a few other things for me to look at after I stopped daydreaming. A print-out of the home page. I was struck again by how oddly familiar the name was to me, but I also couldn't explain why familiarity bred suspicion in my mind. I couldn't help but feel that they must have taken the company name from *Die Hard*. There was a term for borrowing an established name to swindle people that I'd heard before, but I couldn't remember it immediately.

I told the client what I was thinking, but, amazingly, he'd never seen the movie. He was from Singapore, but still …

The *Die Hard* script had at least one line among the greatest 100 movie lines ever spoken, although it's profane. If you haven't seen the movie, let me put the line in context. I know the movie far too well. When I was in college working concessions at the Campus Twin Theatre in Columbia, Missouri, the movie played for six weeks. I've seen it seventeen times.

In the movie, our hero, off-duty cop John McClane (Bruce Willis), is trapped in the Nakatomi Plaza Building after it is taken over by rogue German terrorists. That's why everyone knows the name, Nakatomi. They are led by sociopathic Hans Gruber (Alan Rickman). McClane single-handedly starts taking down the terrorists one by one, but they have no idea who he is or why he's there. He manages to provoke Gruber over a walkie-talkie. The two then have the following exchange:

Hans Gruber: [on the radio] Mr Mystery Guest? Are you still there?

John McClane: Yeah, I'm still here. Unless you wanna open the front door for me.

Hans Gruber: Uh, no, I'm afraid not. But you have me at a loss. You know my name, but who are you? Just another American who saw too many movies as a child? Another orphan of a bankrupt culture who thinks he's John Wayne? Rambo? Marshal Dillon?

John McClane: Was always kinda partial to Roy Rogers, actually. I really like those sequined shirts.

Hans Gruber: Do you really think you have a chance against us, Mr Cowboy?

John McClane: Yippee-ki-yay, motherfucker.

Yep.

Indeed. In this case, I imagined I would be McClane and whoever was running Nakatomi Holdings were yakuza terrorists. Hey, who doesn't want to be the hero?

But if I were McClane, I wondered, did I already have a receding hairline like Bruce Willis at the time? I made a mental note to look at taking Propecia. I'm just as vain as any man in this world. But would that work? Maybe I need Rogaine.

I did know that the first thing I'd need to do was get the company registration. I was working as a subcontractor for another due diligence firm and my supervisor was Tony, aka "Action."

He had arranged the meeting. He called me Kolchak, a nickname he gave me because I reminded him of the nosy reporter in *Kolchak: The Night Stalker* TV series—the *X-Files* of its day. He insisted we use code names, which wasn't a bad idea. People get pissed if you mess with their business.

I called him up, and he had his wife, Monako, go out to get a copy of the documents. Tony had been in Japan many years working physical security, and was well connected to a surprising array of criminals, ex-soldiers, and cops. If he could read and write Japanese he probably wouldn't have needed me; but then again, I did bring something to the table besides literacy. Working fourteen years as an investigative reporter comes in handy.

Chasing corporate criminals or potential criminals in Japan almost always starts with a paper chase. Every legitimate company in Japan is required by law to register their business with the Ministry of Justice. The company registration is public information, although you have to pay to view it or to get a copy. When you know how to read the dense documents, they can tell you a lot about a firm.

Weirdly enough, even the yakuza registered their front

companies—they still did in 2007. The Yamaguchi-gumi head-quarters in Kobe was owned by a real estate company that listed some of the top executives as board members. Of course, this meant that it wasn't hard to figure out that their real estate company was a criminal enterprise, but they obviously didn't feel a need to hide that.

The yakuza had existed in Japan legally since the end of the Second World War, out in the open, with office buildings, business cards, and front companies, some legitimate. But they'd grown so powerful that the government decided to clamp down and in 1992 the anti–organized crime laws went into effect.

The laws were weak and mostly ineffectual, but they had one unexpected side effect: they pushed the yakuza further into the legitimate business world. The laws forbade the yakuza to openly display their crest and organization name in public. The Inagawa-kai, Yamaguchi-gumi, Matsuba-kai, and all of the yakuza groups and their second-tier and third-tier groups could no longer just put the organization name on the mailbox or the door of their offices: they needed a front, or a cover. Front companies soon became a staple of yakuza existence. For example, an office for the Inagawa-kai's third-tier yakuza gang, Takada-gumi, became Takada Enterprises and engaged in "real estate consulting" and other nebulous enterprises. In a way, it was now mandatory to have a legitimate business to run an illegal business.

The yakuza had to incorporate. Incorporation meant creating a company, determining business objectives, putting up capital, and registering all that information—without any falsifications—with the Ministry of Justice. The representative of a company is required by law to list their name and home address on the company registration. And for reporters, what is great about this is that all corporate registrations can be obtained from the Japanese government for a small fee.

Because the representative director of the company is also

required to list his home address on the registration, the address of the company itself and the representative director can then be used to obtain real estate deeds, which can also tell you a lot about a company or an individual.

Real estate in Japan is often collateral for any loan or financial transaction. Once you have the real estate deeds, you can get answers to some possibly illuminating questions. Does the company own its building and property? Has the CEO recently paid off his mortgage or transferred the property to his wife? Which banks and financial institutions are they doing business with? All of these things help you paint a better picture of whom you're dealing with.

The last address of the company is also listed on the corporate registration if the company has moved prior to their current address. If the name has been changed, usually by asking for "closed registrations," you can figure out what the previous name was. On the most current copy of a company registration, anything underlined indicates that it's old and out-of-date information, which helps you trace back the history of a firm.

Thus, there was often a paper trail of sorts. It could be a very long, expensive paper trail to trace a company back to its original owner, the original location, and the original name. It was usually worth doing. Oftentimes, shady companies would make a mistake early on as a business and then cover their tracks later. I am always astonished by how much you can learn from the business records.

CHAPTER TWO

From paperwork to fieldwork

Paperwork can tell you a lot about a company, but it's two dimensional. Most of the time, you're going to have to explore in three dimensions—that means turning off your computer, getting off your ass, and actually going to where the company is located. I'm paraphrasing something I once heard, but due diligence isn't asking if it's raining and then listening to two opposing views and writing it up in a report and calling it a day. It's looking out the window, leaving the office, and seeing whether you get wet or not. Then you know.

The day after meeting with the client, I decided to check out the Nakatomi Holdings offices. The Tokyo Metropolitan Police had drawn up a list of over 1,000 yakuza front companies in the city, including real estate agencies, construction subcontractors, talent agencies, stockbrokers, private detective firms, auditors, importers, and even a bakery. Nakatomi wasn't on that list. Not yet.

The most recent corporate registration for the company had them located in an office building in Roppongi, which wasn't unusual per se. Japan has a number of business districts where certain firms tend to congregate, and Roppongi was a hotbed of foreign investors and funds.

Lehman Brothers Japan had their offices in Roppongi Hills,

which was the hotspot for nouveau riche venture capital. It also contained a giant shopping mall and culture center. The Yamaguchi-gumi, Goto-gumi, and Inagawa-kai Tsukumasa-ikka had been hired somewhere down the development chain to terrorize all the tenants that used to live in the area until they vacated the premises. Many sold their property to the real estate behemoth Mori Building, or agreed to move into the low-rent condominiums that had been designated as a classy ghetto for former residents.

Roppongi used to be called "high-touch town," and no one was quite sure what that referred to, but beneath the glitter was a dark stream of predatory vice and sleaze. So, yes, of course, it wasn't surprising that Lehman Brothers and Goldman Sachs had offices in the area. It wasn't surprising that Nakatomi Holdings would be there, either.

Just a note here. At that time, Lehman Brothers had not yet been infiltrated by a lawyer who had a history of working for Yamaguchi-gumi front companies. That would cost them $350 million in 2008. But that's the price of not doing your due diligence. When Tony, aka Action, publishes his book in 2024, you'll know the whole story.

One thing you learn to look for when trying to determine the legitimacy of a company is what I like to call "territory incongruence". Is the building located in an area where you would expect to find such a business? For example, Nerima-ku is an almost rural and residential area of Tokyo. If a company offering investment-consulting services were located there, that would ring alarm bells.

One of the most important and obvious things you do when checking out a dodgy company is to go to where the company is located. Footwork is almost always the core of any detective work. Japanese police, especially homicide cops, have a saying for this: "The scene of the crime, one hundred times." The meaning is obvious—go back to where the crime took place again and again, because the most important clues and evidence to break the case are probably there.

The offices of Nakatomi Holdings were located on the top floor of an office building three minutes from Roppongi Station. The building was nine stories tall with a basement. I showed up wearing the uniform of a famous Japanese mail-delivery service with a package in my hand. I kind of looked fat in the blue-and-white shirt, but it wasn't a fashion show, it was work. I had a dark navy baseball cap on and was wearing black-rimmed glasses that did nothing but keep out UV rays and looked very nerdy. They also made my face a little harder to remember, and screwed with security cameras. Although nothing could really hide my giant Tengu nose, the baseball cap helped.

I did one more thing before I walked into the building. I took a photo of myself in front of the building, and I sent it as an attachment to an email to Michiel Brandt, who was my research assistant, and Saigo. If something went wrong, there would be at least two people who knew where I was, and that was a bargaining chip.

Michiel was the person I'd trust to contact the police if need be. She knew the cops I was friendly with and trusted, and they'd respond to her if she contacted them asking for help.

Saigo was the muscle. He looked like an anime version of Frankenstein's monster with gray skin and a black suit. Back in the day, he'd been a legend in the underworld: unpredictable, unexpected, and always leaving a tremendous amount of damage in his wake. Tsunami, indeed. When I was nosing around some-place spooky or dangerous, he was good to have around. He himself was an encyclopedia of underworld lore and knowledge. He couldn't be with me on this day — he had other work, and I didn't ask what that was. So I needed to keep a low profile.

If you are going to walk in and out of buildings in Tokyo

looking for clues, it is ideal to be invisible; dressing as a delivery person was the second-best thing. Nobody noticed you, most of the time.

There was a large security camera above the front door that had rusty rivets securing it, but once I walked inside there was no security camera in the room to the left where the mailboxes were located.

Mailboxes could tell you a lot about a business. Some of the mailboxes had the company name embossed onto the metal, giving a sense of gravitas to the firm's presence in the place. Nakatomi Holdings had their name in block letters and printed on a yellow label that was plastered to the outside of their mailbox, one of many in the rows of mailboxes. It looked like it had been made with the TEPRA label maker, and there appeared to be remnants of labels that had been plastered there before, giving the whole mailbox a kind of messy and thrown-together ambience. There appeared to be a bunch of pamphlets and presentation booklets crammed into the mailbox, and at least one had fallen on the floor. While stealing mail is a crime, it's not a crime to pick things off the floor. Being a good Samaritan, I pulled out the overstuffed packet and helped clear some space in the mailbox.

While I was putting things in order, I used my yellow flip-top phone with its own camera to take pictures of the outside of all the envelopes. In 2006, Japanese cellphones were technological marvels, and the iPhone wasn't even a word. Japanese telecommunications giant NTT Docomo released a mobile internet surfing service called i-mode in 1999 that was accessed by cellphones that were way advanced beyond their time. While Japanese people were playing games, surfing the web, and even watching television on sleek flip phones, my counterparts in the United States were still making calls and punching out texts on tiny screens.

However, Japanese phones had their faults.

Almost all Japanese phones are equipped with a shutter sound so that when you take a picture, there is an audible and loud click that is particularly distressing when you're trying not to be noticed. There's a reason for that. Japan has always had a problem with perverts, aka *hentai*, who derive a particular glee from snapping photos of naked women or women's panties.

Just the sight of women's panties sends some men into ecstasy here. Go figure. There's even a word, *panchira*, "a flash of panties," to reference the perverse thrill that glimpse may give to some people. As a reporter, I had written several stories about panty thieves who had amassed massive collections, sometimes sorted by color, size, and lace or non-lace. Men who didn't have the balls to steal panties outright seemed to be happy with up-skirt photos. The old-fashioned perverts went for naked female photos. They soon made "camera phone" (the predecessor to smartphones) a key weapon in their arsenals. Camera phones were deployed to snap up-skirt photos of schoolgirls' underwear, to take sneak photographs of women in bathroom stalls, and, of course, nude photos at Japan's hot springs and public baths. After a B-grade TV celebrity and comedian was caught videotaping the underwear of a woman on the Tokyo subway in 2000, telecommunications manufacturers began including a built-in shutter sound that goes off whenever a photo is taken. That had some impact on cutting down on sneak photography. It also made wielding a phone to snap a picture incognito a pain in the ass. Many digital cameras were also equipped with the same sound function; it's useful to know when you've snapped a picture and hear the nostalgic mechanical sound of a shutter clicking, but it's not helpful in my line of work. I heard there was a place in Akihabara that could kill the shutter sound for a price, but it might have been an urban legend.

I knew it would be quieter if I jotted down the addresses by hand in my notebook, but my handwriting both in Japanese and English is terrible, and I needed to be sure that I had the correct addresses. Photographs are usually better. I just snapped away, hoping no one was around.

I captured my photos, and headed to the elevator. I wanted to see what was on the top floor and to get a sense of the Nakatomi offices. The elevator also had a security camera inside. I couldn't tell whether it was working.

I got off the elevator looking at the address on my package, which was one building off. I had intentionally written a wrong address, and went down the hallways. The Nakatomi office was closed, although there was a nice sign on the solid-metal door. There was a buzzer to the side with an intercom. There was also a camera above the door—very new—and different from the cameras in the rest of the building. The rivets were shiny, and it seemed like a state-of-the-art security camera. It indicated an unusual level of paranoia for a small business, and I made a mental note of it. The door to the office had another mailbox built into it, close to the bottom, I supposed it was for newspapers, periodicals, or maybe a dropbox of some kind. There was a large slot to drop in publications or printed materials, but not large enough for my hand to get in and pull anything out. I had enough for the day, and left. This was a start.

When I got back home, which was a shared house in Nishi-Azabu, I made myself a cup of coffee in the kitchen. I kicked back on my futon and started reading through the materials I'd collected.

The strange alchemy of due diligence at the time was far from an exact science. There was no manual and almost no public sources available to utilize, but there were things that I always checked. You looked for contradictions—contradictions inherent when something (or someone) is not what they claim to be. In order to do this, you have to know what the entity claims to be doing in the first place. I scoured the company's promotional pamphlet for grains of information.

I imagined that my client also had a copy of the pamphlet and it would have been nice to have had it from the start. I had no illusions of friendship or camaraderie with the client, but it would have been in their best interests and made my job easier if they always told me everything they knew when I took the job. The nature of a client was to tell you as little as possible to see what you could dig up or to follow some meaningless "need-to-know-basis" hoarding of information policy. The "need-to-know-basis" way of doing business isn't always a good one. If you're an investigator, the more you know, the better you can do your job, and you don't know what you're going to need to know until way later in the game.

Nakatomi emphasized that it had been established in 1970, showing that it had a long history. However, as I peeled back the corporate registrations, working from the most recent back to the original documents, and followed the company's evolution over time, that founding date became meaningless. The original company had almost nothing to do with the entity I was looking at now.

Nakatomi Holdings KK was allegedly founded in 1970, according to its original website, which had been closed down. The presentation materials noted: "Traditionally, the [company's] activities were focused on the purchase, sale, leasing, management and utilization of real estate, as well as management consulting services and later in the area of hedge fund research and manager selection for institutional investors."

Well, not according to its closed company registration. It was true that the company was established in 1970, on July 1.

However, the company was first called Ryukawa Tosō and registered in Hirosaki City in the Aomori prefecture—one of the northernmost parts of Honshu, the main island of Japan. I like to think of it as the Siberia of Japan. When I was working for the *Yomiuri Shimbun*, it was rumored that if you really fucked up, you would be exiled to the Aomori bureau for a few years.

Yes, this financial goliath was originally in the house- and office-painting business in the North Pole of Japan. *Tosō* means "painting." If you saw a window and you wanted to paint it black, these were the people to go to.

The company was renamed Midori Books on October 29, 1990, and moved to Shizuoka City in the Shizuoka prefecture. According to its corporate registration, Midori Books sold books retail and didn't do much else. Its board members were all Japanese. Okay, so how does a painting company turned bookseller become a consulting firm?

The company pamphlet went on to say:

> Ten years ago, the current senior partners began a collaboration with the company in international private equity investments and hedge funds as well ... As the collaboration expanded, the companies merged in 2002, and the company activities then additionally included a selection of investment vehicles and private banking referrals.

Despite those statements, there was no mention of the alleged merger in 2002 on the company registration.

The pamphlet noted that "in 2005, the original owners of the company retired and the current senior partners took over the company, completing the process in 2006."

This sentence appears somewhat true—according to the company registration on April 11, 2006, all the Japanese board members quit their positions, and the company was renamed

Nakatomi Holdings. Then the current Nakatomi board members assumed their positions on the same day. Its business objectives also changed on that day, and the company suddenly went from listing its core businesses as "sales of books" to "real estate sales, purchase, exchange, leasing and management and management consulting."

The company moved to their current office on May 22, 2006. However, little information was uncovered on the company, except from its website and the company's presentation sheet.

According to its (old) website, preserved in an archive, the company allegedly worked primarily with "non-Japanese domiciled institutional qualified investors" and provided "consulting services on investments in Japan. The company specializes in financial institutions' advisory and secondary transactions with noted hedge funds, private equity funds and direct and co-investments."

The company's explanation of what it did in both English and Japanese made little sense but did include a handful of corporate buzzwords that seemed meaningful.

They did have the business buzzword-laden spiel down well.

"Using its worldwide network of private banks, family offices and asset managers, [Nakatomi Holdings] expanded into advising on strategic expansion strategies of these firms, assisting in facilitating M&A and alliance formations, particularly into the Asian and European markets by financial institutions."

However, there was no information uncovered on the company's clients' names. I looked through G-Search and Nikkei Navi, the two biggest newspaper and magazine article databases in Japan, and came up with zilch. I could find no media coverage of the company from internet and database searches.

I did one more thing. I looked at the companies that had been sending mail to the firm, and checked their addresses against the lists I had of yakuza front companies in Tokyo and beyond. It was a crude system that I had working. It was not a fast system, and it had flaws. In Japan, addresses are sometimes written out with Japanese characters and western numbers, or else completely in Japanese characters, even for the numbers and blocks that make up an address. This meant that sometimes you had to enter variations of the same address to get a hit.

One firm that had sent them an invoice showed up in my search. When I punched the name and address into my database, the listed office address was also the office of the Yamaguchi-gumi Mio-gumi in Tokyo. The Yamaguchi-gumi Mio-gumi, also known as the Yamaguchi-gumi Goryo-kai, was responsible for a billion-dollar loan-sharking operation that had even laundered funds in Las Vegas and Switzerland. And Nakatomi Holdings had been doing business with them. I didn't think that was a coincidence.

All of this led me back to the same question over and over. How was it that a painting company in the Aomori prefecture, the North Pole of Japan, ended up being a financial powerhouse? I imagined the answers would be in Aomori. I was going to need to go there. The best way to really figure out what was happening now was to go back to the start.

I called the client and requested more expense money to make the trip after I gave them an update. They agreed. I also decided to call up Toshiro Igari, who had served in Aomori years back.

I went by his office and had a cup of coffee, and asked him how much of a foothold the Yamaguchi-gumi had in Hirosaki City, because it was already clear to me that they were involved to some extent. Igari, the ever-well-coiffed bulldog, informed me that he remembered the Yamaguchi-gumi as being very weak in that area.

"Jake, I was there in 1983, that's a while back," he told me.

"At the time, there was the Umeva-ikka and the Kyokuto-kai Sato-kai, and they were in the middle of a bloody gang war. Right out of the movies. The Umeya-ikka ended up getting sucked up into the Inagawa-kai, and these days the Inagawa-kai are pretty much under the thumb of the Yamaguchi-gumi. I can't remember what happened to the Sato-kai."

He gave me a brief colorful history of the gang wars there and taught me something I didn't know. The Kyokuto-kai took their name from a private detective agency that had been run by their founder. I thought that might make a nice TV series someday: *Yakuza PI*. Like *Magnum PI*, but with tattooed heroes who were missing fingers instead of Tom Selleck and his iconic 1980s mustache. It wasn't unusual for the yakuza to run private detective agencies—after all, information is money—but I didn't know there was a major mob group that took their name from the front operation.

I explained the case to him so far, and he suggested that the people behind Nakatomi Holdings were probably piggy-backing. "Piggy-backing," he explained, "is when you convince someone of your legitimacy by using a name that they are familiar with. It's like a dubious investment fund taking the name of Sumitomo, Fuji, or even Mitsui. No one really owns the right to those names, so there is no copyright issue, but since people know the names, it gives them a sense of security."

He didn't have anything else to add after that, but he did give me the name of a cop with the Aomori prefectural police who he said would be helpful. Igari said he would make an introduction. I was grateful for the help. It would be nice to head up there with at least one person who might talk to me.

I was a little hesitant about going to Aomori; I didn't know anyone there, and Saigo wasn't going to come with me. He might have if I had paid for the ticket, but I was pretty sure I could handle this one on my own.

Aomori was considered a hardship post for *Yomiuri* exiles for good reason. The winters were crushingly cold, and Aomori City gets about 26 feet—or eight meters—of snow each year. I was just glad that it wasn't winter.

THREE

The North Pole of Japan

To get to Aomori, I decided to take the Shinkansen part of the way, and it felt like a long, long, trip. From Tokyo, you can take the Hayabusa train on the JR Tohoku Shinkansen to Shin-Aomori (3.5 hours) and transfer to a local or limited express train to Aomori Station (five minutes). A one-way ticket costs 17,500 yen and takes around four hours. A train leaves every hour or so. I have a vague memory of it being more of a hassle in 2007, but after fifteen years, I could be wrong.

By the time I got there, it was too late to do much except check into a business hotel and get some sleep. The next morning, I took a taxi to the original home of Nakatomi Holdings. There was a small store where it had been located, and a sign that said Sasaki Painting. The sign itself looked like someone should repaint it.

I walked in, and a forty-year-old man came out to talk to me. He was skinny and dressed in a navy blue suit, wearing sneakers. I gave him my other business card that read *Nichibei Shinyō Chōsa* (U.S.-Japan Credit Investigations), which listed me as an investigator. Sometimes, being straightforward is the best way to go. Most of the time, when investigating a company, you are forbidden to speak directly to the company or anyone who has recently left the company. There are a number of reasons for this, but mostly they have to do with compliance regulations. I never really understood the rules myself, but I had to follow them.

I didn't want to alert Nakatomi Holdings that I was looking into them, nor did I really want to go to the Shizuoka prefecture, which was the home of the Yamaguchi-gumi Goto-gumi and the Yamaguchi-gumi Goryo-kai. So I had decided to only disclose limited information.

"I'm sorry to bother you, but I've been hired to look into a Tokyo firm that does financial consulting," I told him. "And the odd thing is that they started their business right here, where you are located. I'd be grateful if you could help me."

The man, who I presume was Sasaki, grimaced a little bit, but then said, "Yeah, okay. I think you need to talk to my father. I'll call him." He did. He told me that his father could meet me at a coffee shop, *Dote no Coffee-ya Manchan*, in an hour, at 11.00 am.

I left the store and then realized I had forgotten to ask for directions. (Google Maps didn't exist, nor did the iPhone.) I had a map of the city, which listed the coffee shop on it, but I didn't quite know how to get there. I was too embarrassed to walk back in the store and afraid that by asking dumb questions I would blow the interview I had just set up.

The map would have been helpful if I could read the street names, but, as is often the case with names of places and people, the readings of the kanji are very idiosyncratic, so while I could recognize some of the characters, I wasn't sure if I was pronouncing them correctly.

I was in Kikyōno—a place that had two kanji characters I had never seen, *kikyō*, and one I did know, *no*, meaning field— and I needed to get to Dotemachi. I spotted an old man in gray sweatpants and a heavy blue parka walking his dog, and politely asked him how to get to the coffee shop. He looked at me with some surprise when I stopped him, and cocked his head to the side. I repeated myself.

The look on his face was bemused, as if one of his dogs had suddenly begun speaking to him. He answered back rapidly in the local dialect, known as Tsugaru-ben, and I had almost no idea what he was saying.

"Could you tell me that in standard Japanese?" I asked.

He was silent for a second, and then I wondered if I'd hit a nerve by implying that his dialect was not standard Japanese, which was true. You'd never hear an announcer speaking in Tsugaru-ben on NHK, the BBC of Japan. In fact, sometimes when people from the region would appear on television, the broadcasters would put subtitles under their names. There was a *gaijin* (foreign) television personality whose shtick was speaking rural Japanese, but that wasn't me. All this flashed through my head in a moment.

He then just laughed.

"Where's your country?"

"I'm from Tokyo," I answered.

He smiled. He motioned me to follow him, with the standard gesture that is so confusing to many foreigners (who haven't been here a long time) because it looks like the person is motioning you to go away. The movement was palm down with fingers out front. He dragged his fingers inward, toward his palm, and then flicked them back out straight again.

I knew the intended meaning, although I hoped in the North Pole of Japan that the meaning wasn't actually "Fuck off." He walked me there silently, nodding once to a woman dressed in a suit we passed along the street. He opened the door for me and said, "Good luck," and then was gone.

The coffee shop was beautiful, and the coffee was goddamn amazing. The place had a low-lit chill ambience, all wooden floors, and was pleasantly warm. One of Japan's most famous authors, Osamu Dazai, had reportedly frequented the coffee shop in high school. Dazai was a brilliant writer but a total asshole. His book *Ningen Shikkaku (Not Qualified To Be Human)* was a literary classic. I had read the book back when I was attending Jochi Daigaku (Sophia University). It was a great book, but unfortunately it was kind of hard to separate the artist from their art, particularly in his case.

Dazai, a spoiled rich brat and son of a wealthy landowner, was born in Aomori in 1909. He had this habit of meeting women, falling in love with them, convincing his lover to make a suicide pact with him, and then failing to live up to his end. He lived; the girl died. Sometimes, the women lived as well. Eventually, he succeeded in one of his suicide pacts, and that was the end of his career. He turned his life failures into semi-fictional novels, creating the prototype of Japan's "I-novels." (You could even think of him as the James Frey—*A Million Little Pieces*—of his day.) His literary ambitions may have driven him to do stupid things simply so he could write about them. As a result, it's hard to separate his fiction from his real life—as it is with all so-called I-novels.

The strange thing about Japan is that most people don't seem to care how much of an I-novel is true and how much of it is fiction. There are books marketed as nonfiction in the West, like *Yakuza Moon* by Shoko Tendo, that are actually I-novels.

Make no mistake: Osamu Dazai, great writer, total asshole.

As I waited in the coffee shop for the elder Sasaki, reading about Dazai and working on my first book and semi-memoir *Tokyo Vice: An American Reporter on the Police Beat in Japan*, I had this momentary flash of irony and self-awareness. Man, I did not want to be another Osamu Dazai. As I was ordering the apple pie, along came the man I assumed had to be Mr Sasaki, since he saw me, walked over to where I was, and sat down immediately.

He had my business card, which he flashed at me as he sat down.

"I don't know which is your family name. I'll just call you Jake-san, Jake-san. Do you mind if I order a coffee?"

I ordered it for him. He could have been anywhere between seventy and ninety years old. He had a full head of thin gray hair, slicked back, and a face so wrinkled that it looked like his face had been carved into an apple that later dried out. He reminded me of a shrunken head with a smile.

As they brought him a cup of black coffee, he got straight to the point.

"So, my old company is now a fancy stock brokerage in Tokyo. Well, that's a surprise! I always wondered what had happened to it. And now I know," he sipped his coffee. "Why do you want to know the story?"

"That's my job. My job is to figure out whether the current incarnation of your company is a legitimate enterprise."

He nodded and asked if he could smoke. I said, yes, of course. He took out a hard pack of Mild Sevens and lit one. He offered me one. I declined and took out mine.

"You ever gamble?" he asked me.

"Not really," I replied. "I don't like to lose and I hate to lose money on something without getting anything back."

"Smart man. I used to gamble. I liked to gamble. It was a thrill. But I played mahjong, which isn't just about luck. There's skill involved. It's not just a roll of the dice. You ever play mahjong?"

I admitted that I had played in college and sometimes when hanging around the press club as a reporter, and that I was terrible. I barely understood the rules and I always lost.

He laughed, a deep raspy laugh.

"Well, I liked to play poker—still do sometimes, but not for money. And I really liked to play mahjong, but—I guess around

1989 or 1990, I forget—I got in over my head. There was a place you could play, for money, and I went there often. I lost about 2 million yen ($20,000). And that was a lot of money for me."

I nodded.

The mahjong parlor was backed by the Umeda-ikka. They didn't run the place, but they were the muscle and they collected protection money from the owners and debts owed. Sasaki asked the owner of the parlor if there was some way he could settle up. The owner came back to him and said there was a fellow who might be able to help him if he was willing to sign over his business. He wouldn't actually forfeit anything; he'd just be giving the business name and corporate registration to someone else. It sounded like a good deal.

"So, one afternoon, this very well-dressed guy comes into the store who knows my name and offers to buy my company for 2 million yen, in cash. He says he's a *kaishaya*, which isn't a term I'm familiar with, but we discuss it. He already has a copy of my company registration and some forms to fill out. I get my personal seal out of the desk. So we come here, to this coffee shop, and we have a talk. He promises me that I won't be liable for anything and that I just need to sign some forms."

I asked him if he remembered the forms. He vaguely did.

"Yeah, they were going to move the company to Shizuoka or Tokyo—at least on paper. My name was going to be gone and there would be a whole new board of directors. I think they were setting up some retail operations. I didn't care. It all seemed dodgy, but then again, the people who introduced him to me were running an illegal mahjong parlor, so there you are."

"Was there anything about the man that you noticed? Anything unusual? Was he missing a finger?" I asked him.

"Nope. Nothing like that. He was just very smooth. But he had long sleeves on, and you could see a bit of a tattoo sticking out when he folded his arms. So I guess he had been in the business."

Sasaki didn't have anything to do that afternoon and I wasn't leaving until the next day, so we chatted for a while.

When Sasaki got his payment in cash, he went to the mahjong parlor, paid off his tab, and "never gambled again."

I asked him why. He explained succinctly.

"I was running out of luck."

"In what way?"

"Well, here's my theory. Luck is like a deck of cards. You only have so many. There are only so many good ones, and the longer you play the more you run out of your aces and your kings and your jacks, and even the cards get worn out. Maybe if you change places, you can get a new deck of cards. But luck is a finite resource, and I decided that I'd spent as much of mine as I could on stupid things, like gambling, and so I quit playing the tiles. Although I'll admit to playing it online now and then."

"Online?"

"Don't look so surprised, sonny. I'm old, but I'm not so old that I can't figure out how to use a computer. I've got a Mac at home. Very reliable. I'd prefer to buy an NEC or something made in Japan, but Macs are stable. I don't want my computer crashing on me when I'm winning."

We spoke some more. He liked to talk, and I didn't know much about life in Aomori, so I listened to him expound. It wasn't a bad way to spend the afternoon, and I had nowhere else to go.

Before I left, Sasaki pulled a small *meishi* holder out of his man-bag.

"Here," he said. "This is the card of the man who bought my business. You may find it useful."

I took a quick look. The company was named "Business Brain" in English with a katakana name under it. There was a phone number, a fax number, and the name of the representative. I pulled out my state-of-the-art made-in-Japan camera phone, and snapped a picture. I emailed it to Michiel, with a note: "See if you can track this company down."

I thanked Sasaki-san again.

I never forgot that coffee shop, or his anecdotal explanation of luck as a semi-replenishable resource. And it wouldn't be the last time I was to see Sasaki-san. The talk answered most of my questions.

Later that night, I had drinks in a hostess bar with Igari's old friend at the Aomori Prefectural Police Department, Detective Kudo. He was on the edge of retirement and serving as the number two in the Organized Crime Control Division. Igari had made all the proper introductions, so things went smoothly. Detective Kudo told me all about the gang wars that had broken out in Hirosaki City in the 1980s and Igari's role in prosecuting those involved in the first gang war. There had been a second one in the late 1980s after Igari had moved to a new post. I asked him what exactly was a *kaishaya*, which Sasaki had mentioned. I had a vague idea.

He explained.

"They buy and sell mostly dormant companies. *Kaisha* means company, and *ya* is just a genetic suffix for a seller of something. In Japan, the older a company is, the more reputable it appears to be. But there a lot of companies that are basically there in name only, sometimes referred to as *yurei kaisha*, ghost companies or sometimes zombie companies. And they can be useful if you want to save money in setting up your own company, or give the appearance of propriety, or plan to engage in some kind of big or small-scale fraud."

For example, if you were the CEO of a small company and wanted to pay an allowance to your mistress, you could purchase a dead company from a *kaishaya* and put her in charge.

You could then use company money to pay for her services with probably no one being the wiser—payments to a company are rarely questioned.

Purchased companies could be used to embezzle funds, improve sales figures, and evade taxes. The important thing was that there needed to be an actual company so it would be hard to tell what was going on. Kudo told me that Japan was rife with fraud, and in the background of many of these were *kaishaya*. They also helped organized crime groups set up front companies and rent properties. No sane person would rent an office to the Yamaguchi-gumi Kyokushin-kai, but they might rent to "Kyokushin Enterprises," established in 1959.

"Most people, especially real estate agents, are not going to check on the history of a company. So let's say Kyokushin Enterprises started as a toilet paper manufacturer in Chiba prefecture, called Kami Co, with 5 million yen in capital, and then suddenly one day became an investment-consulting firm, changed their name, and moved to Osaka and then Tokyo, upping their capital to 500 million yen. People tend to take what they're given at face value. The most recent company registration is all they look at. And that's why they're often fooled."

He felt that a 20-million-yen purchase price was a reasonable deal in some cases, although the nature of the *kaishaya* was to pay as little as possible and to sell for as much as possible, like any businessman. However, a large purchase would also buy silence from the seller, who would swear never to discuss the deal. Kudo added:

"Most people talk. A year passes; ten years pass. Sooner or later, most people are gonna talk about the strange deal they made, but by then the company has changed places and locations so many times that tracking it down is more work than anyone wants to do, unless they have a reason."

I showed him the company registrations I had with me, and

asked if any of the names rang a bell. None did.

"I'm not a living dictionary of yakuza, you know. If there was a big local boss on here, I might recognize it, but there's no one I know in these docs."

We finished drinking late as he went into great detail about the gang wars here, the stuff of yakuza movies. The next day I headed back to Tokyo, getting in the green car when I could. I had an Asahi Super Dry beer on the train and some rice crackers because it seemed like the thing to do.

There was only one thing left to do for the report. I needed to check out the offices of the yakuza front company, Blue Mountain, that had invoiced Nakatomi Holdings. In a way, Blue Mountain was also a piggy-back. Jamaican blue mountain coffee is really popular in Japan.

Blue Mountain's invoices to the Nakatomi were in the pile of mail that I had benevolently picked off the floor, opened, and then kindly returned. The company appeared to be in the coffee import and export business, but that was a guess, prompted by a cup-of-coffee logo on their letterhead.

I still had plenty of time to do that. I decided to take a break for the weekend. And I also had to check in with Michiel.

Blue Mountain was hard to locate. They'd moved several times, and Michiel was tracking them down by navigating through the labyrinth of real estate deeds and corporate registrations that a shady fly-by-night company leaves behind as they keep moving around.

On the train back, I got a call, and left the green car to take it somewhere quiet on board. It was Michiel.

"I think I've got a lead on Business Brain! The CEO is one Akio Kumagaya, who used to work at Nomura Securities, and they have an office in Ikebukuro."

"Outstanding work," I thanked her. "I'll see you tomorrow at the office."

John Donne once famously wrote: "No man is an island entire of itself; every man is a piece of the continent, a part of the main." I think that holds true for due diligence investigators. It's not a one-man job—you need a partner, a reliable partner. And in my case, Michiel was the one person I could count on, every time. She was my girl Friday, my BFF. I couldn't function without her.

CHAPTER FOUR
Meet Michiel Brandt

Michiel Brandt had been looking at graduate schools in the U.S. She came back to Japan after I'd already started the Nakatomi case, and I was glad she was here. She was my right-hand in due diligence investigations, and I also owed her a night on the town. We had plans to go catch a concert, so meeting up was a bit of both work and relaxation. I didn't want to work her too hard—she was recovering.

She came by the house on Friday late afternoon very businesslike, in a long skirt, a sunflower-yellow blouse, and wearing nerdy glasses. It was a warm October; summer seemed to be lingering around, like a student reluctant to return to classes.

Michiel always looked like an elf to me. She had a cute, round face and big cheeks like a chipmunk. When she smiled, which was often, her hazel eyes crinkled and sparkled; she laughed loudly. She was raised in Japan, so she usually made the very Japanese gesture of covering her mouth when she guffawed, but it didn't do much to drown out the sound of her laughter. She was short but spry.

She showed up that evening with a stack of finished and half-finished reports.

I thanked her for the reports, praised her for tracking down Blue Mountain and Business Brain, and then asked her to put all the reports on my desk, in the next room. We were going to the Blue Note to see Gal Costa perform music by legendary Brazilian composer Antônio Carlos Jobim.

We had a long walk to the nearest station, but she liked to walk.

"Jake, I'm looking forward to tonight. Thank you so much for getting the tickets, *ne*?"

She gave my arm a squeeze as we walked toward Roppongi. It was easy for her to hold my arm, even though I was taller than her. I have long arms, like a gibbon. I didn't want her to feel guilty about the cost of the evening.

"It was my pleasure. It's the least I can do for what you do. Consider it a small bonus on top of your terrible pay."

"How do I look?" she asked. "I dressed up for the occasion."

I pointed at her bright yellow blouse.

"You will look like the most elegant canary in the room."

She laughed, covering her mouth.

"You're relentless."

"You look great. It's a classy outfit. I'm not fit to have you on my arm. Thanks for coming along to make me look good."

She always lifted my spirits. She just radiated happiness. Most people, I imagined, would be bitter and angry at the world if they'd experienced what she had. As we walked to the station, very briefly, we held hands. I tried to think how long I had known Michiel. Because it felt like I had known her my whole life.

It had been at least four years …

I first got to know Michiel when I was still a crime reporter at the *Yomiuri Shimbun*, Japan's largest newspaper, in 2004.

She was an undergraduate at Waseda, a Japanese university,

studying immigration issues. At the time, I was assigned to cover the Tokyo Metropolitan Police Department, specifically vice and organized crime. Human trafficking was becoming a recognized problem in the country. I was invited to participate at a forum on the issue sponsored by the United Nations. At the end, when I spontaneously gave a guided tour of the red-light district to some interns at the U.S. Embassy, she tagged along. That's when I first made her acquaintance. She'd already graduated from UCLA with a degree in political science and international relations. She was researching international labor issues and helping women in need. She was charming, friendly, curious, brave, and intelligent. The enthusiasm she emitted was contagious. Our friendship developed quickly. I'm ashamed to admit that at first I thought of her as a well-meaning muppet. It took me years to realize how substantial she was as a person and as an investigator.

Michiel accompanied me to several conferences, and took detailed notes as well as getting involved with NGOs that fight for the rights of trafficking victims in Japan. After leaving the newspaper in November 2005, I had spent seven months working on an in-depth research project on human trafficking, funded by the U.S. State Department. In the process, I hired Michiel to be my research assistant, because, like myself, she is both fluent in Japanese and English, and she has extensive knowledge of the problem and its dimensions.

And in the midst of doing that she almost died. What almost killed her wasn't anything I could have seen coming, nor could she.

I remember the evening when it started. I had just begun working on the human trafficking report, and Michiel was working with me, doing research and collating information.

She wanted to go out dancing with her friend Cris, from Korea. The only place I knew that was fun to dance in was a club called Yellow, buried in the back alleys of Roppongi. They played techno and trance, and it was so monotonous that even I could dance to it. I asked Special Agent Larry Futa to come join us for the evening. Of course, he said yes. A former intelligence officer and ladies' man, Ken, invited himself. Don't get me wrong: I liked Ken. Even though he had a habit of getting me involved in shenanigans way over my pay grade.

Michiel showed up in jeans and an emerald-green shirt that sort of matched her hazel eyes. Some people told me she had brown eyes, but they always looked dark green to me. Admittedly, I am a little color blind. She asked me, as she always did: "How do I look?"

"Like a sexy M&M."

She punched me in the shoulder.

"Thanks, Jake."

"You're welcome, Mimi."

Everybody called her Mimi. That was her childhood nickname, although I can't remember where she got it.

Larry, holding a martini in his hand, wearing a suit as usual, stepped in.

"Michiel, you look dazzling. Don't listen to Adelstein. He only appreciates pole dancers taller than him."

I corrected him: "They don't have to be taller than me. It's not mandatory. Just a preference."

Larry led Michiel onto the floor. About a little after midnight I was talking to Cris, and Michiel stumbled over.

"Jake, I don't feel so good."

I took her by the shoulders and sat her down. She looked as white as a sheet. Larry and I called her a taxi ,and sent her home. I wrote an email to her parents. Three days later, I heard back, after trying to reach her. Michiel had been diagnosed with leukemia.

It was acute and it was critical. They'd need to start

treatment immediately. I was floored. She'd been diagnosed with Adult T-cell leukemia, a type of leukemia usually found in adults over forty years of age. She was only twenty-three at the time. The doctors told her upfront that she would most likely not live to see the next year.

People like her had a 3 percent survival rate—that's what the literature said. And, when I put aside my wishful thinking, I didn't think she'd make it. Oddly, she never once doubted that she would survive. I visited her in the hospital, and brought her a portable DVD player and a selection of good and awful movies so she could have something to do during those long hours in bed.

In August 2005, she was blessed with a bone marrow stem cell transplant from her brother, Daniel, who tested as a perfect match for her. It was a rarity even among siblings, and by autumn she was discharged from the hospital, in what was a miraculous, speedy recovery.

Here's a weird thing. As a result of her first bone-marrow transplant, she developed curly hair. She looked somewhat like Little Orphan Annie. Of course, I made gentle fun of her. I'm that kind of pal. But I didn't start calling her Annie, because I do possess some discretion, and some jokes are probably only funny once.

She didn't have a job and she wanted to go to graduate school, so I hired her. It was a great deal for me. She was unsure of her Japanese abilities, but it was really a matter of learning the words and concepts necessary for the job. Hell, I was still learning them myself. When I admitted this and she understood, she made flashcards for us.

At first, I did not want to let her do the work, out of concern for her health, but she insisted. Eventually, her zeal wore me down and I relented.

She attended several conferences as my proxy, always

gathering useful intelligence, contacts, and materials. She conducted interviews with related parties, and accompanied me to meetings with government officials. She was indispensable to the project, and she worked extremely hard for very little pay.

I was delighted that Michiel was also a fine due diligence investigator. I hadn't really put her on those tasks seriously until late 2007. Her second bone-marrow transplant was that year, and it was tough on her.

We mostly kept in touch back then by Google Chat. It was a thing.

March 12, 2007 9.06 am

Me: Hey Mimi!
Michiel: Hi! Actually, I'm home! I'm getting a catheter implant tomorrow, so my doctor told me I could go home for a night
Me: Yikes! I've seen those things. For the chemo right?
Michiel: and the transplant
Me: Can I call you Bionic Jaime the next time I see you?
Michiel: Hahaa. Isn't that The Bionic Woman?

The transplant was a success. By November 2007, she was ready to work again full-time. I can't honestly say that everything that had come before crossed my mind as we were walking to the station, but I did get lost in thoughts. Michiel gently squeezed my hand as we got closer, preventing me from walking into a signboard for a girls' bar and bringing me back to reality.

The concert was lovely. I love female singers, and Gal Costa was so on point. We had a nice semi-booth seat and a few tiki-tiki cocktails. In the comedy routines that become part of close friendships, Michiel always gave me flack about how I ordered the most girlie and effeminate drinks on the menu, preferably with a paper umbrella.

I'd always tell her, "Michiel, I spend most of my social life drinking with cops, crooks, lawyers, prosecutors, law-enforcement types, or low-lifes. It's always first a beer, then either sake, whisky, or *shochu* (potato liquor). Maybe, at best, a vodka martini because 007 drinks them. Gotta drink some manly drinks."

"Jake, you could show tremendous courage and order a Malibu Coke. Maybe they'd respect your choice. I do! Truly."

"That's not going to go over well. My street credibility would be completely destroyed."

And if it was winter, Michiel would then point at my DayGlo-colored green (orange, blue, or purple) cashmere sweater, and respond, "Any man wearing those sweaters has already lost any street credibility. Might as well go all in."

It was our little *manzai* act. My love of brightly colored men's cashmere sweaters came from the fact that at the end of winter you could buy them dirt cheap on the Lands' End website. Which she knew.

I was completely comfortable with her. And there was nothing more relaxing than listening to the tones of Gal with Michiel leaning on me and my arm around her.

It was wonderfully chill.

Gal Costa has this siren-like voice, smooth as silk, seductive and vulnerable at the same time. I was hypnotized. It was as if she was a snake charmer, and I must have been the snake. Michiel enjoyed it, too, but she wasn't used to spending a late night out after finishing chemo. She purred a little when she got sleepy.

As we left, Michiel asked if I'd like to head up to Hakone with her and some friends. There was a nice onsen there and the sculpture museum. I would have loved to go, but I had to follow up on our last two leads. She understood. The Nakatomi case was almost done, and we had a hard deadline.

I decided that the most fruitful avenue of exploration would be the office of the *kaishaya*. Michiel did solid work finding their Tokyo office. She'd taken the business card I'd gotten from Sasaki and sent to her, done a corporate registration check, followed up on the clues from that, and then found that they had a branch office in Tokyo. Just to be sure, she'd also pulled the corporate registration for that office as well. The same representative director.

I imagined that a company whose business was buying and selling dubious companies to dubious people would be a treasure trove of information. I wasn't far off.

CHAPTER FIVE

When you want rice cakes, go to the rice cake maker

People seem to think that Japan is crime-free, but they are very wrong. Street crimes are low, but fraud and financial crime are rampant. There is a massive underworld infrastructure that makes ripping off people and businesses much easier than you would imagine. When a company such as Olympus gets exposed for $1 billion worth of accounting fraud, that makes the news, but the other, small-scale financial crimes are buried in the back pages of newspapers, if they are mentioned at all.

Japan's underworld economy is massive. Japan's legal sex industry brings in billions of dollars; the illegal sex industry, probably half as much. For example, sexual massage, known here as "fashion health," amounts to close to 515 billion yen in sales per year. That's all legal revenue. Rip-off bars known as *bottakuri* generate $10 million a year for organized crime. "Wire-me-the-money" fraud accounts for anywhere between $300 million to $500 million in lost savings for civilians each year.

On the corporate level, Lehman Brothers Japan was swindled out of $350 million in 2008, most of it never recovered. In the AIJ investment trust scam, nearly $1 billion vanished. The large-scale crimes couldn't be committed without an underworld infrastructure that supplied pliant accounting firms, fake companies, or old companies repurposed for fraud, sketchy labor-dispatch services, and other tools to make it all come together. A *kaishaya* is one part of that infrastructure.

The suffix *"ya,"* when attached to a business, can also denote the business owner. The suffix *-ya* is often used for that. For example, a butcher in Japanese is a *niku* (meat) *ya* (seller/vendor). A vegetable seller, *yaoya*. A baker or a bakery is a *pan* (breads/pastry) *ya* (seller).

The underworld is full of *ya*s. One of my favorite word niches is the *atariya* ("to be hit" vendor). An *atariya* specializes in getting hit by a moving vehicle (or appearing to) and then shaking down the driver for extensive damages. It's a profitable business until you run into a hit-and-run driver. Then you're probably just dead.

The word is pronounced "atari" like "Atari," the video-game maker that I'm old enough to remember.

There is a modern-day version of this old profession as well: the smartphone *atariya*. The work is a lot less dangerous for the criminal, but also with a much smaller revenue stream. The smartphone *atariya* lurks around station bathrooms, shopping malls, movie theaters, and department stores, looking for an absent-minded sucker to bump into. Ironically, people walking around while looking at their expensive smartphones make the best targets.

The *atariya* will then aggressively bump into you, and "drop" their phone. They will then take out their expensive phone, with a screen that is already broken, and berate you loudly, demanding compensation. Sometimes, they will work as a team—with one person playing the victim and another playing the eyewitness. The cost of repairing an iPhone screen can easily run from 10,000 yen to 40,000 yen, so a demand of 15,000 yen appears to be the sweet spot in which people would rather pay up than deal with the police or stand their ground.

Every now and then, the police arrest one of the perpetrators for fraud, but it's a rare event. The revenues for the smartphone *atariya* are estimated to be several million dollars a year.

The goal of the *atariya* is always to get you to pay them a settlement rather than have to go to court, or risk involvement with the police. He or she may team up with a *jidanya* (agreement vendor) who is good at pressuring people to make a deal. Typically, *jidanya* are also yakuza, or affiliated with them. In recent years, as the number of lawyers in Japan has increased, the number of *jidanya* has gone down as well.

However, in the old days, Japanese civil courts took forever to settle a dispute, the chances of actually getting paid were low, and lawyers were expensive. If you ask the local yakuza to solve the dispute or collect money owed, the matter is settled quickly and you can be reasonably certain that you'll get half of what is owed to you; the yakuza take the rest. However, half of something is always better than all of nothing.

The seller of dead companies or repurposable firms is a *kaishaya* (seller of companies). There are many reasons, as you now know, why it's advantageous to buy a pre-existing company on the cheap. Some of them I didn't know until I spoke to the *kaishaya*. There's a great Japanese saying about Japanese sticky rice cakes, called mochi, which I've always liked.

Mochi wa mochiya. For rice cakes, talk to the rice cake maker.

As a reporter, I've always interpreted the saying to mean, "Ask the experts."

It was time to see the *kaishaya*.

The office was located near the west exit of Ikebukuro Station. The area was a seedy, second-rate Kabukicho (Shinjuku's adult-entertainment Disneyland) that I feel tempted to say had seen better days, but I don't think there had ever been "better days." The office of our "dealer of zombie companies," run by an individual named Akio Kumagaya, had once been located near the west exit of Shinjuku Station, a booming area full of high-rise office buildings, fancy hotels, and expensive restaurants. He had definitely seen better days.

I had Saigo drive me to the office and wait outside. The company was located about five minutes from the station, on the fourth floor of a multipurpose building that looked like it had been built in the 1960s. There was a soba shop on the first floor, and if there was an elevator to the fourth floor, I didn't see one. There were mailboxes easily accessible on the first floor, and I found the one with "Business Brain" pasted on the outside. The sticker looked a little faded, and there were no other labels on it. I walked up to the fourth floor and knocked on the door.

"Come in," I heard a husky voice say, and opened the metal door.

There was a surprising amount of space in the office. The walls were covered with bookshelves crammed with folders, directories, legal handbooks, and even one or two tomes on how to deal with organized crime front companies. It was a very strange layout. At the back of the room was a lone man sitting at a wooden desk piled with documents, and an NEC desktop computer and large multipurpose scanner/fax machine/printer. The windows faced another building, and the shades were down.

There was a fluorescent light in the ceiling, but it was turned off, and instead there was a large standing lamp in the corner and an incandescent desk lamp that lit up part of the place, leaving the rest in shadows. He had good taste in lighting.

The man sitting there was Akio Kumagaya. He was wearing white shoes, a white suit with slightly padded shoulders, a red necktie, and an ostentatious gold Rolex on his left wrist. He had thick, round glasses, which almost seemed to be the shape of his fat, round cheeks. I couldn't tell if he was balding, but his hair was white and crew-cut. He was skinny. He seemed to be thrown together as if God had constructed him out of spare parts and his head had been attached to the wrong doll. Big head, fat face, skinny guy, googly eyes. Maybe he had a thyroid condition. He kind of looked like a ship captain.

I identified myself to him. I didn't make much small talk, but told him straight out why and how I'd ended up there. The honesty seemed to catch him off guard.

We got along. At one point, I went downstairs and bought some coffee from Doutor Coffee for him and me. I also bought a bottle of cheap Suntory whisky from the liquor shop across the street. I poured some in his coffee and mine when I got back up to his place.

As we were chatting, and still beating around the bush, I mentioned that I knew he used to have digs in West Shinjuku.

"What happened? I would think a company like yours would still be doing alright."

He shook his head.

"It used to be a good business, and I made a lot of money back in the day. Ghost companies or zombie companies, or whatever you'd like to call them—they had value. You could take a zombie company and sell it for a steep price. A full-blown corporation with stocks—they were worth the most. Back in the day, to set up a corporation—a *kabushikigaisha*—you'd have to have 10 million yen in capital ($90,000). For a limited corporation (*yugengaisha*) you'd need at least 3 million yen ($30,000). It was expensive to set up a firm unless you already had money. I could sell off a corporation for $10,000 or more, depending on how old it was. But then in 2003, they changed the laws. Now you could set up a company with one yen."

He knew what he was talking about. In fact, in 2006, the

company laws were revised so that the requirement for a mini-mum amount of capital itself was effectively banished. It was great news for start-ups, but bad news for people like him.

I nodded my head, expressing sympathy. He was also a smooth talker, enthusiastic, and clearly erudite. Often, if you shut up and listen to someone who's really into their work, you can learn valuable things. Boredom is your enemy as an investi-gator. If you listen with interest, what you thought were boring things often become interesting.

"Yeah," I said, "there must not be a lot of use for a company like yours these days."

At that, he seemed slightly offended. Maybe I'd wounded his professional pride.

"No, this business, unlike many of the businesses we trade, isn't quite dead yet. Sometimes you have companies that have already gained special permissions or licenses, and that can be useful in starting a business without having to pay the initial set-up costs. In the last few years, I started trading and selling nonprofit organizations, which make great fronts for ... you know."

He didn't say "yakuza." He just made the gesture of a scar running down his face to say it without saying it.

"I'm guessing there's also still a market for established companies for making a backdoor listing. Maybe now more than ever," I said.

His eyes lit up. "Absolutely. Do you know anybody who's looking?"

I felt like we were connecting, but maybe not in the right way. Still, it was good to have a rapport.

A backdoor listing takes place when an unlisted company merges with a listed company (on the stock market) to avoid an initial listing examination, and effectively goes public. Back in 2006, let's say you're a company that makes sex toys that can be activated and manipulated using a smartphone. Let's call your firm Smart Sex Gangu. That's your product—high-tech sex toys. That's not going to get your firm listed on the stock market, but if you can buy up a zombie company with your limited capital, you might have a chance.

Now let's say you buy a firm that made beepers, at a time when beepers were big business. Let's call it Big Beepers, a company that was listed on the Tokyo Stock Exchange Second Section and is now pretty much defunct. You buy it, merge it with Smart Sex Gangu, and now you're a listed company. You can even change the name of the company to something like Big Beeping Smart Sex Gangu. Now you're legitimate. You can get banks to lend you money. That's the advantage of a backdoor listing. For many years, the checks on such listings were nominal at best.

The Tokyo Stock Exchange tends to be very conservative, and its pre-listing checks are very stringent. You need a lot of capital to get listed on either the First or Second Section. But if you smartly utilize a zombie company—in other words, the back door—you have an opening. Guys like Akio Kumagaya certainly could be useful.

Of course, the other use of a backdoor listing is in gaining the confidence and trust of investors to perpetrate large-scale fraud. He was right. His business model wasn't completely dead; it just wasn't going to turn over as much as it had before 2003.

I pulled an envelope full of cash out of my right-hand inner pocket. It was filled with 5,000-yen bills to add bulk, but had a nice amount of 10,000-yen bills at the top and bottom. Altogether, it amounted to 200,000 yen ($2,000). I imagined that would be two months' rent for his dingy office.

I could see he had some reservations. So I tried to put him at ease.

"Before I did this work, I was a journalist. And I carry that ethic with me now. You're a source. What you tell me stays with me, and I'll never tell anyone we've spoken, unless you give me permission. And even then, I'd probably keep your name to myself. I just need to know who you sold the company to—not the name on the registration, but who really owns the company that bought the firm from you."

I put the envelope on the table, just out of his reach, with my fingers on the edges of it.

"Can you promise me I will stay out of your report?"

"Yes, I can. I promise I will keep you out of the report. I just need to know who bought the firm after you."

He seemed convinced. He wrote a name on a pink square Post-it note on top of his desk, and then pulled it off and handed it to me. I looked at it, and then tore it up and tossed it in the trash can next to his desk.

"Thank you."

"Rachi-gumi," he said. "Do you know them?"

I nodded. I did indeed. They were a third-tier group in the Yamaguchi-gumi. The second-tier group above them had offices in the Shizuoka prefecture.

"Do you know anything about a firm called Blue Mountain?" I said.

I pushed the envelope over to him. I could have waited for him to give me an answer about Blue Mountain, but I wanted to make a show of faith.

He rubbed his chin furiously, as if it would somehow fire up his brain and he could pull up information about the company. There was a spark, but the engine didn't seem to be starting.

"Can you give me anything else?"

I showed him printed materials with the company name

and their address that I'd acquired during the job. He went into the back room by a side door near his desk. In the room there were shelves and shelves of notebooks, phone books, company rosters, and files. He came back ten minutes later with a fat notebook. He'd already marked a page with a pink Post-it.

He opened the book and showed me a page. "This address used to be the office of a Mio-gumi front company. Different name. Probably serving the same purpose. That's all I know."

I bowed deeply in thanks. I gestured to the back room full of notebooks and bound printed materials.

"What's all that?"

"*Meibo*. Directories, some corporate, some criminal. That's my side business. I'm a *meiboya*. Names, phone numbers, customer lists. All that information is very valuable."

I didn't say what I was thinking. That information was especially valuable if you were running frauds that preyed upon the elderly. But in order to convince grandpa or grandma that you were their grandson and in desperate need of financial aid, you had to have their name and phone number first.

Kumagaya must have known that, of course. Yet who was I to judge? He sold information. It wasn't his job to know what his customers later did with that data. I briefly glanced at the back of the room. There was an employee directory for the *Asahi Shimbun*. It looked old. I wondered if I still had my *Yomiuri* phonebook, and realized I did. But that wasn't something I would sell to him. That seemed like bad karma and a bad idea. The people in that book were my colleagues. Yet I would be lying if I said the thought didn't cross my mind for a nanosecond.

"Do you have a list of the front companies operating in Tokyo?" I said. That would be valuable, I thought.

"I have one for the Kanagawa prefecture. Those kinds of directories are only put together by the police, you know. You'd have to be a pretty stupid yakuza to make a list of your front companies."

"People are stupid in every walk of life. And people like to track who's who in this world. The police and the yakuza are no exception, even if it's a stupid thing to do," I countered.

He chuckled.

"I'll keep my eye out. Maybe we can do business?"

"I definitely think we could."

I asked if I could take one of the weekly magazines he had laying on his desk, so I could have something to read on my way back.

"Help yourself," he said.

I did.

Blue Mountain was located in a rental office building in Shinjuku Ward, Nishi-Shinjuku, two minutes away from Nishi-Shinjuku Station on the Marunouchi line—the red subway line. I knew that station well because it was the closest station to the Shinjuku Police Headquarters. I had covered the fourth district, which included Shinjuku and Kabukicho, from 1999 to 2001, and spent a lot of time in that police station. There was a police reporter press club on the upper floors where all the newspaper reporters shared spaces and had desks. There was also a large tatami room in the back with plenty of futons so you could take a nap during the day—or at the end of a drunken night before getting up for work. I was tempted to just drop by the club, but I had to remind myself I was no longer a reporter and that those privileges were no longer mine.

Most of the building was filled with small offices for rent. There was a common space on one of the floors with meeting rooms, color printers, and vending machines. Blue Mountain, which was a coffee importer, according to its company registration, was on the fifth floor, office 509. I had picked up a pamphlet at the entrance, so I knew that 509 was one of their bigger offices, but even then the rent was less than $1,200 a month. It was a reasonable fee for a location in that area. People were probably really paying for the prestigious address more than the services. As I'd expected, the guys in 509 had installed a camera above their door. I had a package with me, and pretended to be looking for the right apartment.

The company name, Blue Mountain, was printed on a label and slapped on the company door. The detritus of past labels were still visible on the door. One of them, mostly faded and half-scraped away, read Nakatomi Investments. Not Nakatomi Holdings, but Nakatomi Investments. Yep.

I thought about knocking on the door to see who would come out, and then I decided it wasn't worth the risk. There was no place to hang out where I could wait and see who emerged from the offices. As I was considering what to do next, the door of the office opened and out walked a very tall man, with long jet-black hair, who looked like he had been crammed into a black suit one size too small for him. He was jabbering away on the cellphone he held next to his ear while half-running toward the elevator door. He looked like a yakuza enforcer from Central Casting. I had to assume that, given the police had designated this place an organized crime front company two years previously, it still was one.

The mailboxes in the building were inaccessible, so I left the place, took a ten-minute walk, and went to a café I used to love in Kabukicho and wrote up my report there. I added a few details that had come to light from crunching numbers and data.

When you have a job to do as a private eye and a limited amount of time to do it, in your final report you have to acknowledge what you do know, don't know, and what you suspect. It's color-coding the report in a way: black, white, gray. There was some dark gray data for this one.

There was a possibility that one of the board members who

had resigned in 2005 had been arrested for fraud in 1996. I had done a newspaper/magazine database search of all board members, and there was an exact match for one of them. He had the same name as an individual who had been caught selling fake shares in a listed company, but without knowing more about the man listed on the corporate registration, including his age, I couldn't be sure they were the same person. There were no interviews or articles in Japanese mentioning any of the current board members.

Michiel and I went through the draft report together at my place, comparing numbers to the source materials, and making sure that we had the dates written down correctly. She convinced me to pull some punches in my phrasing.

"Jake, it sounds like you're telling the client, 'Listen, shitheads, stay the fuck away from these people. Are you fucking crazy?' Which you probably do want to tell them. But there's a nicer way to say that."

"As in?"

"Let me write it."

The conclusion was simple:

Nakatomi Holdings seems extremely suspect due to possibly being a front company for the Yamaguchi-gumi, and certainly is, at the very least, involved in business transactions with a Yamaguchi-gumi front company. The lack of information about the firm, and the false claims the company makes on its websites and materials about its history, are alarming.

The firm seems to be targeting foreign investors and using a false history to instill confidence and get them to invest in what they claim is a successful hedge fund with a high return.

There is no evidence to suggest they have ever made a successful business venture.

The board members may have included convicted

criminals. Therefore, any business with the target appears extremely risky and should be avoided.

Just so you know: "should be avoided" is due diligence code for "Stay the fuck away."

Very rarely do you know if a firm is black or white. It would be great if you could always know what a company is really up to, but you can't always know that. There was a slim possibility that Nakatomi Holdings was a legitimate company that just appeared to be as dodgy as hell. I was comfortable with the conclusion I'd reached, and there wasn't time to do more.

I emailed the final report to Tony that afternoon. He was very satisfied with the work, telling me over the phone, "Good job, Kolchak. I think the client might freak." He sent them the report that evening.

Tony was right: the client completely freaked out. After a series of frantic phone calls that night, I agreed to meet our client once more the next day. This time, I met him in the lobby of the Okura Hotel, where we sat in a corner and I briefed him.

I didn't know how deeply involved his firm was with Nakatomi, or if he was already in bed with the firm, but he looked like he hadn't slept at all. Maybe the company had already entrusted a large sum of money to this iffy enterprise. He had seemingly slept in his pinstriped shirt, and, unlike the last time we met, his glasses looked smudged with fingerprints.

I had to take him through the report document by document, and explained the process of discovery, because there are many things, as a rule, that I don't and can't put down on paper. I gave him the original of the firm's brochure as well. I'd already made a PDF copy of it.

When I was done, he asked me if I had any advice.

"Well," I drawled in my best Missouri accent, "the slogan of Nakatomi Holdings is, as you can see in their pamphlet, 'Where

Your Financial Future Is Made Today.' I'd say that today your company's financial future looks pretty shitty."

He didn't laugh. In as few words as possible, he told me that his firm had already signed an expensive consulting contract with Nakatomi. I asked him if their contract with the firm had an organized crime exclusionary clause.

It did not.

I sighed.

I gave him the number and email of ex-prosecutor Toshiro Igari. "You're going to need this guy. When you're dealing with yakuza, or ex-yakuza, this is the guy you call."

I'd never have guessed that, a few years later, I'd find myself in the same position, in trouble with a very unsavory yakuza, and knocking on the door of Igari, asking for his help.

CHAPTER SIX

Occupational hazards

Sometimes you love your job even when you know it might kill you. If you spend too much time reporting on the yakuza or uncovering their front companies, it's easy to forget that violence is an integral part of their culture. Familiarity breeds carelessness. It took a kick in the head for me to remember that no matter how polite, or smart, or friendly some of my underworld contacts were, if they were yakuza, they were always going to be like human IEDs (improvised explosive devices). There is no way to predict what will cause them to explode. I stepped on a landmine in 2010, and I still carry the scar tissue.

I was kicked in the head, by a former yakuza executive, in late January 2010. I think that was when things started to go wrong on the temporal level.

It was bound to happen. If you lie down with dogs, you wake up with fleas. Reporting on the underworld means you will have to deal with brute force, and you may switch from being the observer and the chronicler of events to becoming a victim yourself.

I had an interview with a former member of a Kyushu gang, now retired and working as a nurse—as an act of atonement perhaps. He explained the rationale of his job to me nonchalantly one afternoon. This is what he told me over the course of our very long conversation.

"In general, we don't kill the people in our neighborhood, because that would alienate people and we wouldn't be able to earn any money that way. We are in the business of endurance and enduring pain, as well as inflicting pain, but everything we do is very calculated. Yakuza people come to the yakuza to do things they want to do but cannot. They either don't know how to do it or they are afraid to do it because they are afraid of the repercussions if they do it. Smart yakuza are into financial fraud, but things are different for most of us. Violence is what we sell, it is what we offer; no violence, you just have a bunch of misfits who can't do anything.

"Committing an act of violence requires complex calculations. We are selling violent services, but we also have to consider the costs of providing those services. Let's say someone comes to me and requests that someone be kidnapped, beaten up, and taught a lesson. Maybe they want someone's arm chopped off. They will pay me a certain amount of money for that. Then, if I get caught, which is likely to happen, what crime would I be charged with? Well, we're talking then about crimes of confinement, imprisonment, and bodily harm. You could easily get six years in prison for that. That's not six years of sitting on your ass; that's six years of hard labor. But they're offering 50 million yen. Man, that's a lot of cash. You're basically getting paid 9 million yen ($90,000) a year, for six years, for one crime, when you do the math.

"Consider what the value of an entire year of your life is to you. What about six years in prison? Is the crime worth the time?

"The cost evaluation is also affected by who's asking you to do it. Is it your older brother in the organization? Or is it your *oyabun* (boss)? If your *oyabun* asks you to do it, it's not about the value of your services anymore, it's about your duty. In the old days, if you did it for the organization, they took care of you. You got a bonus and promotion when you got out.

"If you're being asked to do something violent by someone

outside of the organization, then it really becomes a question of which is the best way for both of you to win. Remember, you're not trying to get caught when you agree to perform a particularly violent act or service. When someone hired me to kidnap a man who defrauded them and beat some remorse into him, I didn't plan on getting caught and I didn't get caught. But before you take that deal, think of the worst-case scenario. The worst-case scenario is you get caught and go to jail. Is it worth it then? There's also the worst-case scenario where you accidentally kill someone while trying to beat some sense into them. If you end up getting hung, no amount of money is going to help you. But we're professionals, and we know how much beating is enough to permanently hurt or kill someone, and we stop way before that. Still, anything can go wrong."

I had forgotten that part. Things go wrong. You're dealing with violent people.

Even if there wasn't deliberate violence, anything could go wrong. I had grown overconfident and reckless. I should have been more careful, but then again, perhaps it was an unavoidable occupational hazard.

Here's how it happened.

I had plans to visit Fumio Akiyama (not his real name), a former yakuza underboss. I wanted to interview him. He was a smart man. At one point in time, he was one of the editors of a yakuza news service, for subscribers only, that the Yamaguchi-gumi gave its tacit approval to. The customer base was strictly limited and I had to ask him to secretly forward the newsletter to me. He began to really enjoy writing up stories and analyses of the latest arrests, power struggles, and troubles in the underworld.

Akiyama had been a low-ranking member of a Yamaguchi-gumi second-tier group when I met him in 1999. In the Japanese underworld, he had risen up the ranks before being culled in an event referred to as the "Goto Shock" in late October 2008.

The financial world had what is called in Japan the "Lehman Shock" in 2008, but the Japanese underworld experienced the Goto Shock the same year; it was a large-scale purge of some of the top bosses in the Yamaguchi-gumi.

In mid-October 2008, while the Yamaguchi-gumi executives were debating whether or not to banish Tadamasa Goto from the organization, a group of yakuza bosses sent a letter of protest to HQ. The letter opposed Goto's expulsion and lodged a litany of other complaints. The second-in-command of the 40,000-member organization, Kiyoshi Takayama, responded with a massive purge on October 20. The organization permanently expelled two top-tier bosses, removed five from their rosters, and suspended three others from work. The purge was bloodless, but tensions were high.

Those too close to Goto or who violently opposed his expulsion from the organization were sidelined or removed. It was rumored that Goto had planned to overthrow the organization in a coup, which was part of the reason he was expelled. One more nail in his coffin was his betrayal of the organization to get a new liver in the U.S.

As with many former yakuza, Akiyama had left or been forced out of the group during the Goto Shock, but kept in touch with the organization. He ran a small real estate business out of an office in Shinjuku close to the south exit. He had always had meth issues, and maybe that was part of the reason he was expelled.

When I went to his office, I asked permission to quote him in a book I was working on, *The Last Yakuza*, and permission to share some delicate information he had given me with a third party.

Though it was a formality, I figured it couldn't hurt to ask. Well, I was very wrong about that. Sometimes asking the wrong questions can get you seriously hurt.

He opened the door to his office as soon as I knocked and let me in. There was a reception area and his personal office was behind it. There was a wooden cabinet on the left, a couch near the wall, and a small white sofa to sit on. There was a low wooden table with a crystal ashtray and a crystal jar full of cigarettes and a fat crystal lighter between us. Under the table there were stacks of magazines—weekly magazines, yakuza fanzines, some porno, some business magazines. The ashtray overflowed with cigarettes. The small trash can in the corner of the room was full of empty Coca-Cola cans.

Akiyama looked more like a teacher than a yakuza. He wore a navy blue suit, with a red-and-white necktie, and had a slightly receding hairline. His tiny eyes seemed even smaller because he wore thick frameless glasses. His brown loafers were polished and shiny, but they had a couple of holes. I assumed these were from cigarette ash.

He offered me a Coca-Cola from the mini-fridge at the back of the room, which I gladly accepted and took a sip. He gulped his down like a man in a desert finding a glass of water, then opened another.

He asked, "What can I do for you today, Jake? Or rather, do you have some info on a good piece of property for me?"

Akiyama specialized in problem real estate. When a person dies in Japan, or is murdered at a location, the real estate agent must inform the customer. This reduces the value of the real estate or makes it nearly impossible to rent or sell. Akiyama had a knack for buying up troublesome properties and working around the law to unload them for a greater price than he paid. If there was a murder or suicide on my beat, I would send him the address of the crime scene so he could do his thing. I got information back in return.

"Well," I replied, "I am writing a book about the yakuza's postwar history, to be called *The Last Yakuza*, and I'd like to interview you for it and use your real name if it is possible to do so."

He nodded while listening, drinking his Coke. He kept scratching his arms as I explained what I was working on.

I then said something that may have been the trigger: "There was something you once told me about Tadamasa Goto and I promised not to tell anyone else. While I have respected that promise, I would like your permission to share it with someone who should know about it. I know she will not share it with anyone else. I have my reasons for telling her."

A long silence followed, and then without a word, he reached out and grabbed my shirt, slamming me into the low table. When I tried to roll off the table, he kicked me once or twice in the head with the heel of his shoes—and he didn't miss. I felt a blast of pain. Then, all I could see was black. He landed another kick on my back, yelling, "I'll kill you."

I rolled off the table and grabbed the crystal lighter as I went. I saw him over me and threw the lighter at his head. I hit him square in the face, which was a miracle; I'm horrible at pitching.

The crystal lighter was heavy and had a jagged-edge design. I figured it was like getting a brick thrown into your face.

He fell off the table and onto the couch clutching his face. He was screaming something at me now, but I wasn't really paying attention.

I was up and he was down. I grabbed his leg with one hand and with my other hand I smashed his knee with the crystal ashtray. Cigarette butts spilled all over the floor. And I did it again and again, in a cloud of ash, until I heard something pop.

He tried to stand up, but fell over. He only had one working knee now. He grabbed my arm and dug his nails into it, but I hit him in the face with the ashtray, and he let go.

I'm not a good fighter, but I know that someone with only one knee isn't going to be able to catch up with you if you run away. Over and over, he said, "Traitor, traitor, traitor." I suppose I could have asked for clarification, but I wasn't in the mood to talk. I instinctively grabbed his cellphone when it fell out of his jacket during the fight. For leverage. For information. Or maybe it's just because I'm a bit of a data hoarder. I didn't feel like sticking around. I couldn't focus my eyes properly, and things sounded strange. Like I was hearing them from the room next door.

There isn't a great Japanese equivalent for "What the fuck?" except maybe "*nani nan dayo*"—meaning "What is this?"—and that's all I could think of saying. Akiyama was blabbering something now and making strange noises. I had a headache.

"Akiyama, shut up," I told him.

Rather than screaming in pain, he had his eyes closed and was muttering obsessively under his breath. I was tempted to kick his knee to get his attention. As he stared at the ceiling, his leg hung funny, the good one hooked on the top of the couch.

"Here's the deal," I told him, "I'm going to call an ambulance for you. You're going to say you were attacked and robbed—you don't know who it was, but he looked Korean."

The police always ask this when a foreigner is assaulted—and maybe they ask the same questions to Japanese citizens as well.

They'll ask you, *Did he look Korean?*

Why? Because many cops are racists. If Akiyama said what I told him to say, he'd be giving them what they wanted and they might not ask probing questions.

I continued, "I'm going to get the fuck out of here. If you name me, if you rat me out, not only will I say it was self-defense, but I'll also tell them you tried to kill me and they should give you a piss test because you're high on meth."

I said this in my very serious low-octave-I-am-speaking-Japanese voice. There are linguistic cultural stereotypes here that I have learned. Cute women are supposed to speak with lilting, high voices and serious men are supposed to speak in deep, low voices. I was also trying very hard not to black out. I restated my proposition.

"I'm going to call you an ambulance. If you don't want me to tell the dogs [cops] that you're high on meth—which I suspect is the case—then you tell them the cover story I just fed you, you stupid asshole."

He must have been paying attention. The threat of telling the cops about his meth problem made him spew out a stream of curses in Japanese that would delight any linguist studying the language, which some say has no swear words. They are wrong.

I left the office and went close to the station to find a payphone. I called the fire department, dialing 119, and told them I'd heard a quarrel in Akiyama's office and screams. I also knew the fire department would contact the police. When they asked for my name, I hung up.

My head hurt so badly that I decided to grab a taxi home. I should have gone to see a doctor immediately, but I wasn't thinking straight.

You might ask, why didn't I call the police?

Because Akiyama was and still is a source. You can't turn your sources over to the police. I was pretty sure that he was as high as a kite.

I didn't think it was really anything personal. After doing some research, I was pretty much convinced that he was in the middle of a meth-induced psychosis. I just happened to be there at the wrong time. It was like being hit by lightning. You can't really blame the lightning.

———

From a mutual friend, I found out which hospital Akiyama was taken to and how he was doing. They had to perform surgery on his knee and leg, and on his nose. He was going to be in the hospital for a while. Fortunately, the cops didn't bother to check his urine or blood for drugs. He was treated like a robbery victim.

I went to visit him in the hospital. He was sheepish and apologetic.

"What happened?" I asked him.

"I'm sorry. Things were crazy. You know. I thought you were out to get me. That you were setting me up."

"Yeah, okay, but why? Is it what I asked?"

"I don't remember," he said. "I don't remember much of last week. Because too much of that," he said, making the gesture of injecting himself with methamphetamines.

"I'm sorry about your knee," I said.

"It's alright. Thanks for not turning me in to the cops. I appreciate that. How are you?"

"My head hurts a lot. You kicked it twice."

"Is that so? I'm sorry. Have you seen a doctor?"

"No."

"You should see one. Head injuries are bad news."

The advice was offered in a strangely detached tone, as if I was telling him about being attacked by someone else. We shook hands. We've never discussed "the incident" after that.

He still walks with a limp; I carry around my wounds where they can't be seen.

The beating did some damage to my temporal lobe. My sense of chronology has never been the same. Events from the past seem very recent. I have flashbacks to events long since finished with all the emotional memory and feelings that I had at that time. It makes it a little hard to move on with life.

Because you don't really forget. The past rarely stays the

past. I can only explain it by rephrasing the words of the Teacher in the Book of Ecclesiastes:

> What has been is still happening now
> What has been will be again and be as it is,
> just as it was
> There is nothing new
> Under the Empire of The Sun.

Over and over, I get this feeling that there is nothing happening that hasn't happened before in this world and in my own life.

That doesn't mean it's not worth doing again. And, sometimes, being in touch with your past is useful in the future.

CHAPTER SEVEN

Pachinko wonderland

Pachinko parlors dot the landscape of Japan like giant neon-covered supermarkets. They are found near the exits of almost every major train or subway station. In the countryside, sometimes they are in the middle of rice fields, with nothing else nearby but large parking lots full of Japanese cars. You will see them along every major highway and while the numbers of pachinko parlors decline every year, they still remain, as of 2020, an $18 billion industry with 11 million players. Much of my reporting life has revolved around the peripheral dark side of the pachinko industry.

A Ministry of Health, Labor, and Welfare study found 4.8 percent of the population—over 5 million people—were gambling addicts, many of them pachinko junkies. Many addicts borrow money from consumer loan outfits or illegal loan sharks to feed their habit.

There is a hypnotic quality to the game that can keep people playing for hours at a time. Since the late 1990s there have been repeated reports of children dying while their parents were immersed in pachinko. Parents used to leave their kids in cars in pachinko parking lots for several hours in the summer heat. They'd die of heat stroke. Nowadays, every pachinko parlor has a sign forbidding parents from leaving their children in cars while they play, and employees regularly check to make sure. Even so, there is no end to cases of parents neglecting their children in order to spend a few brain-numbing hours playing vertical pinball.

There is a plethora of varied scandals and crimes revolving around the pachinko business. The gift-exchange shops have always been targets for bandits; there is a lot of cash to be stolen from them if you come at the right time. In the Saitama prefecture, during the 1990s, Sumiyoshi-kai gangsters forged receipts from large pachinko parlors and used them to gain cash from the exchange centers. There were bands of professional thieves specializing in swindling pachinko parlors, called *goto-shi*. *Goto-shi* was a term that was an anagram from the word for "a job" in Japanese: *shigoto*.

Ripping off pachinko parlors was a profession, after all.

The *goto-shi* sometimes worked together with rogue employees to replace components in pachinko machines with altered ROMs to ensure that the machines would strike the jackpot and then the "thieves" would score from the machines in broad daylight.

Yakuza also ran pachinko fan magazines and dubious information services that promised to give players the upper hand in their efforts to beat the machines. One such firm, Ryōzanpaku, became a platform for massive stock market manipulation.

Loan sharks proliferated in the areas next to pachinko parlors. The parlors themselves can invite sketchy behavior as well: there are pachinko players who steal the balls from other customers, sex workers walking the aisles or the vicinity, looking for a customer who has hit the jackpot. Frustrated players sometimes pour coffee into the machines, destroying them in a fit of rage.

And sometimes, the pachinko parlor owners would break the laws as well, by installing altered computer chips into the machines, which would give bigger and more frequent payoffs, which would attract more customers and raise revenues. Yep, letting customers win more can be a losing strategy under Japanese law.

The whole business seemed seedy to me, but not much more seedy than the glittering gambling palaces and casinos in Las Vegas, designed with no windows and no clocks, so you lose track of time, your judgment, and your money.

I never would have guessed that I would end up making a great deal of money myself from the pachinko industry—for one assignment from one of my better clients.

A former spook named William Oldman was my point of contact for the large investment fund that hired me to clean up their portfolio. He was the head of corporate security. When Oldman asked me to investigate one pachinko parlor chain in question, the net worth of the industry was nearly $30 billion.

Pachinko is sometimes called "vertical pinball," but that's a little bit like explaining chess as a more complicated version of checkers. Pachinko in Japan isn't just a game; it's a pastime, it's a culture to itself, and it is a colossal business.

If you've never played pachinko, it's a little hard to imagine how it works. In a sense, it does resemble a vertical pinball machine. But there are dozens of tiny M&M candy-sized balls at play at any one time and there are no mechanical flippers. In the old days, if you were lucky or skilled enough to get the balls into the pay-off holes at the right time, in the right sequence, you were rewarded with an explosion of metal balls, which you would put into buckets and then take to the prize counter to claim your spoils.

At the prize counter, often there would be something that appeared to be worthless, but with a heavy price tag attached. The smart customer would pick that prize, take it around the corner to a "gift exchange" shop and be paid for it in cash.

The first time I ever played pachinko, I lucked out. I walked into a Heiwa pachinko parlor in Ikebukuro, put in my money—when you could still play the game with actual cash—and tried my hand. Bright light filled the room and rows of machines faced each other, loudly bleeping and smashing metal balls together in a way that gave the place a science fiction feel. Noisy, garish, and flashy—I felt like I might have an epileptic seizure.

The game machine was illustrated with a *tanuki* (a Japanese raccoon dog) and had a red circular handle at the bottom. When you turned it, a stream of silver metal balls would shoot up and fall down toward the bottom, some slowed down by the nails on the board—others landing in hotspots to be spat back up again. There was very little you could do to control the balls once you had released them.

God knows how, but I hit the jackpot also known as *ren-chan* or "fever" by some at the time. When the machine started puking out metal balls, I didn't know what to do and they almost overflowed onto the floor, but helpful staff, in suits that made them look like carnival barkers, quickly brought over rectangular buckets to catch the overflow.

After I had several buckets full of balls, I was taken to the gift center. There was nothing that seemed very appealing, but a kindly old man dressed in a shabby suit explained the system to me.

I ended up getting a giant stuffed frog, took it to the gift exchange shop on the corner, which was little more than a small window in a nondescript building, and got 50,000 yen in cash (almost $500).

I vowed to never play pachinko again after that. I know when the odds aren't on my side. I also know that I have an addictive personality. And pachinko is very addictive. It is also not quite illegal. It isn't quite legal, either.

The pachinko industry in Japan is not clearly excluded from

the gambling provisions of the criminal law. Provision 185 in the Japanese criminal code technically bans all gambling for which the gambling establishment can be punished with a fine of up to 500,000 yen ($5,000) or possibly jail time. However, the law also has a loophole that allows for "offering prizes or rewards as part of a one-time entertainment." Thus, in Japan, you can offer a prize to the winner of a bowling tournament, and you can also offer a prize for winning big in pachinko. Admittedly, the only thing pachinko has in common with bowling is that both games use balls.

The Public Morals Law, also known as the Adult Entertainment Laws, categorizes pachinko as a "type seven business." Police have the authority to restrict the value of the prizes and the type of merchandise the pachinko operators can issue at their stores. However, since the 1960s, a "three-party system" has emerged that makes it possible for skilled pachinko players to not just win a prize, but make money. As I've said before, technically, Japan's criminal code bans all gambling.

In practice, pachinko winners take a specially designated prize to a small booth situated close to the pachinko parlor and exchange their prizes for cash, like I had done. Under the provisions of the Public Morals Law, it is considered illegal if this exchange booth then resells prizes directly to the pachinko parlor. It is also held to be illegal if both the exchange booth and pachinko parlor are owned by the same person. It is, however, permissible for the exchange booth to sell prizes on to a third company.

The complicated system contributes to employment in Japan. You need different people to operate the pachinko parlor, the exchange shop, and the gift wholesaler.

The gift exchanges have lots of cash, so they need twenty-four-hour security. This helps give jobs to retired cops. The pachinko parlor actually does "sell" prizes to customers who don't want to cash out their winnings, which helps the supply chain.

And yet the whole scheme is only tacitly accepted now.

For many years, this gray legal area of the pachinko industry made it easy for yakuza to prey upon pachinko parlor owners and extort money from them.

In Tokyo today, almost all of the prize exchange shops are operated by TUC—a consolidation of the industry that was organized by the Tokyo Metropolitan Police Department to push the yakuza out of the industry. This also ensured that the police secured themselves lucrative post-retirement jobs in the industry that they once regulated when they were on duty. The TUC has a number of retired police officers on board. Although it's a taboo to discuss, often veteran police reporters for major newspapers take a job with Pachinko Industry Associations in their media relations division, forming a sort of bridge between the industry, the police, and the media, and in this way help dampen negative coverage in the press.

While the business side of it has become more respectable in recent years, for many Japanese, when they hear the word "pachinko" they think of only three things: gambling, yakuza, and Koreans.

Pachinko doesn't have a savory reputation in Japan—for many reasons—and one of them is that for many years, Korean Japanese residents here with relatives in North Korea have funneled money back to "the Workers' Paradise." Japanese pachinko parlors have long been a source of funding for the criminal enterprise that is the Democratic People's Republic of Korea (DPRK), a menace to Japan and the world.

That was part of the reason Oldman had asked me to look at the new case. The company in question was a small and successful operator of pachinko parlors in the Tokyo area that had come to the fund with a request for a loan to expand operations into Saitama and Chiba. On paper, the company, Wahei Entertainment (a pseudonym), looked good, and it was well managed. It had 1,500 employees and twelve parlors. It was pulling in at least $20 million a year in profits. The company didn't appear to be making payoffs to organized crime, but no one was sure. The question that was of most concern to Oldman was this: was the company and/or its executives sending money to North Korea? If that was the case, it was no deal.

Oldman told me, as he handed me the files, "I've met the vice president of the company, and he struck me as a remarkably upright fellow. I don't quite understand the long history of pachinko parlors here, or the industry, but I do understand why the business unit is hesitant. This company has come to us because Japanese banks are all giving them the cold shoulder. And I don't think that this is based solely on racism. Japanese banks are a lot happier to loan money to the Koreans these days, I hear. Money trumps nationalism."

The problem really appeared to be rumors of a North Korean connection. And the secondary problem was certainly that the owners were the descendants of Koreans who had chosen not to nationalize as Japanese. And the third problem was, of course, that Koreans and yakuza tended to have strange ties.

In fact, 30 percent of the yakuza are Koreans. And to know why that is, you have to know a little history. The first thing you should know is that Japan conquered Korea during its Imperial Expansion and treated the Koreans like shit.

Before the Second World War, the increasing presence of the Japanese settler population in agricultural areas led to a mass exodus of Korean farmers to seek work overseas. Most ethnic Koreans in prewar Japan were farmers from three southern provinces (North and South Gyeongsang and South Jeolla, including Jeju-do), and they engaged in manual and menial work, occupying—along with *burakumin* (Japan's outcaste class) and Okinawans—the lowest tier in the urban market.

It is also arguably true that Korean immigration to the Japanese archipelago was more or less voluntary until wartime mobilization generated enforced migration, *kyōseirenko*, in the 1940s. In the name of eliciting "volunteers," ethnic Japanese and Koreans colluded in the conscription of Koreans to work in factories and mines, which resulted in between 700,000 and 800,000 Koreans being forced to work in Japan between 1939 and 1945.

When the war ended and Korea was liberated from Japanese colonial rule, the question most Koreans in Japan immediately faced was whether to return to Korea or stay in Japan. In fact, the majority—up to three-fourths—repatriated, but some 600,000 remained in Nippon. Most people assume that the majority of those who remained were living in Japan for many years, were pretty much settled (with Japanese-born, Japanese-speaking children), and enjoyed a relatively privileged status compared to the newer immigrants, especially those who came under forced migration after 1940.

The postwar legal status of the Koreans left behind was like a form of purgatory. Although Koreans living in Japan had once been Japanese nationals, the postwar government gradually stripped them of their rights as colonial racism reasserted itself. The Japanese began to refer to them as *zainichi*, and they gradually lost their rights over the next decade.

By December 1945, Korean voting rights were revoked. Things got worse for those left behind. Due to a period of time when Koreans were not under Japanese laws, being treated as "third-party nationals," they had managed to take over the black markets that emerged as the nation rebuilt. In Kanto, Korean yakuza groups such as the Tosei-kai emerged. In Kansai, yakuza groups such as the Yanagawa-gumi rose up and gained power.

The Yamaguchi-gumi learned a lot from the Yanagawa-gumi.

The Yanagawa-gumi went very quickly from running black-market operations to making a business empire. They had their own talent agency. They had a construction company. They also collected money from bars, cabaret, clubs, mahjong parlors, and pachinko parlor prize-buyers.

Bookies for bicycle races, horse races, boat races, and even baseball games all paid them protection fees. If you shined shoes, sold drugs, sang *enka* (the Japanese equivalent of Country and Western, mostly sentimental, ballads), ran a food stall, ran a strip club, or sold pornography, you paid protection money to them. Labor recruiters around train stations and the docks had to pay.

The Yanagawa-gumi itself made money through blackmail, extortion, debt collection, and loan sharking. But even if you were doing that on your own, you still had to pay them a cut.

Pimps had to pay them. Fraudsters gave them a cut. All civil engineering and construction companies paid to work in the area. Every form of entertainment was essentially taxed: baseball, professional wrestling, singing shows, stand-up comedy, boxing matches, street stalls, and ticket vendors. Labor supervision and dispatch companies, gambling dens, bankruptcy liquidation agents, they all paid. Even the flower-sellers and fortune-tellers had to pay *bazen*. Anything that could be found on the street or sold in the area was a source of income, and violence was used if anyone was foolish enough not to pay.

Even before groups like the Yanagawa-gumi rose to power, Japan was already filled with anti-Korean hysteria. This helped foster the 1947 Alien Registration Law, which relegated ethnic Koreans to foreigner status. The 1950 nationality law made patrilineal lines the basis of Japanese citizenship, thus stripping "Korean children" of Japanese mothers of their Japanese nationality. In

1955, all "registered aliens" were forced to be fingerprinted, which was the beginning of a dreaded and demeaning practice that still existed when I first arrived in Japan. Ethnic Koreans were even excluded from the rights enshrined for non-nationals in Japan's postwar constitution; it would take decades of legal challenges and political struggles starting in the 1970s to restore many of those rights.

The Koreans in Japan were barred from all public-sector jobs, and were also excluded de facto from prestigious private-sector employment. The majority of ethnic Koreans had worked in mining, construction, and factory jobs before 1945, but they were expelled from "Japanese" jobs after 1945. Ethnic Koreans therefore were forced to engage in illegal or marginal economic activities, ranging from illegal alcohol production to prostitution to scrap recycling. The Koreans who remained behind became second-class citizens. And that left them few job opportunities.

And so Koreans went into the Korean barbecue business (*yakiniku*), sex work, and loan-sharking. Just like there was a Jewish mafia once upon a time in American history, when Jews were considered unwelcome others, there were Korean mafia groups. Many Koreans also joined Japanese mafia groups. In the 1950s, the yakuza became the temple of last resort for those who didn't fit neatly into the postwar landscape—and those who might not have fit in well before. Japan's outcast class, the *burakumin*, were also welcomed by the yakuza. The yakuza were a meritocracy. If you had loyalty, guts, and drive, you were welcome. The Koreans faced discrimination everywhere, except from the yakuza. Their hungry spirit and toughness were valued by the gangs.

Meanwhile, pachinko also became an industry where Koreans flourished, although it was considered a shady business from the start.

One of the most important reasons Korean Japanese took

control of that market was that they stuck with the business when times got hard. In 1954, a new type of pachinko machine was introduced known as "the machine gun," because it increased the number of pachinko balls that could be shot into the machine at once, sparking a huge pachinko boom, raising the number of parlors to roughly 40,000 nationwide. However, the machines were banned around 1955 by the Japanese government for "encouraging gambling," and by 1956 the number of parlors had fallen to below 10,000. Most of those who stayed in the business were Korean Japanese.

Sometimes, it pays to be the last man standing. By perseverance and hard work, the Koreans managed to make the pachinko industry their cash cow. And who can blame them?

Oldman made a point of telling me that I would have an extra budget for this particular project.

"Think of this as a research effort and not just due diligence. The pachinko industry is a lucrative one, and we would like to invest in it and work with other companies within the industry. But we need context, and we need to understand what the perils are, what the pitfalls are, and how to avoid them."

I was told to take my time, to reach out to many different sources, and to compile a comprehensive report, not just limited to this one case. Over the years, as a reporter, I'd covered many cases involving the Korean Japanese community and crimes revolving around pachinko, but I'd never really studied the whole picture. I was glad to do it, and, what was more, I'd be paid to do it.

CHAPTER EIGHT

Pachinko 101

The first pachinko parlors had humble beginnings in Nagoya in 1948, but had expanded to a scale making it comparable to the casino industry in the United States. In addition, the typical pachinko customer is estimated to put in four times the amount of money as the American casino customer. According to the White Paper on Leisure 2004 compiled by the Japan Productivity Center for Socio-Economic Development, the pachinko market turned over 29.634 trillion yen in 2003. That was the significance of the industry at the time I was first approached to look at it.

Compare that to the figures for horse racing, which made 3 trillion yen, cycling 1 trillion yen, boat racing 1.1 trillion yen, and the lottery 1 trillion yen, meaning the pachinko industry surpassed all other forms of gambling combined. There were good odds of making money investing in that business.

Even as an individual industry it is massive. The automobile industry, including parts, made 41 trillion yen back in 2003, and all forms of health care added up to 31 trillion yen. Pachinko is sneered upon by the upper echelons of Japanese society, but it doesn't change the fact that it was one of the biggest industries, in line with cars and health care. And in 2007, before the iPhone, it was one way for the ubiquitous Japanese salaryman to blow off steam.

The 30 trillion-yen market came from the 6,000 pachinko parlors nationwide. In 2003, 17.4 million customers were spending an average of 112,800 yen playing pachinko, resulting in each pachinko parlor making an average monthly profit of 166 million yen and an annual profit of 2 billion yen. No other industry was making such an enormous profit per store.

No wonder Japan resisted casinos—it already had a casino industry of its own. And pachinko machines had evolved as well. There were pachinko-slot machines now (*pachi-slo*), which seemed like the gambling equivalent of a speedball (heroin and cocaine), more exciting and more addictive.

Many people seek a piece of this 30 trillion-yen pie. The yakuza had been skimming protection money from the shops for decades. The shop owners couldn't do much about this, because they knew they were operating nearly illegal gambling dens. A pachinko parlor owner in Saitama had told me that getting rid of the yakuza had been a nightmare and that it was only after 1992, when the first anti–organized crime laws went on the books, that the police even seemed to give a fuck.

Not only would the local yakuza demand protection money, but they were also sore losers—prone to kick and punch the equipment when they lost, which could ruin an expensive machine. It was considered a worthy investment to pay the yakuza to make sure that they and other yakuza customers didn't frequent the establishments.

Until the mid-1990s, Japan's National Police Agency, which had allowed the industry to exist in a legal gray zone for many years, decided to crack down hard. They were going to help the businesses get rid of the yakuza—and, in return, all they wanted was assurance that the pachinko parlors would offer well-paid retirement positions to select police officers.

While the yakuza have mostly been replaced, the penchant for tax evasion by pachinko parlors has not withered over time. Especially if the parlors are run by North Korean Japanese.

Police sources note: "North Korean–owned parlors in particular feel that rather than paying the Japanese government taxes, they prefer handing over the money to their own government. Although there is high risk in this industry because the police always have an eye on it, its long tradition as the worst industry in tax evasion will not go away easily."

Life as a Korean in Japan has never been easy, and after the war the residents created a support group for themselves that eventually grew into two different divisions: one allied with North Korea, and the other with South Korea.

The Korean war split apart the Korean diaspora in Japan just like it did in Korea itself.

Postwar ethnic Korean organizations arose to combat discrimination, aid fellow brothers and sisters, and engage in politics—like the anti-defamation league for the Jews in the United States. After the end of the war, The League of Resident Koreans in Japan (*zainihonchōsenjinrenmei*), sometimes abbreviated as Chōren, was established. Chōren functioned as a de facto government for Koreans in Japan, collecting taxes, dispensing welfare, and even trying criminals during the period when Japan's government was in chaos. The league had been formed in October 1945, and quickly leaned toward support for North Korea. Initially, its major goals were the repatriation of all Koreans and the teaching of Korean to Korean children in Japan as part of their preparation for repatriation.

Reflecting the Cold War in general and the division of the Koreas in particular, Chōren didn't achieve a united front among ethnic Koreans in Japan. Those unhappy with the communist leanings of the Chōren formed a right-to-center group in 1946, the South Korea–affiliated Korean Residents Union in Japan (*zainippondaikanmindan*), which is now known as Mindan. Mindan's expectation was that Koreans would soon repatriate and, unlike Chōren, it assiduously avoided intervention in Japanese politics, aligned itself with South Korea, and was broadly pro-Japanese and pro-U.S. because of South Korea's pro-U.S. stance.

The outbreak of the Korean War deepened the divided allegiances and oriented ethnic Koreans to homeland politics. In 1955, Chōren evolved into the current General Association of Resident Koreans in Japan (*zainihonchōsenjinsōrengōkai*), usually called Sōren, Chosōren, or Chongryun.

Homeland orientation was the foundation of Sōren ideology, but the organization provided support for ethnic Koreans living and working in Japan. Its two critical pillars were finance and education. At a time when Japanese banks would almost never lend to ethnic Koreans, Chōgin Bank, as Sōren's financial arm, filled a critical need.

There's no question that the Sōren was and is a money-making machine for North Korea. Katsuei Hirasawa, a parliamentarian and former National Police Agency high-ranking officer, discusses this in no uncertain terms, and with surprising empathy, in his book, *A Police Bureaucrat Looks at Japan's Police.*

Hirasawa notes that those (residing in Japan) who have family or relatives remaining in North Korea cannot disobey the orders (from Sōren) to "send money back to the fatherland." It's because their loved ones are essentially hostages. In the past, individuals in the pachinko business who donated more than $1 million were given a merit badge, and their names were published in a magazine as individuals who had contributed to the fatherland. Sōren is essentially a branch of the North Korean government, according to former officers of the organization.

The tax authorities in Japan have been reluctant to collect money from pachinko parlors connected to North Korea.

Once, when a branch office of the National Tax Agency raided a pachinko parlor, Sōren gathered an army of protestors and harangued them. The National Tax Agency was greatly intimidated by this incident.

It was well known that the authorities hesitated to bother the North Korean–affiliated pachinko parlors after this. The Sōren leaders used this to argue that the money saved in not paying taxes to the Japanese government was due to the organization's efforts, and thus the pachinko parlors should kick some money back to the homeland in thanks.

While Mindan and Sōren provided financial assistance to the Koreans in Japan, ethnic education was even more significant. Sōren ideology followed the North Korean brand of communist nationalism and promised repatriation for all *zainichi*. Meanwhile, the South Korean–backed Mindan also set up their own banking institutions and school systems.

It was important to understand the differences between the two, because the CEO of Wahei Entertainment was considered to have been well connected to the Sōren group. When you considered the U.S. and Japanese rules about doing business with North Korea, that association alone could be enough to give the request for a loan a fat thumbs-down.

I met with a corporate investigator from Teikoku Databank, and got hold of a copy of their report on the company. It gave the firm a C+, and noted that the president of the firm, Mr Lee, had been born in Korea and had come to Japan when he was ten years old. He had little more than a high-school education. He liked to play golf. (It seems that every CEO in Japan likes to play golf, even if he doesn't.) There was no mention of any ties to Sōren, but there was a note that Mr Lee had gained South Korean citizenship—date unknown.

If he indeed had Korean citizenship and was also a member of Mindan, that would pretty much exclude him from the ranks of Koreans with North Korea ties, I thought. I knew where I could ask about his Mindan connections, if he had any at all.

CHAPTER NINE

The world according to Mr Lee

I called up Haeng-Yi Kim, who usually went by his Japanese name, Kosuke Kaneda. Like many Koreans in Japan, he used an alias. For Koreans in Japan who wanted to avoid racial discrimination and harassment, or simply wished to fit in better, a Japanese name was indispensable. Kaneda's father ran a pachinko parlor in Saitama, and Kaneda was supposed to take over the firm for him someday. I had gotten to know him while working on a story in the late 1990s, while I was still at the *Yomiuri Shimbun*. From 1997 to 1999, I had doggedly pursued the story of Saitama Shogin, a bank that was a part of a financial network for Korean Japanese, but mostly for Korean Japanese with ties to South Korea or Mindan. The bank had gone under in 1999. Shogin ran its own separate banking systems, but had run into tough times after Japan's economic bubble collapsed.

In the course of working that story, it became apparent to me that Saitama Shogin had failed because of bad loans to dubious entities, including to an Inagawa-kai–backed construction company. It had taken a lot of investigative work to prove what had happened, and the Korean community seemed grateful that our newspaper—mostly me and another reporter—had pursued the case, in some ways forcing the Saitama Police to take action.

In May 2002, the former head of the credit union was

sentenced to thirty-eight months in prison for causing financial damage to the firm by engaging in negligent lending practices.

I really hadn't spoken to Kim/Kaneda since the verdict, but he remembered me. I explained what I wanted without going into too much detail, and he promised to look into it. His father was very active in Mindan; he'd check with his dad, and he invited me to get have a Korean meal with him in Machiya—instead of going all the way to Saitama. I gladly took him up on the offer.

We agreed to meet that Friday. When I got to the little place near the station, I resolved to let him figure out the menu.

He looked a little rounder than when I had first met him; he worked at a dojo teaching Kyokushin karate at the time, which had been founded by a fellow *zainichi*. He still had the solid, hardened look of someone who was used to punching and being punched for a living—and who had a healthy appetite.

Kaneda told me he had taken over the pachinko parlor in Kumagaya from his father. They had opened two other parlors in northern Saitama, and although profits weren't tremendously good, they were in the black.

He complained that the pachinko parlor was cutting into dojo time, but that he was still managing to train and run the dojo, although he was unable to train much himself.

The dinner was delicious. We had *bulgogi jeongol*, a delicious kind of Korean beef stew, *chijimi*—Korean pancakes, several kinds of kimchi, and some grilled pork that was amazing. We drank *makgeolli*, a kind of creamy rice wine, which I have always secretly called "milky death" in my mind. It's sweet and cloying, and it gets you drunk before you realize what's going on.

He had solid intel. Mr Lee had joined the Adachi branch of the Mindan in 2005, and was active in the group. However, at the same time, Kaneda's father had heard rumors that Mr Lee was or had been closely connected to Sōren. The two pieces of information didn't quite match up.

Back in the office, I leaned on a reporter from one of the news services to give me an introduction to a cop in the public security bureau, which he did. The cop could only tell me that Wahei Entertainment was not on a watchlist of firms connected to North Korea or to Sōren currently, but that it once had been.

I looked over all the information I had, and realized I couldn't come up with any firm conclusions. And so I did something that broke the basic tenets of due diligence: I decided to arrange a meeting with Mr Lee himself.

I wrote a letter to Mr Lee, in very polite Japanese, which introduced me and my career so far, and mentioned that I was writing a book, to be called *Tokyo Vice*, which would include a chapter on the pachinko business, but that I wanted to know more about the industry's strong ties to the Korean community in Japan.

It was partially true. I was indeed working on the book, and I did have plans to write a chapter on pachinko-related crime in Saitama. I also sent him a copy of the article I'd written on the collapse of Saitama Shogin.

I don't think I would have been able to find the article at all if Michiel hadn't already been working on the book. Mimi was helping me put years of files in order; she was scanning documents and articles, and sometimes translating short documents to reference later. It was nice to have the due diligence money so I could pay her about the equivalent of a pachinko parlor employee's hourly wage for the work she was doing.

The good thing about the article was that it was one of the few articles in the paper that had my name on it. Most newspaper articles in Japan are uncredited—only special features and editorials or explainer pieces will get you a byline.

To my delight, Mr Lee agreed to meet me. His condition was that the interview would be "on background," and that I would take steps to make sure he couldn't be identified. He felt that advertising his Korean background would not be a plus for him or his family. I agreed. We planned to meet at his office in Adachi Ward. He had an office on the third floor of one of his flagship parlors there.

It had been a long time since I'd walked into a pachinko parlor, and when I got to his place on a Monday at 9.50 am, there was a line outside of men and women waiting to get in. By 10.00 am, the machines inside were already full of players, mostly men in their early thirties or forties.

There were ashtrays near all the machines, and despite what seemed like a top-of-the-line ventilation system, the air was filled with smoke, refracting and bending the bright lights from the machines, as if the neon was leaking out of the cases. There were several rows of the machines, with the players' backs to each other as they deftly, slowly, or rapidly turned the control handle shooting balls up the machine, hoping they would land in the right place and win them a jackpot.

The sound was deafening. The background music, which sounded oddly like trance music, was blaring at full volume. Over and under the music, you could hear the electronic beeps of steel pachinko balls being catapulted into the playing field, and the sounds of the balls pouring into trays when someone hit gold. Off in the distance was the steady chug and clicks of balls being counted in a machine, which would give the player a receipt of his or her winnings. You could feel the wall of sound wash over you. There was the smell of bad coffee and iron in the air as well. I couldn't imagine working a full day in one of these parlors, or even spending a few hours there.

I could see that the floor was immaculately clean. Every machine was polished and shiny. All the low chairs with faux red-leather seats in front of the machines appeared brand new and looked comfortable. I touched one. It felt like memory foam. You could rest your ass on that for hours comfortably.

As I stood watching the staff, checking each machine, and occasionally conversing with a customer—yelling in their ear to do so—I remembered that once, at the Tokyo Metropolitan Police Department Press Club, we journalists had calculated what our hourly wages would be if we divided our paychecks by the amount of time we actually spent chained to the job. Our conclusion was that a low-ranking pachinko hall employee got a much better hourly wage.

I had never considered what a hardship it probably is to work at a pachinko parlor, until I walked into that shop. They deserved the higher salary.

I knocked on the door of Mr Lee's office. He welcomed me in himself; the receptionist was out running an errand. Mr Lee was short, five-feet-two, possibly, but not stocky. He wore a gray suit and a red necktie. His hair was still jet black—possibly he dyed it—and long, and it was slicked back. While he seemed young for his age, his face was so wrinkled that it seemed as though his skin had been made out of Issey Miyake Pleats Please and then glued to his skull. His eyes, however, sparkled with the light of someone who was sharp and shrewd and full of energy.

We went back to his inner office, which was not large. There were bookshelves, a wooden desk made out of wood with a glass top, and a sort of reception area with a low table, a leather sofa against the wall, and two other leather seats on either side of the sofa. I looked at his bookshelf, and saw a few volumes on the law, one or two detective novels, and quite a few books on real estate. The great majority of the books appeared to be works of history, with some historical fiction. There were many books in Korean as well. I couldn't read the titles entirely, but knew *hangul* (the Korean alphabet), and often the Korean books would also have kanji in their titles. There was a crystal ashtray on the small table, with a lighter next to it.

He sat on the sofa, and I sat on the side chair and took notes. He lit a cigarette, after asking me if I was okay with it, and smoked while he talked. He told me that the article I'd sent him had piqued his interest, and that he liked to read books, some historical fiction, but mostly nonfiction and that it would be fun, in some way, to be a part of history.

His voice was gravelly and deep—almost sonorous.

I started with softball questions about the history of pachinko, even though I already knew most of the answers. I asked him about how he dealt with the *goto-shi*. I asked him why there were so many pachinko parlors run by Koreans.

He was a learned fellow, and gave a wonderful exposition. And then I asked him, "I'm told that Sōren, the North Korean association, actually runs ten or twenty pachinko parlors now. Do you know if that's true?"

He froze when I asked the question, and stood up straight. He smushed his cigarette into the ashtray and was silent. Then he raised his head and leaned toward me, his index finger pointing up.

"You should think of the government of North Korea as a giant criminal enterprise, and Sōren as their Japanese franchise. That's all they are. The repatriation movement in the fifties was the largest kidnapping ever committed, and they've made trillions of yen off of it. Then they drained all our savings from the bank system they set up, and as long as we have relatives in North Korea, they will continue to shake us down. They held our families hostage for decades, and now our sons and daughters are also paying ransom for relatives they've never met."

I wasn't exactly sure what he was talking about, but I nodded. He sat back down and leaned against the sofa.

"So, in answer to your question, yes. Yes, Sōren runs its own pachinko parlors. I guess they need to, because people like me are through giving them one goddamn yen."

There are times when asking a question is just a barrier to getting an answer. I decided to shut up and let him talk. The floodgates had been opened. I was almost certain that when he finished speaking, everything would make sense.

During our talk, Mr Lee told me about his brother and the repatriation movement—the great effort to get Koreans in Japan to join their brothers and sisters in "The Workers' Paradise."

In the late 1950s, there was a major repatriation project when Kim Il Sung promised "a new life after their return to the homeland" to celebrate the tenth anniversary of North Korea's founding. The North Korean government sought to relieve a labor shortage and to strengthen its claim as the sole legitimate nation of Koreans. The Japanese government seemed surprisingly eager to help out. Backed by Japanese politicians on the right and the left, as well as by the International Red Cross, the repatriation project dispatched 93,340 people to North Korea, including 6,731 Japanese and some Chinese spouses and dependents.

The repatriation project offered an answer to those in Japan who were disheartened by endemic discrimination and their diminished *zainichi* prospects. They were told that North Korea was a way out of their miserable existence in Japan. The propaganda campaign exploited the meme of a paradise on earth, where every refrigerator was full of beef and pork, and the young could study at Kim Il Sung University and possibly Moscow State University. The project officially ended in 1984, but it had effectively ended by the early 1960s after people learned what was really going on.

North Korea was a horrific totalitarian Willy Wonka's Chocolate Factory. People went in, but no one ever came out.

The project faced only sporadic opposition, primarily by Mindan and the South Korean government, which even sponsored terrorist acts to halt it. In reality, the suffering of *zainichi* in North Korea blatantly contradicted the promise of paradise, and thereby stemmed the flow. *Zainichi* transplants almost immediately became impoverished second-class citizens in autocratic North Korea. Newspapers such as the left-leaning *Asahi Shimbun* share blame for the humanitarian disaster that this sham movement created, shamelessly promoting the repatriation movement, even as evidence emerged that those who went back met a bleak fate. North Korea gained a generation of Korean Japanese as hostages they could use to shake money from the living relatives who'd been left behind in Japan. Whether that was the intention from the start, nobody knows.

Mr Lee's oldest brother had been one of those to go back to North Korea, along with his Japanese wife, in 1962. The older brother had been running a small electronics store in Sumida-ku. Lee had told him not to go, and they had quarreled. His brother had never come back, nor had his wife.

A year after Mr Lee's brother and his wife had arrived in North Korea, the emissaries of Sōren showed up at Mr Lee's store (which he had taken over) with letters from his brother asking for money. And they had been squeezing him ever since. He suspected that only half of the money he sent to his brother and his sister-in-law ever made it to them.

His brother had been lucky. Some of the returnees were regarded with suspicion by the North Korean authorities and sent to labor camps; they never came back alive. Korean Japanese who had fled Japan because of its overt and subtle racism faced the deadliest racism and xenophobia one could imagine from their so-called brothers and sisters.

Mr Lee had last seen his brother and sister-in-law ten years before, when he took the ferry to North Korea, known as *Man Gyong Bong 92*. The *Man Gyong Bong* was a cargo-passenger ferry, named after a hill near Pyongyang. The ship had been built in 1992 with Sōren funds, and had been used to transport passengers and cargo between North Korea and Japan.

When he went, he took cash and whisky for his brother. For his sister-in-law: good green tea, Japanese sweets, and magazines.

"They seemed miserable, and we were only given a short time to speak. My brother looked skeletal. Keiko, his wife, tried to put on a happy face. People were starving to death where they lived; they were alive because they represented money for the kingdom. I felt if they could have gotten on the ship with me and left, they would have in an instant."

The ferry had been discontinued in 2006, when Japan banned all North Korean vessels from entering Japanese waters.

Relations between North Korea and Japan had worsened since Prime Minister Junichiro Koizumi's historic visit in 2002, when North Korea admitted to having abducted Japanese citizens—ostensibly to train spies—over several decades. They allowed some abductees to return with Koizumi when he went back to Japan.

Yes, North Korea had kidnapped over 100 Japanese citizens in and out of Japan over several decades—a horrifying crime that many in the West still don't know about.

There were also reports that the ferry had been used to facilitate some of those kidnappings—carrying the victims as cargo—which hastened a ban on the ship. Other former Sōren members admitted to using the ship for espionage, and there were also reports that it had been used to ferry methamphetamines into Japan, where well-connected yakuza groups, such as the Goto-gumi, sold them to the public.

To the best of my knowledge, the ferry had definitely been carrying meth into Japan. I knew that the ship was also certainly being used to carry massive amounts of cash to North Korea, and I had written an article for the *Yomiuri* on it during my stint covering customs.

That small article had set off some alarms as well.

It wasn't a surprise that, in order to cut off the flow of money to North Korea and the flow of meth to Japan, the ferry had been banned, but it left many families in Japan with no means of contacting their relatives left behind.

Mr Lee knew all of this.

"I can see why Japan hates North Korea. It is a country that threatens Japan with missiles, kidnaps their citizens, and sells drugs that poison the nation. I see all of this—but I also remember how Japan lied to us all—and those who fell for the lie returned home and were abandoned. We were victims of an ethnic cleansing—and the Red Cross helped, and the U.S. looked the other way. I also hate North Korea, but I will never forgive the government of Japan."

Out of sheer dumb habit, I asked him, "Why not?"

He responded angrily.

"Because they knew—they knew that thousands of women and children and thousands of their own people married to Koreans here would be returning—not home to a land of milk and honey, but to a land where people were already starving. And even when they knew that thousands of returnees were being sent to labor camps to die, they stayed silent. Because they wanted to get rid of all of us—all the Koreans who had been slave labor, and all who had come to Japan seeking prosperity under the empire. We were their Jews, and the concentration camp was in North Korea. And they sent us there.

"I didn't go, but nearly 100,000 people did. That is a crime. A deliberate and evil crime. Japan was Stalin with a smiley face and an obsequious bow. They killed us with pamphlets and posters and the Red Cross. All the while, the U.S. smiled and helped them do it because it was expedient."

He almost ran out of breath. He decided to light another cigarette.

"It wasn't a repatriation. It was an ethnic cleansing by Japan and a kidnapping by North Korea. And both sides shook hands on it."

Lee pulled books from his shelf and showed them to me. He had documents as well, neatly bound in color-coded binders. After skimming through a few of them, I understood why he was so fascinated by history.

We talked for hours—because I was interested. I had pretty much gotten everything I needed to know. There was only one question left.

"What happened to your brother?"

Lee paused and said flatly, "He died two years ago. I think he killed himself. I don't know. Keiko, his wife, died before him. Even after he was dead, they didn't tell me immediately. Only when I refused to send more money without proof of life did they tell me he had passed away. Then they demanded money for the funeral. I told them to fuck off.

"There's no point in taking care of the dead—not when it means giving money to the people who killed them."

Lee had severed all contact with Sōren after learning of his brother's death. He joined Mindan to reconnect with other Koreans in Japan who had no ties to North Korea. And that's where he was now.

I thanked him for his time. I went home, and prepared to file my report for Oldman. It took me a day to write it up. I gave the firm a thumbs-up and recommended that they give Mr Lee the loan.

Oldman sent me back a short reply.

"Excellent work and wonderful context. This will prove useful in the future. The history of Koreans in this country is truly a sad affair."

He suggested we meet the following week for lunch, and I suggested a good Korean place. Mission accomplished.

Mr Lee was more or less correct in his harsh assessment of Japan's "final solution" to its "Korean problem." As early as 1955, the Japanese government's foreign ministry was working on plans, in conjunction with the Liberal Democratic Party, to get rid of the nation's poor Korean residents. Prime Minister Nobusuke Kishi, a war criminal and the grandfather of Prime Minister Shinzo Abe, hastened secret talks with North Korea to bring them on board. The U.S., anxious to cut a security treaty with Japan, was prone to giving Kishi what he wanted without a protest.

According to a well-researched paper, "The Forgotten Victims of the North Korean Crisis," the "U.S. Ambassador in Tokyo Douglas MacArthur II [who played a key role on the U.S. side] told his Australian counterpart in 1959 that the 'American Embassy had checked Japanese opinion and found it was almost unanimously in favor of "getting rid of the Koreans.""

At this sensitive moment in U.S.–Japan relations, the state department was clearly cautious of intervening in a scheme that was an obvious vote-winner for the Kishi regime. Besides, MacArthur personally sympathized with the public emotion, commenting (as the Australian ambassador at the time reported) that "he himself can scarcely criticize the Japanese for this as the Koreans left in Japan are a poor lot including many Communists and many criminals."

The irony of MacArthur's remarks comes from willful ignorance that it was Japan's postwar policies that made them poor, limited their job opportunities, and nudged them into criminal activity.

Japan hadn't left them many choices: pachinko; Korean

barbecue owners; love hotel operators. It was either that or a one-way ticket to the workers' paradise, North Korea.

There's a Japanese saying that comes to mind when talking about the repatriation debacle. *"Kiite Gokuraku, Mite Jigoku."* "It's paradise when you hear of it, but when you see it, it's hell."

It's a saying that applies to many things in Japan. What you hear about something and the reality of what it is are often worlds apart.

CHAPTER TEN

Scarecrows

"Are you a poker player, Mr Adelstein?" Oldman asked me. We were drinking Nikka 17 at Lady Jane in Shimokitazawa as he asked this question with a gleam in his eyes. It was a good whisky; it warmed me up. It was a wet, cold night in January, and the bar was chilly as well. A Sonny Rollins album was playing over the speakers, and we were catching up under the giant black-and-white Marilyn Monroe picture on the wall, at the big table. I didn't answer the question immediately.

He followed up by saying, "Perhaps you've never played poker?"

He had a New England accent that made everything he said seem a little like a challenge.

"I don't like games of chance," I replied.

"In reality, it's a game of skill and chance. Both," he said. "I think we should try a real-world round."

He got right to the point.

"I read the report that Tony sent me about Suburban Corporation, and it was convincing.* I assume you did most of the research. The report makes a strong case for declining any

---

* The names and dates in this chapter have been slightly altered to protect the innocent and the guilty. Any similarity to certain bankrupt institutions and yakuza associates should be a hint for you. Or possibly not.

business with the company. Unfortunately, the business depart-ment is not on board. Suburban is huge in the real estate field—they'll do anything to close the deal. Suburban's president said Goldman Sachs made millions on their deals. 'You could too,' he tells them, and they believe, because they want to believe."

I sipped my whisky.

"Whenever Goldman Sachs invests in shady companies, they profit," Oldman said. "The next sucker who does business with the shady company loses his shirt. You can predict it."

The Suburban Corporation was located in Nagasaki and listed on the First Section of the Tokyo Stock Exchange. The company seemed to be doing extremely well, on the surface, with annual revenues near $500 million. Nevertheless, Michiele and I did a deep dive into the company, and found undeniable ties to orga-nized crime. At least until 2006, Tokiyuki Ketta, an individual with well-known ties to organized crime, served as Suburban's special advisor.

In November 1992, Ketta had been arrested along with a member of the Yamaguchi-gumi Goto-gumi for violating the National Land Act in connection with the acquisition of land for a golf course in the Yamanashi prefecture. At the time, he was the vice president of ICJ, a real estate company identified by the police as a Yamaguchi-gumi front company.

After going through corporate records, newspaper filings, police records, and other materials, I made all the connections.

Ketta wasn't just Suburban's advisor. He had a room right next to the president's office with his name on the door; he was an integral part of their operations. His role was to direct the firm's land-sharking efforts. Even though Ketta had been fired from Suburban in 2006, he was still very much lurking in the shadows and still had great influence.

Suburban Corporation also had a reputation for using strong-arm tactics to force people out of their homes and apartments so the company could develop new areas or broker the construction of new buildings.

It seemed cut and dried to me.

Oldman agreed, but he needed to get the business division to back down, once and for all, on the deals they were planning with Suburban. So he asked me for advice.

"Well," I replied, "why don't we invite their representative to a meeting and ask them about what we know, and see how they answer? If they're not straight up, they may have something to hide. Let's see what their anti–organized crime and compliance protocols are."

"You mean, interrogate the company president?"

"Well, at least the vice president," I countered.

Oldman ran his index finger around the edge of his shot glass in clockwise circles for a minute, looking very satisfied and relaxed. Then he finished his drink.

"Mr Adelstein, you and I think alike. I think that may be a splendid idea. That's going to be our poker game. And we will be the house."

Oldman arranged the meeting, made sure that video cameras were in the room, and I made a list of suggested questions. It was a simple plan.

The meeting would be opened by Oldman, who would greet the executive. A young female employee, who was bilingual and attractive, would interpret for him and ask the questions. They would introduce me as an intern who had spent a year in Japan.

Ms Ichikawa, the employee and interpreter, was told that her job was to both distract the guest and put him at ease.

On a very cold afternoon in mid-January, everything went according to plan. Suburban's VP showed up dressed in a dark gray suit, a white shirt, and a white-and-gray–striped tie. Gold-rimmed glasses adorned his face, and his salt-and-pepper–colored hair had been slicked back. He wore a massive gold LeCoultre watch. He got points for good taste in classic Swiss luxury watches, in my opinion.

The interview began with a series of softball questions. Everyone was served coffee. I sat in the corner reading a copy of *The Economist*, looking bored.

"Tell me your vision of the future of Suburban Corporation?"

"Why do you need a loan from our group?"

"Tell us about your REITs [real estate investment trusts]."

And then Oldman lobbed the first grenade.

"Have you or your firm, now, or ever, had any ties to organized crime? In other words, the yakuza?"

The VP waved his right hand dismissively and slicked back his hair.

"Certainly not. We operate under very strict guidelines. The board of directors of our organization includes an ex-prosecutor. We have partnered with Goldman Sachs and other firms that are very strict about compliance. We are confident that our business model will meet your needs."

Oldman nodded and went completely silent after the interpreter translated the answer.

He remained silent for a minute.

You don't know how long a minute can be. With the tip of his finger, Oldman circled his coffee cup clockwise and then counterclockwise, and then he stood up abruptly.

He told the VP, "You'll have to excuse me. I'll have to make a call now. Please wait here for a moment." And then Oldman and his company's interpreter left.

After making eye contact and shrugging my shoulders, I spoke in English, "He may take a while. Do you want another cup of coffee?"

The VP said, "No, thanks."

I went back to reading my magazine. Minutes passed. The VP took out his cellphone and began making a frantic call, speaking in Japanese, in hushed tones.

"I think they know. What do I say? How much do I admit? When did we supposedly get rid of the guy?"

The irritated voice on the other end was shouting, calling the VP stupid and telling him he had failed to fulfill his role. The VP bowed deeply while talking on the phone. His ears started sweating. I didn't know ears could sweat that much.

He hung up the phone.

After fifteen minutes, Oldman came back alone. This time, he motioned to me.

"My colleague will be conducting the rest of the interview," he said with the slightest trace of a smile on his face. He sat down, and I stood up.

I introduced myself in formal Japanese and began the second round of the interrogation. The VP looked very surprised—like a statue in the museum had suddenly begun moving right in front of his eyes. The look on his face also reminded me of the time I'd been discussing what an asshole my boss was at the newspaper, only to realize he was standing behind me.

He was so taken aback that I had to ask him twice, "Are you okay?"

He was very nervous now—possibly because he couldn't remember what he'd said on the phone. People are very bad at remembering what they did and didn't say, if they think nobody was listening. I gave him half the details of what we already knew about his firm and his yakuza associate, Ketta, and then asked him, "Can you tell me what his role was at the firm all those years?"

He didn't answer the question. I hit him with more questions.

"Was your firm not aware of the special advisor's arrest record and criminal history?"

"If they were not aware, why not?"

"If they were aware, why did they think hiring Ketta was acceptable?"

I also made judicious use of long silences. In the middle of our conversation, I pulled out a bright red book from my briefcase and placed it in the middle of the table between us. The title was *Yakuza Front Companies: The Reality and How to Fight Them*. The book had been compiled by the Nagoya Lawyers' Association.

By the end of the interview, he broke down. He apologized for having concealed critical information, admitted that hiring Ketta had been a terrible mistake, and promised that the company had cleaned up its act.

It didn't matter. After the transcript of the interview went up the food chain, the business division's plans were overruled.

A few months after our "interrogation" on June 14, a seventy-one-year-old former *sokaiya* (a professional extortionist who earns a living blackmailing listed companies) sent a letter to the president of Suburban. In the letter, he indirectly threatened to expose the firm's yakuza ties and to ruin the company. The company filed charges, and the old man was arrested, but the details of his threat leaked out at the same time. It was very bad publicity for Suburban, but it was more confirmation that Oldman and I had been right.

Suburban Corporation went bankrupt in August 2008, and filed for protection from creditors under the Civil Rehabilitation Law. This was one of the biggest bankruptcies of a listed real estate company that year. They owed over 255 billion yen, and were eventually delisted from the stock market. Foreign firms that had loaned them money or partnered with them in business ventures lost millions.

Suburban representatives said at a press conference that the firm would seek court-ordered rehabilitation, since it couldn't tie up with other firms for capital. It blamed its collapse on the subprime mortgage crisis in the U.S.

"The panic and credit crunch caused by the U.S. subprime mortgage crisis smashed global financial markets," the CEO told reporters.

In reality, things were probably very different. The firm's main bank was Mizuho Corporation, and the Financial Services Agency (FSA), in an effort to crack down on organized crime in the stock market, told Mizuho to stop funding Suburban or face severe financial penalties and endless inspections in late 2007. Mizuho complied with the request.

Suburban was financially strapped, so it turned to local banks in Nagasaki, but police pressure and government pressure made the local banks turn them down as well.

In the end, Oldman and I had prevented our employers from losing a colossal amount of money. When the other investment firms heard of the bankruptcy, they went into a frenzy. It had a huge impact on the real estate market.

The company made the rare gesture of congratulating Oldman for a job well done, and awarded him a bonus and a commendation. Also, I received a small bonus: a fancy gold-plated Omega watch. I still have it somewhere, I think.

On the day following the bankruptcy, Oldman invited me to Lady Jane for drinks.

"What should we toast to?" I asked.

"The end of the yakuza in financial markets. Possibly the end of our careers. I think our days are numbered."

I didn't expect him to say that.

"What? We saved the company millions. You know how much they were willing to lend to Suburban, so maybe even more."

He laughed. "You have no idea," he said. "Mr Adelstein, the FSA, the prosecutors, the police, the National Police Agency, the National Tax Agency, and other agencies are cooperating for the first time. They're actually sharing information, making a database. Sooner or later, the tattooed fellows will be driven out of the financial markets. And then people like you—"

Making the shape of a gun, he pointed his finger at me.

"—And people like me, with our special skill set, will no longer be needed. We are the best horseshoe makers in town, a few years before Henry Ford starts selling cars.

"And one more piece of information I should share with you. The thing is this—we save the company from losing millions of dollars in bad deals, but we don't make money for them. Most of the executives see us as a nuisance. And the few at the top who realize that doing the right thing pays off, they won't be around forever.

"The work is good. The pay is not shabby. Let's enjoy it while it lasts."

Oldman splurged and bought a bottle of the finest whisky in the bar, and had the bartender put on a Frank Sinatra classic album. It was one from his jazzy days.

The first song up: "The Summer Wind." Just the right music for a hot August night.

Sinatra was so right. The summer wind was a fickle friend, as were our employers, but we had a few good years left, if fate was kind to us. But you never really know how long her affection will last.

CHAPTER ELEVEN

Hanekaeri

The publication of *Tokyo Vice* in October 2009 changed my life; I felt like it validated the work I had done and closed a chapter on the previous sixteen years of my existence. It also made me a little arrogant. With victory comes hubris. And with hubris come mistakes.

I thought when the book started showing up in bookstores that it meant the end of Tadamasa Goto. He wasn't a threat to anyone anymore, right? *I* was still under police protection—but it was police protection without much intensity, the light-beer equivalent of being under guard. A few times a day, a cop patrolled my place to see if I was okay. They often left a note with the Tokyo Metropolitan Police Department mascot on it—Pipo-kun. The mascot has sometimes been the subject of ridicule by U.S. federal law enforcement. You can sort of understand why if you saw him. He is yellow with strange ears, no pants, no gun, and no dick.

The publication of *Tokyo Vice* wonderfully coincided with the one-year anniversary of Goto being kicked out of the Yamaguchi-gumi. An auspicious day. That had to mean something. But I wasn't going to have the last word.

The first inkling I had of the trouble ahead came from my editor at the *Shukan Shincho* in May 2010, when he called me.

"Jake-kun, have you read Goto's book?" he asked.

"I didn't know he had a book," I replied.

"It's coming out soon. I thought you knew or should know if you didn't already know."

Takarajima Publishing, which had published my explanation of Goto's backdoor deal with the FBI, had also just published Goto's biography without bothering to warn me.

The memoir was notable for its use of subtle language that amounted to a yakuza-style fatwa on my life. Before the book was even out, I received another heads-up from a cop.

"Jake, Goto's written his own book. It's like a loaded gun. You'll see. Watch your back."

I didn't know exactly what that meant, but it didn't sound good.

When the book was eventually published, I got a call from a mid-level enforcer in the Yamaguchi-gumi whom I considered a friend, of sorts. In my own head, I called him "Precision Man" because he did everything with such finesse. He wanted to talk to me about that book.

We had lunch a month after Goto's book was published at a Thai restaurant on the edge of the high-rent Nishi-Azabu district—his choice, not mine.

He was dressed like a character from a Michael Mann movie: dark gray suit, white dress-shirt with the top buttons deliberately undone, no necktie, and stubble that seemed like it had been carefully trimmed to look natural, like a bonsai tree. He had some gray hair around his temples that almost matched the dark gray of his suit. Everything about him was precise.

Precision Man had once worked for Tadamasa Goto before a successful transition to another of the Yamaguchi-gumi factions after the Goto-gumi was dissolved. He had a hardback copy of the book with him, in pristine condition with a plain blue cover, and asked me point blank: "Have you read Goto's book?"

"I haven't gotten around to it," I told him.

"You should read his book. He's read yours. Or had someone translate it for him. You're in his book."

He put it in the center of the table near the Thai fish sauce.

I nodded. "Is there anything in there that I should immediately know?"

Precision Man put down his knife and fork ("In Thailand, they don't really use chopsticks," he'd told me with some conviction), and lined them up neatly against each other parallel to the plate. He made a motion like slitting a throat, and looked me in the eyes. I didn't avert my eyes either, but I did feel like I was going to lose this stare-down.

"It's an offer to reward anyone who takes you out. Any yakuza who reads it, and there are some who will read it, will understand." He gestured for me to pick up the book, and told me to turn to a passage on pages 254–55 that was highlighted in bright yellow so evenly that it appeared to me at first to have been printed that way.

It was a quote from Goto that translates roughly like this: "Even though I'm no longer a yakuza boss, if I met this unpleasant reporter, it would be a big deal. He'd go from being a reporter targeted for death to one that was actually dead. (Laughter.)"

The unpleasant reporter was a reference to myself. I didn't quite get how this passage amounted to a fatwa, but Mr Precision did.

"You know a lot about the yakuza," he acknowledged, "but you don't know as much as you think you do. You know the word *hanekaeri*?"

I told him I did. I had learned the word from yakuza writer Atsushi Mizoguchi. He is the godfather of real investigative yakuza journalists. He was a tough weekly-magazine reporter who rarely pulled punches and treated everyone with equal amounts of deference and respect.

Yakuza fan magazines were sold here in the open: three weeklies, three monthlies. They were read by the yakuza, the cops, journalists like myself, and every man in Japan who fantasized about being a gangster. They ran interviews with the current yakuza bosses, but the questions were limited, and there was an implicit understanding that even after the interview was done, the boss reserved the right to edit or scrap it. As one veteran yakuza writer explained to me, "If you violate that rule, there will be harassment and often retaliation."

In 1989, after the gang war between the Yamaguchi-gumi and their splinter group, the Ichiwa-kai, finally came to a peaceful end following four years of bloodshed, Mizoguchi began writing a column for *Tokyo Sports* on the new Yamaguchi-gumi. The post–gang war organization was led by its fifth-generation leader, Yoshinori Watanabe, who looked like a gorilla with a buzz-cut.

Mizoguchi had made a name for himself by taking on stories that no one else would touch. He had written an in-depth investigative exposé about the Soka Gakkai, a powerful Buddhist religious cult that had long used Tadamasa Goto and the Goto-gumi as enforcers to silence their critics and the press. His hyper-realistic and detailed accounts of the gang wars made his works popular, and he was a heavily in-demand writer.

The escalating battle between the Yamaguchi-gumi and the Ichiwa-kai had become a real-life yakuza drama for the public. News about the latest volleys in their never-ending war were food for the morning talk shows, the afternoon variety programs, and the evening news. Some newspapers kept count of the casualties and deaths on each side, essentially a running score of the mayhem. The gangsters themselves would sometimes hold press conferences. Mizoguchi captured all the madness beautifully. However, his column ruffled many feathers.

He portrayed Watanabe as an unfit leader, and hinted that the Yamaguchi-gumi's gorilla was really a puppet for his second-in-command, Masaru Takumi, a brilliant business yakuza and the Professor Moriarty of the Japanese underworld.

In May 1990, when Mizoguchi had just finished his long-running series about the fifth-generation leader, he got a phone call from the group's patriarch, Goto. Goto wanted to meet him immediately at the Hilton Hotel lounge in Shinjuku, located close to the Shinjuku Police Station. I was stationed at that station as the fourth-district reporter from 1999 to 2001.

Before leaving the house, Mizoguchi told his wife, "I'm going to have a talk with Goto, and I'll call you when I'm done. If you don't get a call from me by evening, notify the police."

Of course, when he got to the lounge, Goto was not waiting for him, but two of his thugs were. They told the reporter they would take him to where Goto was waiting. The offer was non-negotiable. They put him in a car and drove him to a nearby office building. Their destination on the thirteenth floor was one of Goto's many front companies. Mizoguchi wasn't happy to be there.

The yakuza boss told him, slyly, casually, "My friends in the Yamaguchi-gumi have a problem with the series you're writing. It's not like you are someone I don't know, but there are loose cannons in the organization."

The word Goto used to describe these so-called loose cannons was *hanekaeri*, which translates as "blowback," but refers to rogue revenge-seekers. It's a handy word in the lexicon of a yakuza boss. It can be used to escape blame for the bad conduct of your underlings. The boss can simply say that his naughty soldiers were acting on their own, doing what they thought would benefit the boss without having received any direct orders from him.

He might shrug his shoulders. "They were *hanekaeri*," he might say, with a slight tone of apology in his voice, as if to say, "Kids these days—ya just can't get them to behave."

And, of course, you can't hold the boss responsible for what his hot-heated kids decide to do on their own, right?

There was some truth to the idea that a young hot-headed yakuza might take things into his own hands to earn fame and glory during a gang war, or when his boss had been slighted. But in this case, the truth was that Goto was really saying, "If you don't listen to me, you will be hurt, and I won't be taking the fall."

Goto continued his speech to Mizoguchi, making a very veiled threat while expressing concern at the same time. "I don't want you to be harmed, and I would like to continue my yakuza life a little longer. From now on, when you're going to write about the Yamaguchi-gumi, why don't you show me your articles beforehand?"

Mizoguchi informed him that the series had ended and that he was now writing a book. Goto wasn't pleased, and asked to see the book. Mizoguchi deflected his request by saying it was dependent on whether he had enough time to show it to Goto … or not. Goto countered by asking him, "Isn't there some way you could stop the publication?" Mizoguchi lied, and said it had already been printed.

Two days later, while Mizoguchi was riding the bullet train, he got a call from the yakuza boss demanding that Mizoguchi either show him the book or cancel it. Goto offered to pay him all the royalties he would have earned on the first printing. Mizoguchi furiously refused. He pointed out that if he took Goto's offer, he would be the laughing stock of the journalism world, and would be finished as a writer.

"Let's say this conversation never happened," he said, and hung up with Goto still on the line.

Several weeks later, Mizoguchi was stabbed in the back by a member of the Yamaguchi-gumi Yamaken-gumi while leaving his office. The assailant had meant to kill him, but missed his vital organs.

In 2006, his son was stabbed by Yamaguchi-gumi members when they couldn't find Mizoguchi. The two men were arrested, but their boss was not. Mizoguchi took the organization and the boss to court, and sued them for damages. He won.

When he talks about the attack on his son, the venom in his voice gets thick. You can feel the outrage, the indignation. The Japanese yakuza aren't supposed to bother the innocent in the straight world. That's something the Italian Mafia or the Russians do. That's against the Code.

I've met him a few times, and interviewed him twice. He's a humble man. His home resembles a mini-fortress, with security cameras and double locks. He's not taking any chances. He once offered me some advice over drinks at a little bar near the Foreign Correspondents' Club of Japan. I think he had coffee and I had booze, or it was the other way around.

He said, "I envy you. You can leave this island. You can go back to America. But I'm stuck here. That means I have to live with the repercussions of what I write. Maybe someday, the yakuza or at least the Yamaguchi-gumi will fade away, and I won't have to watch my back. But until then I can't back down. It's a duty to stand up to them, to let them know they can't win. But I also can't stop writing."

"Why would you want to stop writing? If you stop writing, you'll be bored to death," I joked.

"No," he shook his head, almost sadly. "If I disappear from public memory, if I'm forgotten, or fade into obscurity, then the people who hold a grudge against me will make sure that I really do vanish. Forever."

He raised his eyebrows and shrugged his shoulders, and said, "You should keep that in mind as well. You're already past the point where you're dealing with the worst of them on just the printed page. You're in their world. You're almost stuck there with me."

There's that song, "Stuck in the Middle with You." It started playing in my head as I thought about where I was now in my life. Me and Mizoguchi.

Hanekaeri can be both an action *and* a person. It's the yakuza equivalent of the civilian word *sontaku*. *Sontaku* is a concept in Japanese, almost like social telepathy, that could be translated as "guessing how another person is feeling" or "following an implicit wish of another."

For example, if you're a yakuza underling, and your boss says in your presence, "I'm really troubled by that city council member, Muramoto. He's blocking our company bid on that public works project. The world would be a better place without him."

You would then *sontaku* that the boss wants you to either kill Muramoto or neutralize him, and you would do it. There would be no direct orders that could come back to haunt your boss.

If you were a smart yakuza, like Saigo, you'd extricate yourself from the situation by playing dumb and immediately asking, "So, boss, you want me to whack him?"

To which your boss would get angry, and mumble or yell, "I never said that. No, forget about it. You're so fucking stupid."

The kanji for *sontaku* is made of two parts. The first part means to make a deduction of some kind, and the second refers to the depth of that deduction. The word came into vogue in 2017, after many bureaucrats took it upon themselves to cover up the misdeeds of Prime Minister Shinzo Abe on their own, allegedly, without being ordered to do so. Criminal conspiracies are very hard to prove when they're done with telepathy—and a lot of destruction and alteration of public documents. Japanese publisher Jiyu Kokuminsha even selected it as the New Trending Word of The Year in 2017.

Back in 2010, Goto expressing displeasure with me in his

book was a subtle way of saying, "Will no one rid me of this meddlesome priest?"

It's not a very nice thing for an alleged Buddhist priest—like Goto—to say. Precision Man understood this.

"Well, there's your problem. Goto still has his fans. He has money, connections, and power, and in this book he lays out the proper way of dealing with 'unpleasant' people like you. And he says that, in the past, he has generously rewarded those who dealt with those described as such. It's an invitation to all the *ronin,* ex–Goto-gumi members and literate yakuza, that he'd like to see you dealt with—and that there will be a reward. Except, the text ends the sentence with a laugh—so he can say he was joking."

He leaned in. "I know this grudge-holding geezer way too well. He isn't joking. You should take that as a threat, and take it seriously."

He pushed the book over to my side of the table, "Take it. I don't need 300 pages of his bragging and bullshit. You need to read it."

We talked shop until the check came, and I took the book home. Avoiding my roommates, I went up to the second floor of my house, propped my feet up on my desk, and started reading. If you were to summarize the life of Tadamasa Goto, born on September 16, 1943, the best word would be "unpleasant."

It's a particular Japanese version of the adjective *fuyukai,* which literally means "unpleasant," but also "vile" and "rude." It may seem like a benign description of a man the Japanese police think is responsible for countless crimes and several murders. Goto had never been convicted for murder—at that point—but his underlings had stabbed a real estate agent to death in 2006, and the police were still working the case. He was suspected of having initiated eleven more murders, but there was no solid evidence. Eleven seems like a low number for a gang boss, but then again, how many people do you have to kill before you can be deemed a ruthless psychopath?

Unpleasant.

As I read his self-congratulatory biography, I could see how he had become the man he was. His mother died when he was two, and his father, who was a very honest man, was also an alcoholic who'd erupt into violence after one drink. Although his grandfather had been extremely wealthy, little Tadamasa grew up poor and the youngest of four brothers in a troubled household—a classic juvenile delinquent and a bully. There was one incident that firmly seems to have set him on the dark path:

> When I was 16, I was thrown in jail for a few days with my buddies, for brawling and threatening people. The others in my group, of which I was the clear leader, all ate bento [lunch boxes] provided by their families, who came to meet them when we were released. I ate only the issued jail food and no one came to meet me upon release. I then realized I had no one to depend on and vowed to solve my own problems, run my own life … I also vowed never to suffer from lack of money again. I vowed to keep half of every 10,000 yen that came my way, so that the next time I was thrown in jail I could buy my own bento and change of undershirts. I had been feeling miserable when comparing my situation with my buddies', but this humiliation turned into pride in myself and in my own independence. I have lived by that pride to this day, and have kept my vow to myself regarding money my whole life, even after joining the yakuza, and even now after I have left that world.

Despite his claims of retirement and reformation in the book, Goto was still an underworld crook, according to the U.S. Treasury Department. He was a successful businessman in his prime, with over 100 front companies in real estate, entertainment, and the financial world serving him. Even in "retirement" he was running a criminal empire in Cambodia. A police report from 2007 recorded that at the height of his power, Goto had four mistresses—one a semi-famous actress—and nearly 900 people working for him. At one point, he was the largest individual shareholder of Japan Airlines. He hit upon a winning formula early in his career, and kept it:

> I stayed in my home turf, building up the Goto-gumi through fights with other gangs, taking control of street punks who were young and just pretending to act like a yakuza. We would beat them up and make them apologize, then have them join our gang.

Times changed, but his methods basically stayed the same. He befriended or blackmailed politicians, and did the dirty work for the Soka Gakkai, which conveniently had its own political party, the New Komeito. He helped chase out the locals to build Tokyo's sprawling monument to luxury, Roppongi Hills. Goto moved up in life, but he never moved beyond being a thug.

His memoir, *Habakarinagara* (*Pardon Me, But ...*) was published after he had essentially clad himself in a bulletproof vest by very publicly becoming a Shingon Buddhist priest in April 2009. It was a smart move; even in a generally secular Japan, killing a priest is looked upon poorly. And there were a lot of people who wanted Goto dead; he had enemies. Everyone loves a tale of a badass who becomes a good guy, that universal archetype of redemption, even when it's not true. The weekly magazines, which were all alerted to his "conversion," ate it up. The book's structure consists of a series of grueling interviews by a seasoned journalist. Even then, the book only captures a portrait of Goto that he wants you to see, built from what he is willing to show you. What he unwittingly shows you is that he has no remorse for the pain he's caused.

Most yakuza like to think of themselves as the good guys. What made Goto different was that he didn't need that illusion. He knew he was the bad guy, and he didn't care. As long as he was winning and someone else was losing, all was right in the world with him.

A lot of yakuza hated him, even before his book came out, which wasn't surprising.

If you asked me, "What destroyed the yakuza?" my answer would be two words: Tadamasa Goto. He was almost solely responsible for the criminal empire's destruction. Goto addressed the attack on the director Juzo Itami in his biography. "Of course I didn't order it, but he deserved it because his film made fun of us and was unpleasant."

Fuyukai.

Juzo Itami and myself: unpleasant.

The attack on the director showed the world that the yakuza weren't noble outlaws; they were just tribal profiteers. The incident accelerated police crackdowns tenfold.

Goto was a lucky and powerful fellow. When his liver was about to fail him, he sold out all his fellow yakuza and jumped ahead of hundreds of Americans on the transplant list. Law-abiding, hardworking men and women died waiting for a liver, but the crime boss lived.

However, Goto's fortune came on the back of all the other yakuza he'd thrown under the bus. In his lifetime, the former yakuza boss inspired the two most devastating catastrophes to hit the organization in decades: the organized crime exclusionary ordinances, and the exclusionary clauses in contracts.

I'll admit that while reading Goto's book, I got a queasy feeling. Of course, nowhere in the book did the fake priest address his deal with the FBI, nor express any remorse that other, more decent people died so he could live. At one point, I hurled the book across the room and into the closet where I kept my futon. He was an arrogant motherfucker and a braggart to boot, but his jabs at my own work without bothering to name me pissed me off. I didn't need journalism tips from a lying sack of shit. Of course, after hurling the book into the closet, I had to get up and sort through the pile of unfolded towels, clothes, socks, and my aikido *dōgi* (uniform) to find the damn thing and continue reading.

I'm neither particularly brave nor faint-hearted, but I could sense the intention in Goto's words. I figured that the best thing to do was to get help from his legal nemesis, Toshihiro Igari. Maybe I could have the threat removed or the distribution of the book stopped, and possibly have my own rebuttal inserted among the pages. I had a vague idea of what might be done, but Igari would know what could be done. I decided to write him an email and outline the problem.

I was drafting the letter on my Mac in early July 2010 when one of the police officers from the Kitazawa Police Station Organized Crime Division, who were responsible for keeping me alive, dropped by the house. It was Officer Osaki. He looked like a walrus with bad eyesight that had been turned into a human being, and he walked like one, too. Despite the walrus exterior, he had a solid reputation as a detective, and was well known for his ability to get people to give up more information than they should. Maybe that was because he seemed so harmless—people underestimated him. As soon as he came in and flopped down on the couch, he got down to business.

"Have you read Goto's book?"

"I have," I replied.

"Then you know. There's a threat not so cleverly concealed in there. It appears to be a sort of threat. You want to press charges?"

I sighed.

"I'd like to, but read it closely. The part where he makes a threat notes that he's laughing. So he could say it was a joke."

I pulled out my copy of the book and showed him the page. He read the lines a few times, his finger tracing the words. He looked disappointed.

"These were interviews, right? If we have the tape, we can prove the intent was different. Maybe."

I nodded.

"Well, what should I do?" I asked.

He cocked his head and thought.

"We're talking about this in the department at headquarters. Don't do anything for the moment. But watch your back. And lock the door when you leave."

I nodded.

"And when you're home," he added.

I have to admit that at the time I was pretty bad about locking the door. There were many people who never bothered to lock their doors, but I shouldn't have been among them.

"And also, sort the plastic bottles and the cans better. Plastic bottles are on Saturday. Cans are on Friday. Your neighbors complain."

I agreed to do that, too. I was going to offer to spend more time brushing my teeth as well, but that might have seemed like sarcasm. Sarcasm in Japan just comes across as being rude. Parody works; irony is appreciated. Mockery does not go over well in a society where losing face makes people lose their cool.

There were good things about being under police protection in Japan. You did feel secure. You had someone who cared where you went and when you were coming home. Every day, sometimes at night, sometimes in the morning, there would be a little yellow note in the mailbox with a picture of Tokyo Police mascot Pipo-kun on it, letting me know if anything was out of the ordinary. Usually, everything was just fine.

Heion Buji was the phrase. Of course, I also knew that when you called the police and asked them if there was anything happening in the area that you should be reporting on, they'd always reply, "*Heion Buji*," even if nine headless bodies had just been found in an apartment. But it was peaceful and quiet where I lived, as far as I knew.

Later that same month, the walrus started returning with his supervisor. They never seemed to call or make an appointment. They would just show up during the day, which was fine with me. One time, over coffee, they explained that they could take a criminal complaint from me, but the prosecutors were unlikely to back them up. Goto was no longer a yakuza. He had allegedly had a change of heart and had become a priest. And as I'd pointed out myself, the threat in the book was punctuated with a notation, "laughter," meaning it could all be dismissed as a joke.

I thanked them for their efforts, and asked them to give me time to think it over. I'd never written to Igari, and now I felt it was the time to do it. I rewrote my email and explained the situation. I finally sent it on August 5. The reply from his office was immediate.

Dear Jake,

This is Suzuki from Igari's office. He is currently overseas at the moment and will be back on the 8th and then taking a vacation on the 11th. He can meet you on the 8th, the day he returns. Please let us know if that works.

I saw him on August 8. It was a Sunday; he had come back from Brazil and gone directly from Narita Airport to his office to meet me. I had spoken to him earlier that summer to see if he would cooperate in a yakuza documentary I was working on for a television station owned by NewsCorp. He was tanned, looked healthy, and was in great spirits. He was still wearing a suit, even in the midst of Japan's unbearable summer, and a crisp, white shirt that looked like it had just been taken off the rack.

It was a relief to see him with that bulldog face and black hair slicked back. In his deep, booming voice, he welcomed me into the office. He had a copy of the book with him. There were bookmarks and Post-its coming out of the sides, as though the book was exploding with colored paper.

"I need your help to deal with the fallout from the book," I said.

He understood. I was worried that maybe I was overreacting. It was just a book, after all.

"It's not just a book," Igari said. "He impugns your honor, your work, and he threatens you. It's a slap in the face. You were right to come to me. He's done everything possible to avoid criminal prosecution in the wording, but I doubt that's what he originally said. We will find out."

After much discussion, he and his two colleagues came up with a plan. Igari knew people at Takarajima Publications. He'd take it up directly with them to remove the threat and correct the false information, and if they wouldn't, he'd sue the publisher. He pointed out that because of the way the book was written, suing Goto would be more difficult than suing the publisher. He suggested I sue for one yen. I asked him why.

"It shows that you aren't doing it for the money, and it also shows that you think the book is a bunch of worthless shit. One yen is the right amount."

I laughed.

His parting words to me were: "It'll be a long battle. It'll take money and courage, and you'll have to come up with those on your own. But we'll fight."

On August 27, I sent a follow-up email to his office to see how things were progressing. The next email came from one of his colleagues. He regretted informing me that Igari had died in the Philippines. What he could tell me was that, on August 27, his body had been found in his vacation home in Manila with his wrists seemingly slashed. The time of death was unknown.

Igari had been working on his final book, *Gekitotsu* (*Collision*), prior to his death. It's an amazing work that pulls no punches, using the real names of the yakuza and the politicians and individuals connected to them.

Before leaving for Manila on vacation, he had told his editor, "I'm nosing around in dangerous places. I don't know what's going to happen to me. Let me sign the publishing contract now."

I went to Igari's offices in September to pay my respects; there was no funeral. There was a little shrine for him in his office, but everything was pretty much as he'd left it. On his desk was a heavily notated article about the Sumo Association's match-rigging. His secretary told me, "Igari-san was really happy to take your case. He laughingly bragged to everyone, 'I'm representing a reporter from *National Geographic*—that makes me an international lawyer!'" I could visualize him saying that with his deep, rolling laugh.

Grief is a funny thing. Seeing his empty desk, I got a little misty-eyed for the first time. I just couldn't believe that he would kill himself, especially after that roaring pep talk. That wasn't the man I knew.

Igari's partners picked up his case, and they helped me draft a letter to the publisher as a prelude to taking legal action. I wasn't sure that they would have my back if things went forward, and I didn't blame them. I was the last client he had ever had, and after taking my case he was found dead. Sometimes you really are on your own.

I asked around about what happened to him. I couldn't find anyone who had a solid reason for him to kill himself. There were a few newspaper articles speculating that he had been murdered and that it had been covered up, but nothing substantial. I spoke to his editor. I spoke to his friends. I spoke to his law partners.

There was a rumor he had gotten into trouble with a young female lawyer and that she was going to sue him for sexual harassment. I could never verify the rumor. It would have been a very yakuza way to kill someone. They invent a scandal that might justify a suicide, and then they kill their target and make it look like suicide. In Igari's case, there was no note left behind—not even one written on a word processor and printed out.

I was still in a bind. I was going to need help, because I was lost. I hated to ask yakuza for favors. I hated to owe anyone anything, because I generally feel an obligation to repay my debts, no matter how long it takes. Well, maybe I wasn't going to ask for a favor, but I was going to ask for some advice; asking for advice and asking for a favor aren't the same thing—although, to be honest, I know that in the yakuza world it often is the same thing.

It was never easy to reach the Elder, who was sort of my benefactor in the organization, but I did reach out to him anyway. On September 11, I went to the payphone that had been designated to me, and he called right on schedule.

The first thing he said to me was, "I heard your lawyer is dead. Igari was a pain in the ass, but he was a brave man. I'm sorry for your loss."

He always seemed to be one step ahead of everyone else, or at least me.

"Yes, he has passed and that's why I'm calling. I have a quick question for you: have you read Goto's book?"

There was a short pause at the other end of the phone.

"Yes, we've all read it. He's a cheeky bastard. What is that Italian thing called?"

I didn't immediately follow the conversation, "You mean Mafia stuff?"

"Yeah, that code of silence thing. Omeletta, or something like that."

"Omerta."

"Yes, well, he has no idea of that. We are at a loss as to what to do. If it was only his business he was screwing up, that's one thing. There are things in there that no one is supposed to know. But since it's a bestseller, shutting him up might draw a lot of attention. And he's a priest now. It's his confession, right?"

"Yeah. I don't read much remorse in there."

"He takes a few pot shots at you. And you know that there is certainly an implied threat."

"I know. I hired Igari-san to address the problem. He was going to demand a retraction from the publisher, and then we were going to take both of them to court."

It was such a long silence on the phone that I thought we had been disconnected.

"When was this? When did you hire him?"

"August 8. I was the last client he had."

If it was anyone else, they might have asked if I thought that Goto was responsible for my lawyer's death. Of course, I had considered the possibility, and, of course, so did he. I didn't even need to say it, because I knew that he understood.

"Let me look into this. In any event, the council would like to have a word with him, and so would I. I am coming up to Tokyo next week. Can you meet me at the Grand Hyatt on Sunday?"

Of course, I agreed. At the time, the Grand Hyatt was still one of the few places that seemed oblivious to having a yakuza boss stay there now and then. Either they didn't know who their clientele was, or they didn't care. The room wasn't booked in his name, but his Tokyo lieutenant met me at the French Kitchen, on the second floor, in the smoking section, and took me up to the room. There was a pack of my cigarettes waiting for me, some *yatsuhashi* (a popular souvenir snack from Kyoto), and him. Maybe it was because it was a Sunday, but he wasn't in a suit. He was lounging around the room in a dark bathrobe, and barefoot. The room was huge, in two parts, and it was dominated by a long table. I stood until he motioned me to sit down.

We chatted about the changing world. The crackdown on yakuza in the stock markets was still going full-force, and the Democratic Party of Japan had supposedly gained the support of the Yamaguchi-gumi, a subject on which he conversed with me wryly, pointing out that everyone knew that one of the Kansai DPJ members was in their pocket. I didn't bring up the elephant in the room, because I knew that he would. He did not disappoint me.

"Your lawyer was looking into a lot of things that make people uncomfortable. He was looking at our involvement in sumo, our involvement in baseball, and his book will likely ruffle many feathers as well—if it's ever printed. I will tell you that I know he did not die a natural death, and that's really all I can tell you. Your concerns about Goto are noted, and as you know I have no fondness for the man. I've made it clear to him that it would not be in his best interest if anything happens to you. So you can breathe easy, for the time being."

And that was that.

I did eventually get a copy from the Philippine police of the autopsy performed on Igari. He had been found dead in his hotel room in Makati City at 3.00 p.m. on August 27. Beside his body was a utility cutter, a cup of medicine that might have been sleeping pills, and a glass of wine. He was found face-up on the bed. There was a laceration wound on his left wrist. The autopsy found the cause of death to be a myocardial infarction. Suicide was not determined to be the reason for his demise. His brother, Tetsuro Igari, identified the body, and he was cremated. The ashes were flown back to Tokyo. Jaime Masilang, chief of the Homicide Section, made notes on the report.

The laceration wound on the left wrist seemed odd. It wasn't enough to bleed to death, and who would try to kill themselves with a cutter knife? But if you're going to stage a suicide without getting blood everywhere and possibly on yourself, maybe that's a good way to make the attempt.

I once asked Igari-san over wine, "Have you ever been threatened? Do you ever fear for your life?"

He didn't answer my question directly.

"I became a prosecutor because I wanted to see justice done in this world. When I quit and became a lawyer, I didn't go to work for the yakuza, like many ex-prosecutors do. I continued to fight them. Not all yakuza are bad guys, but 95 percent of them are leeches on society: they exploit the weak, they prey on the innocent, they cause great suffering.

"If you capitulate, if you run away, you'll be chased for the rest of your life. And if you're being chased, eventually whoever is chasing you will catch up. Step back, and you're dead already. You can only stand your ground and pursue. Because that's not only the right thing to do, that's the only thing to do."

And so I stayed. Igari-san wasn't an investigative journalist, and he wasn't a saint. But he fought for justice and for truth, and as an investigative journalist, I've always believed that's what our job entailed. Forgive me if that sounds naive. I believe that if no one stands up to the anti-social forces in the world, we all lose.

I expected that, when I called Igari's editor to find out more about why Igari felt his life was in danger, he would be reluctant to speak with me. That wasn't the case. He knew who I was. "Igari said you were one of the most trustworthy, crazy, and courageous journalists he knew."

It was the first praise I'd ever received from the dead, and it was more than I deserved. But it made me feel obliged to live up to those words. Sometimes, the best way to honor the dead is to fight for what they died for. That's the only way I know how to mourn. I wrote an obituary about him for the Committee to Protect Journalists. His life was spent as a prosecutor, but he died as a damn-fine investigative journalist. In the afterword to his book, Igari wrote the following. I have translated it as best I can, referring to what I remember from the earlier draft he had been kind enough to show me:

I have tried to write this book using real names (not pseudonyms) as much as possible. I know that this is a great risk for me.

I know that there are risks involved. But I wanted to write as frankly as possible about my struggle against the absurdities and injustices of society. To do this, it is only natural that we should write about our opponents by their real names.

Have we become too insensitive to the absurdities of our society? Have we become too inward-looking, too concerned only with what others think of us? Are we being swayed by the powerful? Do we pretend to be indifferent to the injustices around us for fear of upsetting the powers that be?

I don't give a damn whether anyyone likes me. I never flattered anyone. I've always lived that way.

Because I lived a stupidly honest life, there were many unforeseen circumstances, disadvantages, and great losses. But there is no point in regretting it now.

In my own way, I wanted to appeal to people that there is

meaning in life only when we confirm our existence and live with conviction. If even a few readers can relate to this or learn from my experiences, it would be an unexpected delight.

Before I began writing what you are reading now, I read those words many times. Even after he died, Igari had a lot to teach me. These days, his book is out of print. I still have a copy. Perhaps there comes a time when fate is inescapable, but I am certain that we have a great deal of choice in our lives. I knew that Igari would never choose to die as he did. His mysterious death in Manila is not the ending he would have envisioned for himself. Maybe he knew it was coming. Regardless of how he lived, he wrote the final chapter of his life in his posthumously published book. We all desire to be the master of our own destiny, and sometimes we do so by any means necessary, no matter how painful that may be.

PART II

THE MELTDOWN

CHAPTER TWELVE

The envelope

March 11, 2011

If you don't really want to know the answer, don't ask the question. Many people think they want the truth, or ought to know the truth, but when you tell it to them, they act as though you've personally assaulted them. Sometimes their reaction is to try to punch you, so learn to duck … or learn to fight.

If people don't like the message nowadays, they attack the messenger. The messenger and the message are treated as if they were one and the same, especially in journalism, and maybe it's always been that way for private investigators. Sometimes, you get hired by a client to determine whether the firm they're doing business with is actually a yakuza front company, and when you tell them that is indeed the unfortunate case, they will fight you every step of the way when you try to turn in your report.

It's a hard world when doing the job you were hired to do gets you nothing but trouble. Sometimes, the people who hired you to make sure they're complying with the law and not doing business with anti-social forces don't want an answer; they just want an alibi.

It was in 2011 that I began to have doubts about whether I wanted to stay in the business of finding out the truth.

———

In 2011, the world as I knew it started to melt down: physically, metaphysically, metaphorically—everything I thought I'd accomplished seemed inconsequential. I had been playing a winning hand for years, and suddenly the dealer at the upper table called my bluff, I had to fold, and the house had won. Maybe it was time to cash in my chips and get the hell out of Japanland.

It all started on March 11. I was in New York City, not Tokyo.

The Hardest Men in Town was the title of the yakuza film festival sponsored by the Japan Society in New York City, and I had been invited there to speak about the difference between yakuza films and the reality of the yakuza.

I even was lucky enough to have lunch with Paul Schrader, writer of *Taxi Driver*, directed by Martin Scorsese. Schrader had also written a wonderful and unusual film called *The Yakuza*, directed by Sidney Pollack in 1975, which featured Robert Mitchum and iconic yakuza film star Ken Takakura. Schrader enthralled me with tales of why his film *Mishima*, about Japan's literary genius turned right-wing bodybuilder revolutionary, Yukio Mishima, was never shown in Tokyo. He said that Ken Takakura had accepted the part, but later had to apologetically bow out, saying, "The people I work for will not allow me to be in this film. I hope you understand."

Mishima was homosexual or bisexual. It wasn't something people in Japan felt comfortable seeing on screen. Still, I was surprised to know that Takakura had even considered the role.

After finishing lunch with Schrader, I knew I had work to do. I had a few outstanding cases in my inbox—some corporate reports. I went up to my room late in the day to call my boss in what would have been his afternoon in Tokyo. We made chit-chat for a bit, and then I heard some rustling.

"I think we're having a bit of an earthquake," he deadpanned.

The rustling grew louder. I could hear people in the office talking to each other in gradually louder tones.

"Is everything all right?" I asked.

"The whole building is swaying. This is quite the earthquake."

"Maybe you should get out of there. Please let me know you're safe when you can."

"Shall do," he said. And he hung up.

I had no idea what the hell was happening. I called up NHK News (the BBC News of Japan) on my iPhone, which had been introduced to the world a mere three years before and had quickly become the phone of choice in the land of rising technology. The first reports were coming in of a massive earthquake. I tried calling my roommates back in Tokyo, but all the phone lines were busy or dead.

I spent the next hour watching a disaster unfold in slow motion—from across the ocean.

At 2.46 pm a 9.0-magnitude earthquake (the fourth-largest in recorded history) occurred off the coast of Japan. The earthquake started a geological disaster, like hitting the jackpot on a pachinko machine, but with nothing good coming of it. The tremors unleashed a massive tsunami, taller than Tokyo Tower, which reached Japan within half an hour. Cities were wiped out. Thousands of people died or simply vanished into the pounding waters.

And those waves went on to crash into the Tokyo Electric Power Company's Fukushima Daiichi nuclear plant. There were reports that the plants were in critical condition and that there might even be a nuclear meltdown.

It was bad news upon bad news. I hopped into a small coffee shop near the Japan Society and asked them to turn on their TV, and I watched. I started emailing friends. At least email was working. Twitter was working. Facebook—kind of. But I couldn't get anyone on the phone. In those days, I still called people instead of texting them. I didn't know anyone or have any friends who lived near the epicenter of the earthquake. That was something of a relief, but if I didn't feel the tragedy personally yet, it didn't mean I didn't understand the depth of the calamity.

For the first hour, I dealt with the news with detached calm. I made a checklist of people to contact. And I went through that list, one by one. I'd done this before, but it was a different kind of looming disaster back then.

Slowly, I started to feel a gnawing in my gut, as if I had been so busy that I had missed eating lunch and dinner, and there was no food in the house. I had a Zagnut bar in my luggage and took a bite, but I wasn't hungry. All I did was leave toasted peanut butter and coconut debris on the counter of the hotel room. I went back to the computer, typing away.

People started writing to me, calling me. It was the worst disaster to happen in the decades I'd spent in Japan, and I wasn't there. Normally, that's where I was all the time. In some ways, I suppose the timing couldn't have been better, because it must have been a terrifying week to be there.

I wanted to go back and make sure the people I loved were safe and sound, but the airports had shut down. Getting home would turn out to be an odyssey.

March 18, 2011

The only flight that would take me home left from San Francisco. It was a short flight, compared to going back from New York. The plane was nearly empty. Three of the nuclear reactors at the Fukushima Nuclear Plant had already probably melted down.

The authorities had evacuated the entire area around the plant, which had become a forbidden zone. There were rumors that a radioactive cloud was drifting from Fukushima to Tokyo. The situation didn't seem under control.

Had I survived a natural disaster only to fly back to a man-made disaster—was I doing the equivalent of taking a flight back to Chernobyl? The information available was contradictory and not encouraging. Was there another even bigger earthquake on the horizon?

I tried not to think about it.

I had a row to myself on the plane—rows upon rows to myself. I walked the aisles and thought about what I needed to do. The plane had a skeleton crew.

The flight attendants would vanish now and then, and it would seem like I was on a ghost ship. There were no crying kids in the seats, and the lights were low. When we approached Tokyo and started to descend, it looked like the whole country had gone dark. Could a few nuclear reactors going off the grid have crashed the electrical system? All across Japan, the lights were dimmed; there were only tiny points of light. We floated down into a field of fireflies.

The first thing I did when I got off the plane in Narita was find a place to have a smoke, and as soon as I lit up, I felt both a sense of relief and a weird, sweet kind of dread. It had taken me a week to get back from New York.

I was lucky enough to have someone pick me up. Saigo, my reliable ex-yakuza driver and bodyguard, showed up on time in his black Mercedes-Benz, the gas-guzzling monster he insisted on using for work. On my way home from the airport, we drop-ped off a bag of supplies (toilet paper, diapers, instant ramen, and blankets) to an Inagawa-kai yakuza boss who I knew would take them where they were needed.

It had been hard to get all the bags onto the plane. United

Airlines could have charged me for excess baggage, and almost did. The man at the check-in asked me why I was carrying so much, and I told him I was bringing relief supplies because of the earthquake. He said to me, "I am from Chile, where we had a terrible earthquake years ago. I think it's wonderful what you're doing." He didn't charge me. It was a nice moment.

When I got back to my house at 11.00 pm, on the wooden shelf in the entranceway was the white A4-sized envelope with the results of my very expensive medical check-up that I'd had done before I had left for New York. I had all but forgotten about it.

I opened it up. It was not good news. They had found a 3.6-centimeter tumor in my liver, probably cancerous: "Please come in for a follow-up examination as soon as possible."

I read the letter twice. I looked at the data twenty times—the pictures, the charts, the scans, the numbers. What did it all mean?

I felt confident that if there was a fortune-telling Magic 8-Ball in my hands, the answer floating in the murky waters would be "Outlook Not So Good" over and over. For a fleeting second, I thought about writing bad poetry, or maybe a haiku. But then I remembered the immortal words of Basho, the great poet, who once said the following:

How witty is he,
who sees a flash of lightning and does not say,
"Life is fleeting."

I took the results up to the tatami bedroom of my rented old Japanese house. I was too tired to deal with turning on the light; I touched the TaoTronics lamp on the desk, which lit up barely a quarter of the room. As I did so, I caused a minor paper avalanche.

Camille—my French flatmate, a redhead we all called Kami-sama (as if she was a god)—had piled up some of my mail and two weeks' worth of newspapers on my desk. She had stacked them neatly, and I had quickly and casually knocked them all over the place while fumbling for the light. I shuffled briefly through the newspapers: the *Mainichi*, *Yomiuri*, *Asahi*, *Sankei*. It was amazing how similar each newspaper's coverage of the nuclear disaster was; no one was calling it a meltdown yet, and everyone knew that it was.

I stole a glance at the *Yomiuri*'s coverage—they were pulling their punches. I had worked at that newspaper for twelve-and-a-half years, and I knew that Tokyo Electric Power Company, as one of its biggest advertisers, always got a certain amount of slack.

I searched my desk drawers for a pack of clove cigarettes, found one, and lit up, sucking in the sweet smoke and listening to the crackle of cloves and tobacco. The lit end of the cigarette sparked a little, and I was careful not to set the examination results on fire.

My grasp of Japanese medical terminology is not good, but I was certainly familiar with liver cancer, having seen documents that pertained to the liver cancer of one particularly bad man. Yakuza often have Hep C or other liver problems due to their tattoos, or the dirty needles and awls used in the tattooing process, or their histories of using methamphetamines via injections.

I definitely knew the characters for liver disease, in all its variations. The character for liver in Japanese is an important one. There's even a compound word in Japanese using the character for liver that means "what is really important." Literally: liver and heart. Those were important things.

Well, what else was important? After reading a single sheet of paper, everything that I was doing and had done seemed unimportant. In fact, I had been thinking on the long, nearly empty plane ride back that while the yakuza were a social evil and a menace to Japan and perhaps the world, there were worse things than the yakuza. One of them was the Tokyo Electric Power Company, which was lying through its teeth about the nuclear disaster and what they knew—as, possibly, were people in the Japanese government who had let them run amok for decades. I was thinking that really evil people might not necessarily have a tattoo. I chain-smoked a few cigarettes, trying to figure it all out, oscillating between self-pity, anger, hope, and fear.

First of all, there was no mystery here.

The probable reasons for my getting cancer were right in front of my face, between my fingers, and yet I kept smoking. I can't say that I was surprised. You're not going to stay well if you smoke all the time, drink excessively, put yourself in stressful situations, exercise rarely, and never get enough sleep—or only sleep when you can find enough sleeping pills to put you out for a few hours.

At least it was not prostate cancer. I might die, but I could at least enjoy fucking around for a few more months, or so I figured. Sex was the only extracurricular activity I enjoyed anymore. I distracted myself by looking at the rest of the results. Other than cancer, I seemed to be in relatively good health for a forty-one-year-old—very soon to be a forty-two-year-old—man.

I tried to calm myself. It wasn't a definitive diagnosis; it was only a preliminary diagnosis. I started looking at the words I didn't know in the document, one of them being "cancer marker." And when I checked what that meant—that it was an indicator of how likely it was that you had cancer—and what my cancer marker was, and the qualitative value of the figures I was seeing, I felt a sort of turbulence. Maybe it was another aftershock, a seismic one.

I wasn't sure what to do next. I wasn't sure who to tell. I

decided quickly that I wasn't going to tell my estranged wife or my kids. Why give someone something to worry about when there was nothing they could do about it? I don't believe that sharing is caring when it comes to personal crises. Sometimes, you just hand someone a burden without any way of alleviating that burden, just to make yourself feel better. The more someone cares about you, the more likely they are to worry about things like this.

They can worry, but they can't do anything else.

I would talk to my father. He was a pathologist and a coroner. He understood cancer and death. And he had a good sense of humor about those things.

I went for a walk in the neighborhood, still smoking away. The 7-Eleven was open. The lights were half off, and the shelves were nearly empty. As I expected, there was no toilet paper. When disaster strikes, the first thing that people in Japan hoard is toilet paper. Cue the Freudian "anal retentive" jokes. No one is sure why this happens, except that it has happened before. Japanese tradition.

I bought some chips, and I almost bought a bottle of Zima, "the malternative," but then I decided to just buy a bottle of Mitsuya Cider.

I was glad I had toilet paper at home. I thought about the shortage as I was walking back, and came to one conclusion. It wasn't just a Japan problem. Maybe it happens all over the world—crisis turns people into selfish assholes, and the first thing they think about is taking care of their own asshole.

For some reason, I remembered that when I started working for the newspaper in 1993, I was told that a wise reporter never drinks alone—it's a gateway to becoming an alcoholic, and I already had one vice that was bad for me. Now, there were 10,000 thoughts in my head. I couldn't think straight. I wanted some sort of sign from the universe as to what I should do next.

I decided not to go straight home from the 7-Eleven, but to go and drink down at the Hachimangu shrine. The huge stairs going up to the shrine from the park were always a good place to sit and think late at night. I could go buy a fortune, if they were open. I'm superstitious, and I wanted metaphysical reassurance.

The shrine was closed; there were no signs from the stars to be had. I sat on the concrete steps, shivering a little in the cold, finished my cider, and smoked a cigarette. When I got back home, I had only an occasional sense of swaying and dizziness; there were still tremors every day and every night. They weren't so bad, Camille said; they had been much worse while I was gone. "This is not my lucky year," she told me.

Yeah, this year was turning out to be an unlucky one. Unlucky for everyone. Maybe I just needed a lucky charm to ward off the diagnosis if I could find one before going back in for a follow-up consultation on Monday. That made no sense, but that's magical thinking for you.

I was sure I had a lucky charm somewhere, maybe pinned to my wooden desk, perhaps under the newspapers. It was either the one that warded off evil or guaranteed victory. I wondered if luck was a replenishable substance. I had a vague recollection that you were supposed to replace the protective talismans and other knick-knacks every year. Clearly, I had not been paying proper tribute to the gods.

I was still looking for it when I saw the placard. I've never been a huge fan of inspirational literature, but I did have a quote from my Zen master—although I thought of him more like a Zen big brother—written in Japanese calligraphy on a small placard taped to the wall.

I'm not sure that he was the person who said it originally, or if he was paraphrasing someone else, but I had been moved by the words when he had said them to me earlier in the year:

It's never too late
to be what you might
have been.
... Or wanted to be.

Yeah, it was a lovely sentiment, but maybe it wasn't true. Maybe sometimes it is too late to be the person you wanted to be.

I put the placard in my left hand, and I stepped onto the balcony. It was eerily quiet; there were no sounds of people chatting, no cars passing in the distance, no trains running. It was as if someone had pressed "mute" on the remote control of the world. Many people had already fled Tokyo, thinking that the nuclear accident might get even worse, that a cloud of deadly radiation might waft down to us in the metropolis. Massive numbers of *gaijin* had left Japan for safer places, earning the ridicule of those who had stayed behind, calling them "flyjin."

Well, I didn't consider them cowards or foolish. No one knew what the hell was going on in Japan. I'd only come back because I had work to do and people to take care of.

I had two cigarettes left. I put the second-to-last one in my mouth. There was a blue plastic bucket of water in the corner of the balcony, next to a faucet. Out of frustration, or in a kind of existential temper tantrum, I took out my lighter, and I set the placard on fire and dropped it into the bucket after it had almost completely burned to a crisp. I had second thoughts about what I was doing, but, of course, once you set fire to something, it's a little too late to have second thoughts.

I wanted to listen to depressing music, maybe early Miles Davis, while I smoked the last cigarette of the night, but the batteries in my headphones were dead, and I didn't want to go downstairs to look for new ones. In the hush of the night, I smoked my Gudan down to the stub and tossed it in the bucket. I went inside, closed the door behind me, and took two sleeping pills—Halcion to knock me out, and Nitrazepam (Nerubon) to keep me asleep.

As I felt the Halcion kick in, dragging me down to sleep, I couldn't stop thinking about the placard. Maybe it really was too late to change anything at all.

CHAPTER THIRTEEN

How to make a percutaneous ethanol injection cocktail

March 28, 2011 was a Monday. On that day, I celebrated my forty-second birthday by undergoing an MRI and receiving a diagnosis of liver cancer; I wondered if I'd have a forty-third birthday. I had also had a CT scan that day—it was like icing on the cake.

Actually, the day started off with a cupcake. Camille, my remaining roommate, had put a little frosted red velvet cupcake on the table with a candle on it for me. It was a sweet gesture, even if she spelled my name Jack. She still called me Jack, now and then, after months of us living together. I didn't mind. Maybe there weren't many Jakes in France.

As I packed my bag and looked for my suit that morning before going to the clinic, I felt a strange sense that the year had gone astray. This wasn't the year I had planned. Had I wound up in the wrong universe?

The year had started well. In 2011, I was still enjoying the fruits of *Tokyo Vice* being published. I spoke at universities. I spoke to investment bankers—for a fee. I traveled back and forth between the United States and Japan often. I even went to San Francisco to see Michiel. She was happily enrolled at the University of Monterey. She was in remission. It looked like leukemia had lost the battle with her, although I knew I shouldn't use that metaphor; it always seemed like a stupid thing to say. Cancer isn't intelligent, and it's not an opponent.

Michiel and I had a great time while I was visiting; it was like the good old days. We had a wonderful evening at the San Francisco Night Museum. There was music, booze, and access to the aquarium. Michiel and I danced at a little mock disco. At the aquarium, she did a hilarious impersonation of Ariel from *The Little Mermaid* drowning to death, which was probably in poor taste, but amusing to me at the time. We all sang a few verses of "Under the Sea" together.

But, as my father had told me, nobody is lucky forever.

In February 2011, after I had been in Japan for a few weeks, Michiel wrote to me: "Jake, you'll never guess what? Actually, you'll probably guess. The leukemia is back. I may have to return to Japan, because insurance may not cover it all this time."

She seemed chipper in writing, but when we talked on the phone, I felt a tinge of despair. I assured her it would all be good. She was a survivor.

"Hey, you'll always have a job with me," I told her. "Think of it as a great chance to get back to work and earn some serious due diligence money."

The due diligence business was still good. The Lehman Shock had wiped it out, but, by 2011, people were investing in Japan again. There was plenty of work for me to do. Plenty of work to share with Michiel. Except she would be in the hospital.

In February, I didn't think I'd also be spending a lot of time in the hospital myself.

So there I was, at 6.00 pm, on my birthday, on the table in a dimly lit room of a very fancy clinic, listening to three doctors discuss the best possible way to remove the 3.6-centimeter tumor from my liver. It was close to a major artery, almost poking out, so they felt that the sooner they could keep it from going mainstream, the better the chances that it might not metastasize—if that wasn't already the case. As often happens in Japan, none of them seemed to be aware that I spoke and understood Japanese.

I didn't go out of my way to make them understand that I understood Japanese perfectly. I wanted to know the unvarnished truth. Japanese doctors used to never tell patients they had cancer. They had reasons. Doctors feared that if you told a patient the truth, they'd kill themselves out of despair—even though treatment might be possible. They worried that the word *gan* (cancer) itself would rob the patient of all hope. And, oddly, the families were told before the patient. That had been the case with my father-in-law, but I wasn't my father-in-law. I wanted to know exactly what was going on and what my options were. So from the moment I walked into the clinic, after making an appointment days in advance, I had more or less kept my mouth shut and made every effort to only speak in English.

It had been a long morning. Many decisions had to be made.

How does one dress for a visit to a doctor when you're reasonably expecting a terrifying diagnosis? I decided to go with a dark suit, plain white oxford, and blue necktie. Japan is still a country where wearing a suit means people take you seriously, or that you're socially aware enough to know that donning a suit and tie means you're aware of the gravity of the situation. The act of putting on the suit, buttoning the shirt up, and pulling a well-made noose around my neck made me feel like I was somehow in control.

There are many ways to tie a necktie; I only knew the Oriental Knot. The name of the method to do this has probably been changed to something less archaic, but it's the simplest

way. You start with the reverse side out, and the wide blade of
the tie is lower than the narrow blade. Pass the wide blade under
the narrow blade, loop it up, pass the intersection. You pull the
wide blade down through the slipknot, and adjust accordingly.

Most of the time, I can only do it right if I don't think about
it. I was about to leave the house when I looked in the hall
mirror and realized that my tie was a strange gift from my time
at the *Yomiuri Shimbun*, with a Yomiuri Giants logo built subtly
into the pattern; you could see it if you really looked and the
light refracted off it. I thought about changing ties, but it was
too late. I was going to carry my past around my neck anyway.

All of Tokyo had decided to conserve energy after the nuclear
disaster—and maybe we all believed that with a few nuclear
reactors offline, we'd run out of power. For reasons that I never
understood, everything was kept dark. When I got out of the
elevator on the clinic floor, it appeared to be shut down. There
was no one in the immediate reception area; no one waiting for
an appointment. The vending machine in the corner of the foyer
in front of the clinic was the only thing emitting light. Had I
turned up at the wrong place?

As I stepped into the reception area, the motion sensors
turned on one of the lights, illuminating a woman behind the
counter in a classic nurse's uniform with even a hat on. The only
nod to modern fashion was the blue sweater over her uniform.
She said my name.

"Adelstein-san, we've been expecting you."

The facility was empty. As we passed down the hallway,
lights went on and off on our way to the room where the doctors
were waiting for me. I could hear my footsteps, the clack of the
nurse's high heels, and the click of the lights turning on and off.

It had been weeks since the Fukushima reactors had exploded, and the Japanese press and the government were still refusing to acknowledge that there had been a nuclear meltdown.

I understood the decision made by people who decided to flee Japan or get out of Tokyo. I never really saw that as a choice, but maybe I would have considered getting out had the situation been different.

When I opened the door to the examination room, there were three doctors waiting for me. I guess that was lucky. There were no other patients at that hour, or maybe even that day, and so with time on their hands they were there to greet me. There was a senior doctor with a white beard and a lot of pomade in his black-and-white hair. There was a middle-aged doctor with short hair who was wearing a polo shirt underneath his open lab coat, and who looked like he had spent a lot of time at the gym. The young doctor was tall and thin, and had square wire-frame glasses and a faux Beatles haircut. Quite a crew. The middle-aged doctor, perhaps only a few years older than myself, greeted me in good English, and I responded. The other doctors nodded their heads.

They explained the findings so far and what they were going to do next. I went through a battery of tests.

I thought about the possible outcomes. What if I needed a new liver? Holy fucking Buddha, that would be irony for you. What would I do? I was a poor candidate for a liver transplant, and I wasn't a politically connected and wealthy gangster. Could I blackmail Goto's surgeon into bumping me up the list? The blackmailing-a-rich-doctor thing I was okay with, but jumping to the head of the line might mean someone more deserving of a liver would certainly die.

I thought about this, sitting in the park during the lunch break, freezing my ass off, drinking a hot can of Boss coffee and wishing I had someplace to go. The park was mostly concrete, and whatever leaves had been on the two trees in it had withered away. I was the only living thing in it.

When I got back, I was told that they had decided that I should have a CT scan to be absolutely sure it was a tumor, and I agreed.

There was a discussion of whether performing a biopsy was a good idea or not. The Elder doctor stroked his beard and said, "The AFP blood test, CT scan, and MRI all indicate HCC. The other test results are typical of HCC, and look at this thing—it's huge."

I wanted to ask my father what all this meant, so I took notes in my head. AFP. CT. MRI. HCC. All those years of getting drunk with cops and crooks, and mentally taking notes so I could write them down later, was coming in handy. I had it all down in my brain.

I knew what a biopsy was, of course. My father has been a pathologist for most of his career, and worked at the Ellis Fischel Cancer Hospital for a few years; he was still doing "frozen sections" when I was in college. Anyway, not doing a biopsy sounded good to me. The less surgery, the better. HCC, well, that stood for hepatocellular carcinoma. I had no idea what AFP meant.

And so I listened as they discussed all the options. The Elder thought an operation was the best plan.

The tumor still appeared to be in one place in the liver, and to be the primary tumor. A skillful surgeon could do the resectioning with minimum damage to the liver. The Younger was gung-ho on radiofrequency ablation, even though he wasn't sure it was the thing to do for a tumor this size. The Elder was not convinced. "I don't think that has a proven track record yet. It's fancy, but will it get it all?"

The Jock doctor interrupted them both as they were jabbering: "Let's do a percutaneous ethanol injection. It's perfect. Not invasive. It's fast, and he seems to be the perfect case. I've done it before, and it worked well." He appeared very confident.

And that's when I raised my hand and spoke in Japanese.

"The percutaneous ethanol injection thing sounds great to me—what is it?"

And at this, the Elder and Younger did a doubletake. It was the classic, "Oh, look, the dog can speak!" expression of bemusement and surprise. Andrew Morse, a reporter at *The Wall Street Journal*, had coined the phrase to describe the reactions he got when querying bureaucrats at the Ministry of Economy, Trade, and Industry in Japan.

The Jock doctor was not surprised; he just laughed. He switched to speaking to me in Japanese immediately.

"What we do," he said, gently poking me where my liver was, "is inject 100 percent pure alcohol into your liver, where the tumor is. That's ethanol. The tumor dies, but the surrounding tissue is unharmed. We take a very thin needle, we use ultrasound or something like it to guide it—and we inject the booze into your liver through the skin. It usually takes about five or six sessions."

It seemed like a crazy idea, like homeopathic medicine. When you consider that consuming large amounts of alcohol probably was part of the reason I had liver cancer, treating it with direct injections of alcohol seemed wonderfully ironic. It wasn't the equivalent of treating lung cancer by smoking cigarettes, but it sure sounded like it.

Amy Plambeck once told me that they treat methanol poisoning with ethanol, which is weirdly funny. One letter of the alphabet can be the difference between life and death.

I wound my head around the idea some more. In Japan, they say that sake is the all-purpose medicine, that it cures ten thousand ills. I guess if it's taken as pure alcohol, maybe it could.

"Is it painful?"

He cocked his head. "Not normally. Your tumor is sort of surrounded by scar tissue. If it doesn't leak out of the target area, you should feel nothing. Even if it does leak onto the surface of the liver, maybe you'll have a fever and some pain. It certainly won't hurt as much as surgery."

The Elder nodded. As the Jock doctor explained a little more to me, the Younger "Let's blast it with radio frequency" doctor made a small objection with what normally would have been huge repercussions.

"The Ministry of Health, Labor, and Welfare only allows for percutaneous ethanol injection for tumors with a diameter of less than 3 centimeters," he said. "He doesn't qualify for this procedure."

At that, there was silence. A thousand things crossed my mind, but all of them boiled down to a crude realization: *I'm probably fucked.*

And then something extraordinary happened.

The Jock doctor pulled up the MRI, the CT, and the other files, and took a look at my file and my data. And he looked at both the other doctors and said, "Well, you know, in light of what we know now, I think we should recalibrate our findings."

And as he typed data into my file on the computer screen in front of him, with a light touch and a clickety-clack, suddenly the diameter of my tumor was a mere 2.9 centimeters. He showed both the doctors the screen. They shrugged their shoulders, and nodded. The Elder doctor smiled and said to me, "Well, it's just barely under the guidelines. We will need to start therapy as soon as possible. There's a hospital we can introduce you to. Can you go there next week?"

The Jock looked at me at the same time and raised an eyebrow, as if to say, "Last chance, kiddo."

I got it.

"Yes," I said, "I've got nothing going on. Schedule me in."

And that was that. I thanked them all profusely for their time. They asked me what I did for a living, and I told them. We talked about baseball, the nuclear accident, energy conservation, the fleeing foreigners, and the Tokyo Electric Power Company. The Younger doctor scuttled off to another room, and the Elder doctor left after him. I attempted to thank the Jock doctor for going out of his way to make sure I qualified for treatment. He seemed to sense what I was going to say. He cut me off.

"There are many ways to cure cancer," he said. "Almost all of them work. The only problem is that in curing the cancer, the treatments usually kill the patient. I know this treatment works—and hopefully it will work for you. That's the best-case scenario. But you can't miss a single appointment, and you need to listen to what the doctors at the hospital tell you. Check in with me any time."

He gave me his card. I gave him my card.

It didn't take long for the nurse to give me the bill for the day. It was around 11,000 yen ($110) for the MRI, CT scan, bloodwork, and time spent with the doctors. Japanese public health care is amazing. I couldn't even imagine how much that would have cost me in the United States.

I left the clinic with all my data on a CD, and my next appointment printed on my clinic card. When I got home, I copied the data and the photos, and sent them to my father for a second opinion. He agreed. Percutaneous ethanol injection was the best treatment. There was no guarantee that it would work, he said, but it was unlikely to hurt me. It was the best possible option.

After I'd read my father's replies, I took off my necktie and hung it on the coat rack, crawled up to my room, and turned out the lights. I hadn't done anything, and I was incredibly tired. It seemed to me that I could still feel the CT ink swishing around in my veins. I was tired, but sleep would not come.

I sat up on my futon reading a book of sayings attributed to Dōgen Zenji, the founder of Soto Zen Buddhism. I had been reading the book hoping it would help me find some of that Zen master calm and equanimity in the face of what seemed to me a rather premature death. I had marked a few passages that resonated:

All things are impermanent
What is born will also die
There is no meeting without parting
What has been gained will be lost
What has been created will be broken
Time flies past us like an arrow fired into the void
All is evanescent

Tell me—
In this world, is there ...
Is there anything that is not transient?

Nope. The answer is a big fat, no. Dōgen, you make a good point.

There are many ways to enlightenment, or so I have read.

Remember the favorite of Californians, Tantric Buddhism, where you free yourself from desire through desire. That always sounded appealing—to defeat sexual desire by having lots of long, slow sex.

There was something tantric about this cure that they were offering. Think about it: they were going to cure my liver cancer by injecting alcohol into my liver.

Fight fire with fire. Fight poison with poison. I was willing to try anything at this point.

I'd spent so many years worrying about getting killed by an angry yakuza that I'd never really prepared to deal with my worst enemy: myself. But thanks to the article I'd written on my way home, I suddenly found that a great many yakuza no longer regarded me as an enemy; they regarded me as a friend. Funny how that worked out.

CHAPTER FOURTEEN

Yakuza to the rescue

The most important thing is to help the weak. Duty and kindness follow. Then the third would be: don't betray others.

—SHINICHI MATUSYAMA, CHAIRMAN OF THE KYOKUTO-KAI, ON WHAT IT MEANS TO BE A YAKUZA MEMBER

Maybe it has to do with living up to the slogans that the yakuza profess. Or maybe it's about getting a stake in the reconstruction of Japan. Construction is a big business.

—SUZUKI TOMOHIKO, FORMER YAKUZA FAN MAGAZINE EDITOR, AND AUTHOR OF YAKUZA AND THE NUCLEAR INDUSTRY

Sometimes, bad people do good things, but that doesn't mean they've suddenly become good people. Sometimes, kind people do cruel things, but that doesn't mean they've become cruel people, or were cruel bastards all along. Adversity brings out the best and worst in people.

The yakuza have always professed to be good Samaritans, fighting the strong, protecting the weak, and coming to the aid

of the struggling in times of calamity. The period after 3/11*
was one of those rare times when the yakuza were a benefit to
society.

I remembered that after the Kobe earthquake in 1995, the
Yamaguchi-gumi had been faster than the government in getting
help to the people that needed it. They provided soup, warm
blankets, makeshift beds, diapers, and other living essentials
faster than the Red Cross. It helped that they had huge amounts
of money available, made from squeezing local businesses and
illegal enterprises nationwide. They could afford to be generous.
They also benefited from strong leadership, deep connections
in the logistics industry, and no red tape. No receipts needed.
No approval required. No bureaucracy. Kobe was their turf,
and they took the opportunity to show the community that they
were part of it—not just parasites, but sometimes providers. Of
course, there was a calculated public relations aspect to that
selfless work, but there was also genuine concern for the welfare of those who lived there.

I went to cover the Kobe earthquake in 1995. I'd talked to
some of the Yamaguchi-gumi members there about the work
they'd done, and to the locals. I also remembered that in the
chaos that followed the earthquake, some Yamaguchi-gumi
factions killed their criminal rivals and buried the bodies in the
rubble. When opportunity knocks …

Aside from a few inter-yakuza murders, the Yamaguchi-gumi
had mostly done a great job of helping the residents. These
charitable acts were, of course, milked for years to justify their
own existence, but it doesn't mean the thugs at the ground floor
weren't sincere in their work.

---

*   "3/11" has become shorthand for the series of disastrous events that rocked
Japan, starting on March 11, 2011: the earthquake and tsunami that devastated
the country and the nuclear reactors in the Fukushima prefecture. Just as 9/11
is self-explanatory in the U.S., in Japan, when you say 3/11, everyone knows
what you mean.

A few hours after the 3/11 earthquake, I figured the yakuza would be running to the rescue again. I figured correctly.

Right after the meltdown, while I was still in New York trying to find my way home, Lucas Wittman from *The Daily Beast* sent me an email. He knew my editor, Timothy O'Connell, at Random House/Pantheon. *The Daily Beast*, which was still vaguely part of *Newsweek* at the time, wanted coverage of the disaster—including anything I could bring to the table. I pitched him "Yakuza to the Rescue."

I told him on a phone call, "You need to know the yakuza's standing in Japanese society to understand why they'd play a useful role in preserving peace and providing humanitarian relief."

I told him they had 80,000 members, and when you added up their front companies, affiliated industries, and associates, they were almost a second army in Japan. And as unlikely as it might seem in the aftermath of the disaster, they might be among Japan's first responders.

I was in touch with Saigo and a few other sources back in Japan, and, sure enough, the yakuza were doing their part to aid in the disaster relief. It took phone calls and emails to catch up. Twitter was working, even while the phone lines were not. The internet was definitely a more reliable communications network.

The Inagawa-kai—which had 10,000 members, offices all over Japan, and a foothold in the Fukushima area—was divided up into blocks, and the Tokyo block (known as Kanagawa) was doing the heavy lifting. They were already dropping off a lot of supplies in Fukushima and Ibaraki. This was the beginning of their humanitarian efforts. Supplies included cup ramen, bean sprouts, paper diapers, tea, and drinking water. The drive from Tokyo to the devastated area took them twelve hours. They went through back roads to get there. They traveled through the highly radioactive forbidden zones. They were going into radiated areas without any protection or potassium iodide. Typically, 100 to 150 members would go per mission with a minimum of twenty trucks.

On the micro-level, the Kanagawa block of the Inagawa-kai sent seventy trucks to Ibaraki and Fukushima, dropping off supplies in areas with high radiation levels. They didn't keep track of how many tons of supplies they moved. The Inagawa-kai as a whole had already moved over one hundred tons of supplies to the Tohoku region.

I didn't doubt the people I was speaking to about their efforts in bringing aid, but I needed some proof for my editor. I called up a boss of a low-ranking yakuza group in Tokyo, Mr Purple, fondly beloved by all. That is, unless you were on his bad side.

"Hey, I think what you're doing out there is awesome. I'd like to write it up. Do you have any photos I can use?" I asked.

"Photos? Maybe. Maybe I can send some video. But you can't use it. We'd be so fucked. We're trying to keep this on the down-low, so the cops don't get in the way."

"I think they'll figure it out pretty quickly."

"Yeah."

There was a long pause.

"You gonna run this story immediately?"

"No, a few days from now. Will you have time to do what you have to do as the first responder?"

"Perhaps. I'll send some footage. It's really cool! Some guys were even wearing Inagawa-kai jumpsuits to help out. But that was a little too conspicuous. You get what I mean?"

I had seen the tracksuits, so I knew. I sent the footage to Lucas with strict instructions about how to handle it. I began documenting the yakuza aid efforts from across the ocean with help from sources, cops, locals, and, surprisingly, a great number of yakuza as well.

It was important for me to get a granular sense of the yakuza's role as first responders in the rescue effort. I had footage of their efforts in one city and talked to people who had gone on the run. Also on the scene was a friend of mine, a local reporter.

It was at about midnight on March 12, less than a day after the devastating earthquake struck the Tohoku region, that trucks carrying roughly fifty tons of supplies arrived in front of the Hitachinaka City Hall in Hitachinaka, in the Ibaraki prefecture. A hundred guys in long sleeves and coats started unloading the boxes right away. They weren't the Red Cross. They were part of the Inagawa-kai. All of them tried to hide their affiliation.

The sleeves were rolled down to hide the ornate tattoos that marked so many of Japan's yakuza members. Those who had missing fingers wore gloves. There were no gang badges with bushels of rice and Mount Fuji in the background, like the Inagawa-kai symbol. The yakuza group's corporate emblem wasn't displayed. Some yakuza members have the logo tattooed on their chests; it goes without saying that no one was bare-chested that night.

They came under the cover of night because they didn't want their donations to become a public affairs issue. Since Takaharu Ando, the head of Japan's National Police Agency, declared war on organized crime on September 30, 2009, things had been tough for regulated but not illegal organized crime groups in Japan. The Inagawa-kai knew that any high-profile operation, even one with charitable intentions, might invite harsh crackdowns from the police.

Hitachinaka City Hall employees knew who they were. One of them videotaped the delivery, but they didn't turn down the supplies; nobody else seemed willing to supply them. The main roads had been uprooted and split in half, electricity had been knocked out, and sewage lines had exploded. The historical museum had collapsed, over 1,000 houses were damaged, and, on March 13, over 9,000 people were crammed into sixty-eight shelters in the city.

During the video I was shown, gangsters unloaded blankets, water, instant ramen noodles, bean sprouts, flashlights, batteries, paper diapers, and toilet paper in front of the still-standing city hall. They were loud, but they moved quickly. City officials watched as they nodded at them and then left. The next day, 200 Inagawa-kai members arrived at Kasumigaura City Hall in the Ibaraki prefecture with 100 tons of food and supplies in thirty trucks. They brought twice as many blankets this time. They took two hours to unload their supplies in front of city hall, and then they left.

It was remarkable.

The earthquake shook the country at every level: political, economic, and social. The Japanese government's slow response to the crisis and the criminally inept response of the Tokyo Electric Power Company (TEPCO) made the nation shake with anger.

Yet while the Japanese cabinet was trying to figure out what to do, spurning U.S. help and failing to use Japan's de facto army, the Self-Defense Forces, the yakuza were picking up the slack.

In sparsely populated areas of rural Japan, where police were in short supply after the disaster and even before it, they also served as a police force. The reports of the disaster from Japan and abroad were full of stories about the absence of looting, theft, and crime in the wake of the chaos. In reality, that wasn't entirely true. ATMs were ripped out of empty convenience stores, smashed open, and the money taken. In the large, poorly lit shelters housing the refugees, there were fights, thefts, and sexual assaults.

Technically, yakuza aren't allowed to commit street crimes. Rape is not allowed either.

The yakuza frown on stealing purses, and on robberies, break-ins, and muggings: all the crimes that make the general populace uneasy. However, blackmail and extortion are generally acceptable. I once asked an Inagawa-kai boss, "Why aren't blackmail and extortion banned?" His reply was, "If you have something to be blackmailed about by us, you deserve to be punished. That's social justice."

Yakuza are brutal peacekeepers on their own turf. That's in their self-interest, too. If people are reluctant to visit the areas where sex shops, illegal gambling parlors, strip clubs, and hostess clubs are located, the operators lose money. It pays to keep the peace. Yakuza groups in Tokyo, Fukushima, Miyagi, Chiba, and other areas in Japan already had soldiers patrolling the streets, keeping an eye out for criminals, looters, and profiteers. The yakuza were the most visible "police presence" in sparsely populated parts of the Miyagi prefecture.

By sending out 960 members to disaster-affected areas, including Iwate, Miyagi, and Fukushima, the Yamaguchi-gumi acted as a second police force to maintain order within the shelters and devastated areas. They were referred to internally as the Yamaguchi-gumi Peace-Keeping Forces. To deter the common criminal and/or sexual miscreant, members were asked to show their tattoos and to walk around the shelters, making it very clear that they were yakuza. Yamaguchi-gumi were more prevalent at the shelters than police until March 21. By the beginning of April, officers from the Tokyo Metropolitan Police Department and others were dispatched to disaster areas. It is somewhat ironic that one of the very first roles of the yakuza in the post-quake chaos was to enforce the law.

Every yakuza group began to mobilize to help out: the Sumiyoshi-kai in Tokyo opened their offices to those stranded in

Tokyo; the Matsuba-kai rounded up 100 trucks and 121 drivers to carry water, blankets, and other essentials to the stricken areas; and Kyokuto-kai members sent food supplies and went themselves to the areas to provide hot meals.

Matsuyama Shinichi, the chairman of the Kyokuto-kai, said about the rules of being a yakuza, "The most important thing is to help the weak. The second is to fulfill your duties, obligations, and stay true to your feelings. The last thing is not to betray anyone."

During his three visits to the earthquake zones, a Kyokuto-kai member echoed those words, saying, "We can only do what we know. We're the guys cooking fried noodles at the festivals. It is tragic to take the equipment and food items we use for happy occasions like the Sanja Festival, and set them up for those mourning their loved ones and their homes. Not a joyful occasion. No words. A hearty welcome seems out of place, as does silence."

Of course, the most efficient and fast-moving group in the relief effort were the Yamaguchi-gumi, who have a history of post-disaster humanitarian work. Their experience as emergency responders dates back decades.

A third of the Yamaguchi-gumi organization is said to have been mobilized during 1964's Niigata earthquake to provide food, water, radios, and medical supplies to the area.

In 1995, after the great Kobe earthquake, the Yamaguchi-gumi, which has its headquarters in Kobe, gathered supplies from all over the country and brought them into the devastated city, dispensing hot food from their offices. As they patrolled the streets to prevent looting, they were lauded for delivering supplies to those who needed them more quickly and efficiently than the government did. They provided hot-food stands in the headquarters premises and daily essentials to all visitors. One of their more bizarre efforts was drilling a well on the headquarters grounds and supplying fresh water. In the end, it was a tremendous effort that gained the goodwill of the people of Kobe. It was also an incredible PR campaign.

On July 16, 2007, after the Niigata Chuetsu earthquake that resulted in the TEPCO nuclear accident that preceded the Fukushima meltdown, there was nothing that the Yamaguchi-gumi could do about the radiation, but they did make sure there was no starvation.

The Yamaguchi-gumi sent trucks and people to the area after 3/11 as well. They set up soup kitchens, and provided blankets, water, and food. The local merchant's associations and emergency shelters, even school principals, responded by sending thank-you notes to the yakuza.

In contrast to many government agencies in Japan, where staff rotation destroys continuity and accumulated knowledge, the Yamaguchi-gumi was able to learn from the mistakes of the past. In the Clinton era, when the Federal Emergency Management Agency (FEMA) was still a highly functional agency and a model for emergency responsiveness, one of its senior trainers went to Japan to share the agency's expertise. He remarked that his efforts were somewhat futile when it came to training Japanese government staff.

"I train staff, and just when they are familiar with protocols and how to respond, they're transferred to somewhere else. Sometimes they are transferred to an entirely different organiza-tion. There is nothing to build upon."

In that respect, the Yamaguchi-gumi was like a Clinton-era FEMA for Japan.

A Yamaguchi-gumi boss who personally drove two trucks into the Ibaraki prefecture, with tons of water bottles and enough food supplies to feed 800 people, proudly showed me pictures of himself cooking *yakisoba* for people near one of the shelters. He elaborated on why the Yamaguchi-gumi was able to be an effective first responder.

"You have to know what the people need. Here are things that were lacking: infant formula, diapers—both for babies and adults. There is a huge elderly population there."

Based on past disasters, the organization made a list of the essentials that were needed: food, water, warm clothing in all sizes, and sanitary napkins. Tampons, too, though most Japanese women do not like them. Allergy-prone children needed not only regular powdered milk, but also special brands. They collected raincoats, down jackets, kerosene heaters, and kerosene. Spring arrives late in Tohoku.

The foot soldiers were told to not just buy from large supermarkets, but to also visit local shops in the area and make purchases from them. They were instructed not to buy so much that the local shops would run out of merchandise. A delicate balance had to be struck.

Yamaguchi-gumi under police scrutiny used *kyoseisha* (cooperative entities) for much of their work. The gang members who went to help out all took great care to hide their tattoos and their missing fingers, just like the Inagawa-kai. Most of the support was organized by the Takumi-gumi faction's acting leader, Tadashi Irie, who was a financial genius and a good planner. Yamaguchi-gumi members distributed cushions, first-aid kits, shoes, socks, and garbage bags to stricken areas. The Yamaguchi-gumi Okuura-gumi leader in Osaka chartered several trucks with supplies, sending all 200 of his subordinates to disaster-stricken areas, including allegedly setting up temporary baths in the Miyagi prefecture and providing hot meals. The boss himself cooked food and served it to the displaced.

I asked several yakuza, both low-ranking and high-ranking, "Why are you doing this?" Some answered along the lines of, "Because I was told by my boss to volunteer." Others had more thoughtful answers. One Sumiyoshi-kai executive, a member of the Kato Rengo faction, and a full-time gangster who was adept at extortion, explained the efforts simply: "In times like this, societal divisions have no meaning. Yakuza and civilians, or foreigners and Japanese, do not exist. We are all Japanese. We live here together. Certainly, there is money to be made down the road. Right now, it's about saving lives and helping each other. Most yakuza are human garbage. Only 5 percent follow the rules. For now, we're all doing our best. It's one of the few times when we can be better than we usually are."

Even a senior police officer from Ibaraki, speaking on the condition of anonymity, agreed. "I have to give it to the yakuza. They have been on the ground since day one, providing aid where others cannot or do not. Laws can be like a double-edged sword, sometimes hampering relief efforts. Outlaws can sometimes be faster than the law. It happened here."

Other police officers saw things differently. "There is an element of this that involves fund raising," an Osaka detective in the Organized Crime Control Division said. "Yakuza members raise money for funerals and other events. They ask all the lower-ranking members of the franchise to chip in, and thus collect large sums of money. This is what they have been doing as well. This is one of the best ways to collect huge amounts of money right under our noses. I don't believe all the payments collected are going toward relief. Some 10 percent of it ends up in the accounts at headquarters, or in the pockets of some bosses. There's an element of money-laundering."

I didn't doubt it.

The Daily Beast published my article on March 18. It was an enormous hit—far more than I had anticipated. For me, the yakuza's disaster response wasn't unexpected, but if you didn't know Japan, it would have been surprising and a compelling read.

The Japanese media followed up on the story, and the foreign media did as well. I think it took time for some outlets to get confirmation. The police certainly didn't want to tip their hats to the yakuza. And the yakuza, already on the bad side of the cops and the government, didn't want to piss them off further by showing they were more competent than both.

One Inagawa-kai boss who had helped me write the article was summoned to Inagawa-kai headquarters by Kazuo Uchibori. Uchibori was angry about the attention that it was bringing, and my source thought he might have to offer up a finger as an apology. I felt terrible. I couldn't see that one coming. But I got someone to whisper into Uchibori's ear, "Isn't this good PR for us? In the end, isn't this what we're supposed to be doing?"

And my source, who didn't give up my name, despite the fact that pretty much everyone knew we were acquaintances, didn't have to lose a finger. Instead, he gained some rare praise from Uchibori and only a verbal reprimand not to talk to the press too much.

As for me, my article was translated into Japanese by people I didn't know, and then two versions showed up all over the internet. Tomohiko Suzuki, in the monthly yakuza fanzine, *Jitsuwa Jiho*, interviewed me and wrote a three-page article (published April 17, 2011) about my reporting on the yakuza coming to the rescue. He even noted my role in getting Tadamasa Goto kicked out of the yakuza—something that I thought would be cut from his article. It was still a touchy subject.

I wasn't used to being praised in a yakuza fanzine as being a fair and equitable reporter. I'd have to say that the spontaneous translations and the attention from the article changed my life. Both were widely read. I've never had more than twenty good sources in or connected to the yakuza in my career. But they all read the article, and they all liked it. Although I hammered home the point that the yakuza were merely returning some of the money they'd squeezed out of the locals over the years, everyone seemed to skip over it. Perhaps even the yakuza are prone to confirmation bias. The bad guys are always the other guys.

On March 20, the one yakuza I trusted the most, the Elder, called me from Osaka. This was two days after *The Daily Beast* article. At the time, the Yamaguchi-gumi hired people to keep track of what was written about them. No one should be surprised by this. He had been given a translation.

"Good work, Jake-san," he said over the phone. "We kept a low profile this time, but honestly, the publicity didn't hurt us. In fact, it helped us." He laughed at his own joke. "We can't be considered publicity hounds either ... but you might be." Both of us laughed.

I was thanked for bringing some attention to the good done by the yakuza. I pointed out to him one passage that argued a little differently in the article.

Ninkyo(do), according to yakuza historical scholars, is a philo-sophy that values humanity, justice, and duty and that forbids one from watching others suffer or be troubled without doing anything about it. Believers of "the way" are expected to put their own lives on the line and sacrifice themselves to help the weak and the troubled. The yakuza often simplify it as "to help the weak and fight the strong," in theory. In practice, the film director Juzo Itami, who was attacked by members of the Yamaguchi-gumi Goto-gumi because of his films depicting them harshly, said, "The yakuza are all about exploiting the weak and disadvantaged in society, and run away from anyone strong enough to stand up to them and their exploitive extor-tion." He was primarily correct, I think ... of course, most yakuza are just tribal sociopaths who merely pay lip service to the words.

The Elder just laughed. "Goto was and is a walking piece of dick cheese. He's the worst of the yakuza. However, you also wrote something thoughtful. You said that we valued *giri* (reciprocity)—at the least the best of us, and you yourself know that sometimes that is true."

He was right. The main reason I was still alive because he watched my back. I never asked for it, and he never directly offered such protection, but I understood.

"I do know that's true," I said, "I get it. That's why the article throws you and all the other yakuza a bone."

As we talked, we discussed the situation in Tokyo and Fukushima. When I told him about my reporting on TEPCO, he was interested. "They are a thousand times worse than we'll ever be," he said. This was difficult to disagree with. It crossed my mind to mention my battle with liver cancer, but I decided not to. Chemotherapy was harsh, but it was my burden. Additionally, the whole thing might have been seen as a request to get a new liver, and really, that wasn't something I wanted to ask for.

He asked me a question, "When are you going to write about TEPCO and the disaster at Fukushima?"

I thought about it for a second, "As soon as I know enough to write something about it. I don't know anything about nuclear power. I'll need to know more."

"Well," he took a deep breath, "you should know that the yakuza and the nuclear industry here are deeply in bed. And there was a time when TEPCO paid us a lot of money to make sure journalists like you didn't do their job and write the things they didn't want written."

I was intrigued, but, without missing a beat, said to him, "But of course, and no disrespect to your profession, for decades you people were also happy to look the other way in exchange for TEPCO advertising money. Nuclear energy corrupts and spoils everything it touches. Yakuza, TEPCO, corrupt politicians, we're all part of that dark empire. I hope you can shed some light on it."

I was certainly going to try.

CHAPTER FIFTEEN

The dark empire

Normally, if you're running a power company and your criminal negligence causes a nuclear meltdown, you're going to go out of business. Would Tokyo Electric Power Company be dismantled? Was it responsible? What did the future hold for the company? A lot of foreign investors with shares in TEPCO wanted to know—and so did Oldman. Within a week of the disaster, I was asked to do a massive due diligence job on the company. Except this time, I insisted that I be allowed to write about what I learned for publication as well. Oldman wasn't thrilled about this idea. He told me as much in a coffee shop a station away from his office.

"Jake, that would be highly unusual."

"Well, these are unusual times. I need to write about this. It's important."

"I get it. I'll convince the penny-pinchers and power brokers upstairs that there is a method to your madness. I will tell you that there will be some stipulations."

The rules turned out to be simple: after they had received a final report, I would have to wait two months to write an article. They had "an exclusive." It seemed like a fair deal to me. It was going to take a lot of money to finance this investigative journalism, and so I agreed. Over the years, investigative journalism has fallen into a decline in the U.S. and even in Japan—because it takes money to do the work, and newspapers don't have that money. It's much easier to lead with stories of violent crimes and celebrity gossip—at no risk and often very little cost. I was glad that I had the financial backing to take a deep dive because the client wanted to know if TEPCO was going to fall apart. This was a lucky case of synergy.

The biggest obstacle I would face in reporting what really happened at Fukushima was that I didn't know anything about nuclear power. I didn't understand how a nuclear power plant worked, and I didn't understand how a meltdown happened. This is one of the joys and challenges of being a reporter: having to learn about things you don't know anything about.

And the fact that I felt terrible most of the week also helped. I couldn't socialize very much. The percutaneous ethanol see- med to have worked, yet my cancer marker hadn't gone down. So, although the tumor appeared to have been wiped out, I had been given the option of making sure that any lingering cells were decimated. I took the option, and was undergoing chemo- therapy by late April.

If I had been offered the option of radiation therapy, I don't know if I would have taken it. I was already spending a lot of time learning about radiation, and I didn't want to live it 24/7.

I bought a few books for children on nuclear energy and the pitfalls of the industry, which I found to be well illustrated and well written. I searched for articles critical of the nuclear industry and past accounts of disasters that had preceded the Fukushima accident, some of which I remembered reading about before, if only briefly.

It was while scouring Amazon for something meaty that I found an entry for a tome called *Tokyo Electric Power Company: The Darkness of an Empire*. It had apparently sold only 3,000 copies. There were no reviews on the site, and it was out of print. I ordered a used copy.

It had been published in October 2007 and was by Katsunobu Onda, a journalist born in 1943 and a veteran reporter. He had been following nuclear power matters for the *Weekly Gendai* and other publications for thirty years. Those documents were valuable resources, as they contained facts about TEPCO and testimonies from nuclear power professionals that Onda has chronicled. There were several parts of TEPCO's response to the Niigata Chuetsu offshore earthquake that seemed to suggest the company had anticipated the Fukushima Daiichi nuclear accident. In many ways, Onda prophesied the next disaster before it happened.

There was one more thing about the book that was fascinating. It was almost a biography of TEPCO as a human being. There was a documentary called *The Corporation* that made the point that many corporations had a personality, and that their personality was almost always sociopathic. In the U.S., the Supreme Court ruled that corporations have the same rights as individuals, but in Japan it seems like they are granted more rights than human beings. The corporation is a demigod.

TEPCO almost seems to be an embodiment of callous cruelty, greed, and evil. Over and over again, Onda documented how the company covered up fatal mistakes and mishaps and went out of its way to make sure that even its employees didn't really know what was happening.

Onda had three decades of experience covering TEPCO and nuclear energy in Japan, so there was no way I'd learn more than him in such a short time. I wanted to hear what he had to say. I reached out to his publisher shortly after the disaster in a very politely written letter, and they set up a meeting.

Onda, at first sight, was the grayest man I had ever met. His hair was gray, his skin was gray, and the rims of his glasses were gray. It was as though he had met a succubus who had sucked out his life force, leaving him barely alive. He was wearing a dark suit and a patterned polo shirt, and I hesitated to shake his hand for a second, as if he might accidentally drain the life out of me as well. But as we sat down and he began talking about his book and his research, his eyes lit up, and he came alive.

It was during our talk that I first heard the words "nuclear mafia." The term didn't refer to the fact that yakuza or ex-yakuza were often doing the grunt labor at the nuclear power plants or the hiring of the workers. The term referred to the collusion between the company, politicians, private security forces, and other large corporations with vested interests. The United States has its own military-industrial complex, which Eisenhower warned us about before fading out into the sunset, and I quickly learned that Japan had a nuclear-industrial complex—in other words, a nuclear mafia. It is so deeply entrenched in the country that it's hard to imagine it will ever really go away. Or maybe it will last as long as it takes to clean up the Fukushima disaster—another fifty years.

I praised Onda's book, and I asked him point blank why it hadn't sold more copies. He crossed his arms, leaned back in his chair, and spoke to me the way you would tell a small child that Santa Claus doesn't exist. "Because no newspaper would carry an ad for the book. No major magazine would review it. There was no television coverage. Do you want to know why?"

I did.

"Because TEPCO is one of the biggest advertisers in Japan. The mass media here is part of that nuclear mafia—they are parasites on the TEPCO budget. The figures are phenomenal. The mass media here played a central part in making the public accept nuclear power, and they have done their best to gloss over every accident, every disaster, every inhumane act or crime involved with the nuclear industry here. TEPCO alone spends the equivalent of $300 million in advertising every year—-the bulk of that goes to the press. That's not to mention the wining and dining of reporters like yourself, back in the days when you worked for one of the national papers."

As he said this, I recalled eating a very good Kobe steak at a dinner with TEPCO flacks in Saitama around 1998. They had paid; I had chewed. I'd written something in return.

Well, I had eaten off the platter, and now it was time to make amends. I knew which publication I'd write the first article for. I just didn't know when. With Onda's help, I started to prepare for that day. I met former nuclear workers. I located an American who'd blown the whistle on malfeasance at the Fukushima plant. I spoke to nuclear engineers who'd worked on the plant. And I talked to yakuza from several factions. The yakuza were supplying the labor for most of the nuclear power plants in Japan. And Saigo helped me locate a worker who had been on site the day of the earthquake and at the start of the meltdown.

I was going to write all this up in an article for *The Atlantic Wire*. I'd never really written about Japan's nuclear problems before, for any publication, so this would be something new for me. I was excited about it.

It was a strange time to be in Japan. Every evening, NHK would announce the radiation levels for major cities in the country as regularly as it presented the weather report. Another news staple was that TEPCO would admit to more problems every night, and then apologize for them. Each subsequent day brought more news of radiation leaking from the plant, along with reports of mistakes, cover-ups, and corporate malfeasance by TEPCO. Slowly, voices within and outside the Japanese government were beginning to suggest that it was time to dismantle the company and put its nuclear plants under government supervision. Books highly critical of the firm were becoming bestsellers.

No one republished Onda's book, but used copies were

selling out, and he was hired to write a new book on the nuclear industry. He was inspirational and prescient.

We agreed: TEPCO had become a symbol of everything that was wrong with Japan: cronyism, collusion, gentrification, corruption, weak regulation, and entropy. Despite being in the spotlight for the worst nuclear disaster since Chernobyl, TEPCO continued to engage in questionable labor practices, managed to escape bankruptcy in closed-door meetings with politicians, and, by denying its culpability, shifted part of the reparations burden onto taxpayers—deeds that testified to the extent to which TEPCO still had plenty of political power, if not as much nuclear power.

For months, TEPCO had been insisting that the cause of the nuclear disaster was the "unprecedented" tidal wave that had flooded the emergency generators, delaying cooling.

TEPCO, originally a public utility until it went private in 1951, had enjoyed over half a century of lax government regulation, a de facto monopoly status in the power industry (and the security that accompanies such a position), and finally an increasingly untouchable image, fortified by every scandal that had gone virtually unpunished. The headquarters must have been constructed from Teflon.

Despite its many accidents, TEPCO had managed to shield itself over the years from rigorous investigation and censure. It had done so, in part, by wining and dining the Japanese media. It was spending nearly a half a billion dollars in advertising each year. It hired retired National Police Agency bureaucrats and former officials from the Ministry of Economy, Trade, and Industry (METI) as "special advisors." Using political connections, threats, and a complacent press, they have managed to stay in business.

There were many signs that TEPCO was incompetent and corrupt long before 2011. In June 2000, Kei Sugaoka, a

Japanese American engineer who had worked at the Fukushima reactor, blew the whistle on decades of TEPCO's cover-ups and dangerous practices in a letter to METI.

Onda had written about this, and I managed to track down Sugaoka and get hold of a copy of his original letter. The letter, which details some of his work at the Fukushima plant as an inspector for General Electric (GE), which helped build the plant, states:

> I was performing a visual inspection on the steam dryer [a critical part of the nuclear reactor] at the Fukushima site Unit 1 for TEPCO; the dryer was inspected and found cracked to the condition to where it was required to be replaced by a new one at an extensive cost to Tokyo Electric Power Company. I have inspected numerous BWR (Boiling Water Reactor) steam dryers and never discovered a dryer damaged to that extent.

Then came the most damning evidence:

> We submitted [video] tapes to TEPCO that were going to be sent to METI, edited with visual cracking intentionally omitted per TEPCO request.

Sugaoka proved to be a valuable source in finding out everything that was rotten in the TEPCO empire. I first interviewed him on the phone on May 23. Sugaoka refused to comply with the request to edit the tapes himself, noting that this was a criminal offense. "I wasn't willing to lie," he told me. "That made me a troublemaker. Lying was standard practice at TEPCO, and maybe for most of the nuclear industry."

This letter did not prompt action by the government until 2002, when an investigation revealed that, for over two decades, the utility company had been consistently falsifying data at its nuclear power plants: specifically, there were twenty-nine instances of altered data pertaining to cracks in devices in the core structure of at least thirteen nuclear reactors. Regarding the delay, the METI minister at the time remarked lamely, "Taking two years [for the government investigation] is too long in light of common sense. It should have been done more swiftly."

After the 2002 scandal, the nuclear reactors were shut down for inspection. Unfortunately, this was about the extent of the action taken to address TEPCO's delinquency. The Nuclear and Industrial Safety Agency (NISA), which was part of METI, didn't file any criminal complaints against TEPCO on the suspiciously irrelevant grounds that the cracks had been fixed. It was the police equivalent of letting someone go on charges of attempted murder because "they didn't succeed in killing the victim."

The president, vice president, and chairman resigned over the scandal—a sacrifice that seems less weighty when considering that they all then went on to serve as advisors to the company. At that time, the earliest cover-up was thought to have dated back to 1986; however, in a later, 2007 investigation, TEPCO admitted to an additional 199 occasions "involving the submission of false technical data to authorities." Unfortunately, whatever reforms had been put in place after these investigations were too late; as examined in Onda's book, only a few months later on July 16, 2007, a powerful earthquake hit Japan's north-west coast, causing malfunctions at the Kashiwazaki-Kariwa plant. The quake caused radioactive leaks, burst pipes, and fires, for which the facility was inadequately prepared. TEPCO later admitted that the company knew the fault line under the plant was capable of causing a 7.0-magnitude quake. The plant was created to sustain one up to a magnitude of only 6.5.

Beyond the usual media posturing and the occasional

sacrificed executive, TEPCO had not been held accountable
for these incidents, as the power industry is subject to only
a three-year statute of limitations on such offenses. METI
dealt with the bad publicity by placing full-page ads in major
newspapers on March 29, 2007, promising that Japan would be
the safest and most secure nuclear nation in the world. Akira
Amari, the minister of METI at the time, credited himself with
making TEPCO own up to its past fabrications and lies. In
fact, his name appeared in a font almost as large as the one for
the ministry. The ad promised that all improprieties would be
settled, further falsifications and lies would not be allowed, all
information in regards to trouble and accidents would be shared
with concerned parties, and safety would be the number-one
priority in future. By March 12, 2011, we all knew that the ad
was also a lie, and an expensive one at that. The ministry spent
an estimated 30 million yen (about $300,000) to send out that
message.

Onda had told me that he had felt a strange sense of déjà vu
when listening to the claim that the 2011 accident was "unforeseeable" at the initial press conferences. "It was the exact same
phrase trotted out in July of 2007," he noted. "The possibility of
a tidal wave causing a nuclear meltdown was not unforeseeable
either; members of the Fukushima Diet (the local legislature)
had warned the company as early as 2007."

Sugaoka scoffed at the company's use of the word "unprecedented" when describing the recent disaster. "TEPCO
knowingly used a defective, misaligned piece of equipment for
over a decade, and doctored video footage showing massive problems. Is it any surprise that the reactor would eventually break
down? The containment vessel was never designed to withstand
an earthquake. Unit 1 is forty years old—it should have been
shut down ten years ago. What was the Japanese government
thinking when they gave the firm permission to extend the

reactor's life for another ten years? And that TEPCO had the audacity to ask should tell you how close their ties are to the Japanese government."

The TEPCO that Sugaoka knew was an organizational mess at every level. "The plant had problems galore and the approach taken with them was piecemeal. Most of the critical work, construction work, inspection work, and welding were entrusted to subcontracted employees with little technical background or knowledge of nuclear radiation. I can't remember there ever being a disaster drill. The TEPCO employees never got their hands dirty."

Sugaoka also said he saw signs of yakuza ties among his colleagues at the facility. "When we'd enter the plant, we'd all change clothes first. The clean-up crews were staffed with guys covered with typical yakuza tattoos, a rough bunch," he said. Police sources confirmed that one of the companies supplying the plant with workers, M-Kogyo, headquartered in the Fukuoka prefecture, was a front company for the Kudo-kai, a designated organized crime group. A former yakuza boss noted, "We've always been involved in recruiting laborers for TEPCO. It's dirty, dangerous work, and the only people who will do it are homeless, yakuza, banished yakuza, or people so badly in debt that they see no other way to pay it off."

The regular employees were given better radiation suits than the often-uneducated yakuza recruits, although it was the more legally vulnerable yakuza and day laborers who typically performed the most dangerous work.

I spoke to one TEPCO executive, speaking on conditions of anonymity, who described the TEPCO working hierarchy as being something akin to that of plantation owners and slaves. The staff employees working at the nuclear reactors

enjoyed special benefits, safer conditions, and more stringent
radiation-level checks, while hired workers at the power plants
were considered subhuman.

"If you voice concerns about the welfare of temporary workers at the plants, you're labeled a troublemaker, or a potential
liability. It's a taboo to even discuss it." He told me that TEPCO
had roughly 10,000 employees staffing the nuclear facilities,
and 70,000 part-time workers doing the grunt work. That didn't
match the official figures I had at the time, but I'd already begun
to understand that TEPCO's official figures didn't mean very
much.

TEPCO had not handled the nuclear disaster well, neither
in the real world nor on the PR front. Initially, TEPCO denied
that any meltdown had occurred. On May 12, they confirmed
the suspicions of outside experts that a meltdown had already
taken place, and that it had probably happened within the first
few days after the earthquake.

This was only prompted by the notification that members of
an International Atomic Energy Agency investigation team were
coming to Japan to conduct their own investigation. TEPCO
"discovered" that not only had a meltdown occurred, but that
there had also been a "melt-through." (Fuel rods had melted and
also breached the containment vessel.) The company's former
president, Masataka Shimizu, resigned "to take responsibility."
Jumping in a nuclear reactor would have been a better way to
do it.

The extent of the damage was tremendous. Already, 90,000
people had been evacuated after the 9.0-magnitude earthquake
and subsequent tsunami created the nuclear crisis; the number rose again as radiation "hotspots" outside the 20-kilometer
evacuation zone emerged. Although 30 percent of Japan's
energy is generated at nuclear facilities, the consequences of
the disaster spurred talk of abandoning the country's nuclear

programs altogether. Many in Japan were asking to what extent they should continue to entrust this private corporation with highly dangerous energy sources.

It even seemed that TEPCO might finally face some serious consequences for their screw-ups. A few months after the disaster, the Special Investigative Division of the Tokyo District Public Prosecutors Office had begun a preliminary investigation into TEPCO on charges of criminal negligence resulting in death and/or injury. Meanwhile, the Labor Standards Bureau was investigating the company for violations of the labor laws. A Ministry of Justice source close to the investigation said to me at the time, "It seems very clear that TEPCO knew that an earthquake would probably damage the reactors and result in a meltdown. They failed to take preventive measures, and their response in the aftermath was negligent and insufficient, and, under Japanese law, they will be held criminally responsible. The question is who will take the fall and how far the investigation will go."

Of course, that was an optimistic assessment.

There was still one mystery left for me—and it had been bothering me from as early as late March 2011, when I began tracking down workers who had been there at the time of the disaster. Before the tsunami arrived, workers said the quake left its aging Unit 1 reactor crippled—and it was possible that the meltdown had started as soon as the earthquake hit.

Here's something you should know about Japan, if you don't already. Japan is located smack dab in the Ring of Fire—and that's not a reference to the Johnny Cash song. The Ring of Fire is a long, horseshoe-shaped area that is seismically active and dotted with earthquake epicenters, volcanoes, and tectonic plate boundaries on the fringe of the Pacific. Because of its location—which is subject to massive earthquakes, eruptions, tidal waves, and natural disasters galore—Japan is a terrible place for nuclear power plants.

It's the geographical equivalent of a recovering alcoholic spending his nights working in Golden-Gai, Shinjuku's densely packed city block of tiny bars and drinking dives.

There is no question that Japan is a bad place for nuclear energy, but the big question that was unanswered in 2011 was this: how much damage had the earthquake done to the reactors? It was the great mystery of this continuing nuclear disaster. I don't use the word "continuing" loosely. Fukushima is still a nuclear accident in progress. Watch what happens if they are unable to pump water into the core for a day.

The second big question, a refined version of the first, was this: how much of the damage did the March 11 earthquake inflict on Fukushima Daiichi's reactors in the forty minutes before the tsunami arrived? Everything depends on that answer. If the quake alone did so much structural damage that a meltdown was unavoidable, then every other similar reactor in Japan is at risk.

I had sources that indicated this was indeed the case. David McNeill, a reporter for *The Independent*, had similar information as well. We decided to combine forces.

Throughout the months of official lies and misinformation, one story had stuck: "The earthquake knocked out the plant's electric power, halting cooling to its reactors," the government spokesman Yukio Edano said at a March 15 press conference in Tokyo. That story, which has been repeated again and again, boils down to this: "After the earthquake, the tsunami—a unique, unforeseeable event—washed out the plant's back-up generators, shutting down all cooling, and starting the chain of events that would cause the world's first triple meltdown to occur."

Every time TEPCO and the Japanese government discussed the accident, they would repeat the word *soteigai* (unforseeable) like some sort of mantra or magic spell. It was as if, by uttering that magic word, they couldn't be held responsible for the disaster. And, of course, the disaster was defined as the "unforeseeable" tidal wave.

But what if the recirculation pipes and cooling pipes had burst, snapped, leaked, and broken completely after the earthquake hit, long before the tidal wave reached the facilities, and long before the electricity went out? This would not have surprised people familiar with the forty-year-old Unit 1 (Reactor One), the grandfather of the nuclear reactors still operating in Japan.

We spoke to several workers at the plant who recited the same story: there had been serious damage to piping and to at least one of the reactors before the tsunami hit. All requested anonymity because they were still working at the plant or were connected with TEPCO. One worker, a maintenance engineer in his late twenties who was at the Fukushima complex on March 11, recalled hearing hissing and leaking pipes. "I personally saw pipes that came apart, and I assume that there were many more that had been broken throughout the plant. There's no doubt that the earthquake did a lot of damage inside the plant," he said. "There were definitely leaking pipes, but we don't know which pipes—that has to be investigated."

A second worker, a technician in his late thirties who was also on site at the time of the earthquake, narrated what happened:

It felt like the earthquake hit in two waves. The first impact was so intense you could see the building shaking, the pipes buckling, and, within minutes, I saw pipes bursting. Some fell off the wall. Others snapped. I was pretty sure that some of the oxygen tanks stored on site had exploded, but I didn't see for myself. Someone yelled that we all needed to evacuate, and I was good with that. But I was severely alarmed, because as I was leaving, I was told and I could see that several pipes had cracked open, including what I believe were cold-water-supply pipes. That would mean that coolant couldn't get to the reactor core. If you can't sufficiently get the coolant to the core, it melts down. You don't have to have to be a nuclear scientist to figure that out.

As he was heading to his car, he could see that the walls of the Reactor One building had already started to collapse. "There were holes in them. In the first few minutes, no one was thinking about a tsunami. We were thinking about survival."

A third worker was coming in to work late when the earthquake hit. "I was in a building nearby when the earthquake shook. After the second shockwave hit, I heard a loud explosion that was almost deafening. I looked out the window, and I could see white smoke coming from Reactor One. I thought to myself, *This is the end*."

He didn't think about fleeing. Not yet. There was work to do. When the worker got to the office five to fifteen minutes later, the supervisor ordered them all to evacuate, explaining, "There's been an explosion of some gas tanks in Reactor One, probably the oxygen tanks. In addition to this, there has been some structural damage—pipes have burst. A meltdown is possible. Please take shelter immediately."

However, while the employees prepared to leave, the tsunami warning came. Many of them fled to the top floor of a building near the site and waited to be rescued.

The reason for official reluctance to admit that the earthquake did direct structural damage to Reactor One is obvious.

Onda explained it this way during our conversation: "If TEPCO and the government of Japan admit an earthquake can do direct damage to the reactor, this raises suspicions about the safety of every reactor they run. They are using a number of antiquated reactors that have the same systematic problems, the same wear and tear on the piping."

Onda notes, "I've spent decades researching TEPCO and its nuclear power plants, and what I've found, and what government reports confirm, is that the nuclear reactors are only as strong as their weakest links, and those links are the pipes."

During his research, Onda spoke with several engineers who worked at the TEPCO plants. One told him that, often, piping would not match up the way it should, according to the blueprints. In that case, the only solution was to use heavy machinery to pull the pipes close enough together to weld them shut. Inspection of piping was often cursory, and the backs of the pipes, which were hard to reach, were often ignored. Since the inspections themselves were generally perfunctory and done by visual checks, it was easy to ignore them. Repair jobs were rushed; no one wanted to be exposed to nuclear radiation longer than necessary.

Onda adds, "When I first visited the Fukushima power plant, it was a web of pipes. Pipes on the wall, on the ceiling, on the ground. You'd have to walk over them, duck under them— sometimes you'd bump your head on them. It was like a maze of pipes inside."

Onda believes it's not very difficult to explain what happened at Unit 1 and perhaps at the other reactors as well. "The pipes, which regulate the heat of the reactor and carry coolant, are the veins and arteries of a nuclear power plant; the core is the heart. If the pipes burst, vital components don't reach the heart, and thus you have a heart attack: in nuclear terms, a meltdown. In simpler terms, you can't cool a reactor core if the pipes carrying the coolant and regulating the heat rupture don't get to the core."

Tooru Hasuike, a TEPCO employee from 1977 until 2009, and a former general safety manager of the Fukushima plant, also noted: "The emergency plans for a nuclear disaster at the Fukushima plant had no mention of using seawater to cool the core. To pump seawater into the core is to destroy the reactor. The only reason you'd do that is if no other water or coolant was available."

Problems with the fractured, deteriorating, poorly repaired pipes and the cooling system had been pointed out for years.

In September 2002, TEPCO admitted to covering up data concerning cracks in critical circulation pipes, in addition to previously revealed falsifications. In their analysis of the cover-up, the Citizens' Nuclear Information Center wrote:

> The records that were covered up had to do with cracks in parts of the reactor known as recirculation pipes. These pipes are there to siphon off heat from the reactor. If these pipes were to fracture, it would result in a serious accident in which coolant leaks out. From the perspective of safety, these are highly important pieces of equipment. Cracks were found in the Fukushima Daiichi Power Plant, reactor one, reactor two, reactor three, reactor four, reactor five.

The cracks in the pipes were not due to earthquake damage in 2011; they came from the simple wear and tear from long-term usage, with signs of disrepair having become apparent over a decade earlier.

On March 2, nine days before the meltdown, NISA gave TEPCO a warning over its failure to inspect critical pieces of equipment at the plant, which included the recirculation pumps. TEPCO was ordered to make the inspections, perform repairs if needed, and give a report to NISA on June 2. The report appears to have never been filed.

Before dawn on March 12, the water levels at the reactor began to plummet, and radiation levels began rising. Meltdown was taking place. A TEPCO press release issued on March 12, just after 4.00 am, stated, "The pressure within the containment vessel is high but stable." There was a note buried in the release that many people missed: "The emergency water circulation system was cooling the steam within the core; it has ceased to function."

According to the *Chunichi Shimbun* and other sources, a few hours after the earthquake, extremely high levels of radiation were being recorded within the Unit 1 building. The levels were so high that spending a full day in the building would have been fatal.

The water levels of the reactor were already sinking. After the Japanese government forced TEPCO to release hundreds of pages of documents relating to the accident in May, Bloomberg reported that a radiation alarm had gone off 1.5 kilometres from the Reactor One on March 11 at 3.29 pm—minutes before the tsunami reached the plant.

TEPCO would not deny the possibility that there had been significant radiation leakage before the power went out, but it asserted that the alarm might have simply malfunctioned.

What we do know for certain was that on March 11, at 9.51 pm, under the CEO's orders, the inside of the reactor building was declared a no-entry zone. Around 11.00 pm, radiation levels for the inside of the turbine building, which was next door to the reactor, reached hourly levels of 0.5 to 1.2 mSv. The meltdown was already underway.

At its 7.47 pm press conference the same day, TEPCO's spokesman—in response to questions from the media about the cooling systems—stated that the emergency water-circulation equipment and reactor core isolation cooling systems would work even without electricity. Oddly enough, TEPCO later insisted that the cause of the meltdown was the tsunami knocking out emergency power systems.

Sometime between 4.00 and 6.00 am on March 12, Masao Yoshida, the plant manager, decided it was time to pump seawater into the reactor core, and notified TEPCO. Seawater was not pumped in until hours after a hydrogen explosion occurred, roughly at 8.00 pm that day. By then, it was probably too late.

On May 15, TEPCO went some way toward admitting at least some of the above claims in a report called "Reactor Core Status of Fukushima Daiichi Nuclear Power Station Unit One." The report said there might have been pre-tsunami damage to key facilities, including pipes. Shaun Burnie, an independent nuclear waste consultant, commenting on the report, noted that, "It raises fundamental questions [about safety] on all reactors in high seismic risk areas."

As Burnie points out, TEPCO also admitted a massive fuel melt—sixteen hours after loss of coolant, and seven to eight hours before the explosion in Unit 1. "Since they must have known all this, their decision to flood with massive water volumes would guarantee massive additional contamination— including leaks to the ocean."

No one knows exactly how much damage was done to the plant by the quake, or if this damage alone would account for the meltdown. However, eyewitness testimony and TEPCO'S own data indicates that the damage was significant. All of this, even though the shaking experienced at the plant during the quake was within its approved design specifications.

It turned out that TEPCO would tell the truth—accidentally and years later. And it should also be noted that the unfore-seeable tidal wave was something it had foreseen years before the accident. Its senior staff ignored the warnings and then lied about it—again and again.

In October 2012, in a report about the accident, the company admitted it had been afraid to examine the risks of a large tidal wave. In a bid to gain trust for its newfound honesty, the company said it had been afraid that any admissions of such a risk would result in public pressure to close the plants down. That was a calculated lie. They feared a public backlash, but they had, in fact, examined the risk of a large tidal wave—they had just decided to do nothing about the risk. As residents of the area sued TEPCO for damages, more and more of the truth came to light.

On January 29, 2018, the *Mainichi Shimbun* ran a report that showed TEPCO had refused to even look at the threat of a tsunami in 2002.

In 2006, NISA had told TEPCO to plan for a massive tsunami that exceeded the company's expectations. The company refused. It finally did a risk assessment in 2008 that concluded waves of up to 15.7 meters might hit the Fukushima plant, but failed to take any action. Court documents also suggest that TEPCO executives were aware that a tidal wave could knock out the low-level generators, but decided it was too expensive to move them.

Hiroyuki Kawai, a humanitarian lawyer who established the National Network of Counsels in Cases Against Nuclear Power Plants, told me, "TEPCO knew about the possibility of a large-scale tsunami, and did nothing about it. The idea that if it's not easily foreseeable, no one is responsible, is mistaken."

He felt there was a way to make sure individuals were held accountable: hold nuclear plant operators criminally liable for negligence. The threat of jail might help them take their work seriously and to think twice before cutting corners.

Of course, that never happened. The Fukushima nuclear disaster wasn't the first time that negligence at a power plant resulted in injury and death. In 1999, two employees died in an accident at the Tokaimura power plant run by JCO, a nuclear-fuel-cycle company. Six of the company's executives were later charged, and pleaded guilty to criminal charges of negligence resulting in the deaths. They were all given suspended sentences. None of them went to jail.

I never let go of this story, because the nuclear mafia here and the impetus to reopen the remaining nuclear plants remains a clear and present danger to everyone who lives here. No tidal wave of disinformation can hide that truth.

In the summer of 2021, I felt that my worst fears had been confirmed.

What if I told you that Japan's post-disaster nuclear safety measures were basically meaningless because the government and the regulatory agencies had failed to examine "the black box" containing critical information about the accident? Because TEPCO hid it from them?

"There is a very strong possibility that there will be another nuclear disaster in Japan, and TEPCO cannot be trusted," Toshio Kimura, a former nuclear engineer who predicted Japan's 2011 nuclear disaster six years before it happened, told me in the summer of 2021.

What he has to say means that most of Japan's post-earthquake safety measures are meaningless. A parliamentary investigation committee declared in 2012 that, "although triggered by these cataclysmic events," the disaster was "profoundly manmade," and could be attributed to "a multitude of errors and willful negligence that left the Fukushima plant unprepared for the events."

That legacy of negligence has continued for a decade now. Not much has improved.

In the spring of 2021, Japan's Nuclear Regulatory Authority (NRA) effectively banned TEPCO from restarting its nuclear power plant on the Sea of Japan coast after the complex was found to be riddled with major security flaws, and after inspectors discovered a cover-up of security breaches. The NRA gave a de facto order to suspend operations at the Kashiwazaki-Kariwa plant until "the company reaches a state where self-sustained improvement can be expected."

"It's just another example of this company covering up misdeeds, as they always do. It can only be said that [TEPCO] is not qualified in any way to be running a nuclear power plant," said Kimura. In his new book, *How Nuclear Energy Will Destroy the Nation: A Discussion*, Kimura points out that TEPCO's persistent cover-ups have resulted in nuclear safety regulations that are fundamentally flawed.

Kimura asserts that while there is a strong possibility that the tsunami caused the meltdown in two of the reactors, the meltdown began in Reactor One long before the tidal wave hit. For many, his book confirmed the suspicions that any sensible person would have.

After the 3/11 disaster, TEPCO did an in-house investigation of the accident, and released an 800-page report, along with 2,000 pages of data. When Kimura examined the report, he found that *some of the most important data had been omitted.*

"There is a device that measures the flow of water in the reactor core, and none of that data was included. If we were talking about an airplane, that device would be the equivalent of a flight recorder or a voice recorder, and its data is critical." TEPCO claimed it had released all the data about the accident, but they were lying.

It was only after Naomi Hirose became president of TEPCO

in the summer of 2012 that Kimura was able to access the information. After analyzing the data, Kimura realized that within one minute and twenty seconds after the earthquake, coolant stopped flowing into the reactor, and that it was impossible to cool the nuclear fuel.

"It's what is called 'a dry-out.' The logical conclusion is that in the over-forty-year-old reactor 1, the cause of the meltdown was not the tidal wave, but the shaking of the earthquake itself."

One minute and twenty seconds after the earthquake, the meltdown in Unit 1 was already starting.

Nuclear physicist Ryoji Okamoto, in an article published in the March 2013 edition of *The Journal of Japanese Scientists*, cites multiple sources indicating that the earthquake alone played a substantial role in the nuclear disaster. He asserts, "If the influence of the earthquake [on the meltdown] is important, then we need a fundamental re-evaluation of the guidelines for seismic resistant nuclear plants—and thus creating new safety guidelines is unavoidable."

Fundamentally, all of Japan's post-3/11 nuclear regulations were made without consideration of an earthquake alone causing a nuclear meltdown—because critical data was hidden from investigators and the Japanese parliament.

Keep in mind that, at the time of writing, a thin majority of the Japanese public, 53 percent, is opposed to restarting the nuclear reactors. It's the nuclear mafia that is hell-bent on returning things to pre-2011.

The situation is so dire that two former prime ministers, from rival parties, held a joint press conference in March 2021 calling for Japan to abandon nuclear power.

However, this is no longer Japan's problem alone. On schedule, Japan started releasing into the ocean radioactive waste from its 2011 nuclear accident in late August 2023. While Japan assures us that the water will be safe, can we really trust it? While the government in its announcement claimed that the tritium levels in the water were very safe, they neglected to mention that much of the on-site "treated water" contains lethal levels of other radioactive materials.

What happens to the people of Japan and to the countries that share their ocean when the next nuclear accident happens? It may only be one earthquake away—and recent events seem to indicate that neither TEPCO nor the government that should be regulating it can be trusted.

The biggest lie the Japanese government ever told was that nuclear energy was safe and secure. The second-biggest lie was that the tsunami caused the meltdown at Fukushima by knocking out the generators, which resulted in the loss of power. It wasn't the loss of electricity that started the meltdown—it was the earthquake itself, at least in Reactor One. What this means is that, despite all the new post-tsunami regulations, nuclear power in Japan still isn't safe. The country's vulnerability to earthquakes hasn't been factored in. All over Japan there are nuclear plants that are like deactivated time bombs. And the corrupt old men that run this country are hell-bent on starting up these time bombs once more—to benefit themselves and their cronies. They are guessing that they may not live long enough to see it all go wrong—once again. Maybe they just don't care.

The problem with historical revisionists is that they never learn from their mistakes because they're too busy rewriting the past to pay attention to the present. Japan's ruling elite are dragging us into the future ass-backwards. That won't end well.

But then again, very few things end well.

CHAPTER SIXTEEN

Who goes there?

All things come to an end, and, fortunately for me, by late August 2011 I stopped having chemotherapy. It wasn't all bad. Every cloud has a silver lining, and I wouldn't say that about cancer or chemotherapy with a straight face, but there were surprising, weird benefits.

I lost a lot of weight; I don't think I'd been able to fit into a pair of size-33 jeans for years. I had a lower libido, which also kept me out of trouble. The doctors also warned me there was a chance that chemotherapy might make me sterile, and they were right. Think of the lifetime savings in condoms! *Banzai*.

My writing output dwindled from a flood of articles to a small stream. I had been writing for *The Atlantic Wire*, *The Daily Beast*, *The Japan Times*, and sometimes for *ZAITEN*, but between March and August 2011 my output declined drastically. I didn't have the energy. To finish one article took me weeks.

I went home to Missouri between chemo sessions and my due diligence work that I had to keep doing because it paid the bills. I spent time hanging out with the family. Beni and Ray were great kids, still pre-teens and feisty, but never getting into trouble. They had essentially grown up in the U.S., but the due diligence gigs provided the means for to me travel back home often. I was grateful for all of that. I had decided not to tell them about the cancer. I had many low-energy days, but I tried to time my trips when I was at the tail end of a chemotherapy session before the next one came.

But things being what they were, I had to spend a lot of time in Japan. And I spent much of it with Michiel.

After a while, I've noticed, there is a sickness fatigue that settles in among the friends of those who are ill. Fewer people come to see them. Maybe they write, send postcards, or promise to drop by, but they don't. This didn't bother Michiel in the least.

We spent a lot of time in her hospital room at St. Marianna University School of Medicine in Kawasaki. I knew the hospital very well. After another relapse of leukemia, she was there for a large part of 2009. As a matter of fact, I still knew her room number in the blood diseases ward by heart.

Whenever I walked into her room, she was doing yoga on the bed. All over the world, hospitals have an unpleasant over-sanitized smell. It conceals the smell of the dead, dying, and sick. One summer, I volunteered as an orderly at the Harry S. Truman Veterans Hospital, where my father was the chief of pathology. After a while, I began to recognize the scent of the terminally ill. It wasn't nauseating, but it wasn't fragrant either. Michiel never had a room to herself, and people came and went. Sometimes, they were very ill.

Due to chemo, she developed some allergies. Air fresheners made her sick. Gluten made her nauseous. Every time I came back from my travels to Japan, I brought her bags of gluten-free cookies, cereals, and snacks. She was always outrageously grateful, but it was never an act. Mimi was always like that.

I decided I was going to make her an organic air freshener. I found a recipe in a New Age magazine called *Real Simple*, but it was still a bit complicated. The recipe called for coffee grounds (dry), cinnamon, dried ginger, and sandalwood chips. The

sandalwood was pricey, but I knew someone who had some—
Ryōgen, my landlord from decades ago and my Zen master. I
dropped by without notice, and he didn't seem to mind.

He had met Michiel once, and was saddened to hear about
her condition. Upon entering the temple, he invited me to his
room on the first floor before the main seating area and diagonally across from the stairs. His hot-water kettle and his green
tea pot were on the long table, as usual. Papers, newsletters,
and envelopes were piled up in semi-orderly piles. I explained
my plan to make Mimi some homemade air freshener.

He had me wait while he went into the back of the temple,
behind the Buddhist altar, and rummaged around for some
sandalwood.

"It's really nice of you," he told me. "Hospitals are sad places,
and the air is horrible. Sandalwood will purify the air and give
her some peace."

"Yes, I hope so."

"Here you go," he said, handing me a bag full of sandalwood
pieces.

"Thank you, very much," I said, taking them with a bow.

My response in normal Japanese would have been, "No,
that's too much" or "Are you sure?"

But that fake formality annoyed Ryōgen immensely.

If you asked, "Is it really okay?" he'd probably respond, "No,
it's not okay. Give it back."

Or, "I wouldn't offer it if I didn't mean it. Just say thank you
and take it."

I knew the drill.

"What's going to happen to her now?" he asked.

"She's probably going to get a bone-marrow transplant from
her mother. The theory is that the last transplants from her
brother were too good. Because he was such a perfect match,
her immune system was not stimulated to fight off the next

leukemia invasion. That's why they hope this one will work. Her white blood cells have to be removed prior to the transplant, so that the transplant takes well."

"How many bone-marrow transplants has she had so far?"

"I think two."

"Ah."

"Ah?"

"Then she will probably die this time. Her time in this incarnation may be over. I hope that she lives."

He said it as nonchalantly as he might say, "It looks as if it might be a cold and windy day tomorrow. Wear your good coat." That was just the way he spoke.

"I hope she survives as well. She's survived three relapses. Miracles happen."

"Sometimes," he said, averting his eyes, and pouring me a cup of tea. I drank it down, and thanked him again and left.

It was a very short walk to the station. Ryōgen never really minced words. He was brutally honest, which was unusual in Japanese society. But being brutally honest didn't mean that he was always right.

Though I'm not much of an artisan, I was able to grind, smash, and pulverize the ingredients by following the instructions to create a pleasant potpourri. But there were rules about these things at the hospital, so I ended up putting it in small scent bags. In Japan, these are called *nioi bukuro*. Mimi loved the homemade air freshener. She kept one bag under her pillow, and secretly put one into the air conditioner/heater so that the scent wafted from it gently. It made the room seem subtly more pleasant.

Usually, I took a taxi up to see her, and sometimes Saigo drove me. While on the road, I learned how to fight off car sickness and write well. Also, I worked on the way back. When I took the train up, I timed it so I could get a seat and either read or write.

However, I had to give the hospital props for finally getting wi-fi. Back in 2009, Mimi and I had only been able to communicate by texts on her cellphone, which was a far cry from a smartphone. Eventually, I resorted to buying her a mobile router so she could communicate with her friends and, of course, me, and we were finally able to become Facebook friends. Thanks, Zuck.

But in the spring of 2011, nearly two years later, here we were again. There was a sort of déjà vu to it all, like a dream that was repeating. As I got better, Mimi alternated between getting better and getting worse. There were drugs keeping the leukemia at bay, but the underlying condition had to be addressed.

We played board games, shared books, and watched movies. She started preparing for her master's degree. I remember one afternoon in May we snuck out to a nearby park and spent the afternoon discussing her future. She seemed a little downbeat.

"What's up, Mimi?"

"Jake," she said, exhaling, "I'm thinking of changing my area of focus in graduate studies. I don't think I'm going to focus on human trafficking in Japan anymore. It doesn't seem as relevant as it was when I started."

"Okay," I said. "I think that's probably wise."

"You're not disappointed in me?"

"No, not at all. I get it."

A lot had happened since I'd written a recommendation in March 2007 to support her application to the Monterey Institute of International Studies Graduate School of International Policy Studies. In her essay to apply for the graduate school, Michiel had written:

I aspire for a career at an international organization such as the IOM (International Organization for Migration), where I can fight for my all-time passion, combatting human trafficking. [Not only do I find it personally abhorrent, but intellectually, it] is a terrible exploit of labor that robs women, men and children of their freedom and dignity. In fact, human trafficking is too polite of a term. "Modern slavery" is a more apt expression. Perhaps if portrayed by this term, more people would share my vehemence to combat it.

I [have done] fieldwork with a nongovernmental organization called The Asia Foundation, assisting rescued victims of human trafficking in Japan by guiding them to shelters, getting in touch with their families, and arranging flights home if they desired it.

I have also taken the approach of public awareness. In order to decrease the demand in Japan, I helped organize seminars with the Foundation to make the current situation public. The majority of Japanese do not have the faintest idea that they live in the largest destination country for victims of trafficking.

Worse, most look down upon these foreigners with menial jobs, having no idea that they were tricked into coming to Japan, their passports taken away upon arrival, forced into debt, not paid for their services, and threatened with the death of their families if they were to run away.

And that was still true in 2007. But now it was 2011.

In my own way, I'd been waging a war on human trafficking in Japan, and she had been a sister in arms. And when I thought about it, it wasn't "I"—it was "Us." She had helped me get hold of a copy of the International Labor Organization (ILO) report on human trafficking in Japan in 2005. The Japanese government had paid for the research, but when they read the report, they told the ILO to bury it and not release it to the public.

It was a scathing indictment of Japan's lack of interest in helping human trafficking victims and of its consistent failure to prosecute the cold-blooded criminals running the operations. This passage, in particular, brought it all home:

> Japan's commitment to rigid migration policies and its strong position against illegal migration may have informed its hesitancy to recognize and deal with trafficking in general. Some difficulties arise in clearly defining human trafficking, people smuggling and illegal immigration when dealing with actual cases, largely because of the clandestine nature of these activities. Similarly, victims of trafficking may be perceived to be voluntary participants in illegal immigration, which thereby removes their right to protection.
>
> While there is international consensus that trafficking victims should be treated as such and should receive proper protection and rehabilitation, in practice they still are very often arrested, detained, and deported as illegal immigrants.
>
> Victims frequently bear all costs of the deceptions they have undergone, while the traffickers retain their profits and are rarely prosecuted.

Michiel and I had read the whole thing on a tight deadline, picked out the most important parts, and translated them. I wrote the article for the *Yomiuri Shimbun*, and it landed on the front page. It was such an embarrassment to the government of Japan that they delayed their announcement of planned anti-trafficking measures, and as result strengthened them.

Michiel had been an incredible help in drafting the report on human trafficking in Japan for the U.S. State Department from 2006 to 2008. It made me think of how long I'd known her and what a stand-up ally she was in all things. I remember how she had chewed out a U.S. State Department representative who didn't understand that most sex work in Japan was legal, and that to label all sex work as human trafficking was a tremendous disservice to real victims and sex workers.

We'd done good work. But things had changed.

Human trafficking—at least sex trafficking—hadn't completely vanished, but it had been mostly shut down in Japan by 2011. The cost for organized crime was too high, so, for the most part, they moved out of the business of exploiting foreign women. Zengeiren, which was effectively a human trafficking business lobby, stopped having board meetings at the Liberal Democratic Party's headquarters. Some of their meetings were chaired by former prime minister Shinzo Abe, which tells you how well connected they were to the government. So-called entertainer visas were strictly monitored now, and rarely issued. Immigration raids had put the fear of God into the seedier clubs. Even Polaris Project Japan had to change its focus to domestic trafficking.

The future wasn't what it used to be.

I gave her a hug as we sat on the bench.

"Michiel," I told her, "look at it this way. We sort of won. Polaris Project Japan. Asia Foundation. The U.S. State Department. The HELP organization. The cops, and the few legislators that actually gave a damn. Our efforts actually changed things."

She gave me a high-five.

"Yes, I guess you did. You changed things. You made a difference."

"No, you were with me every step of the way. We changed things. We did it. Not that I'd ever want to quote George Bush, but more or less, 'Mission Accomplished.' There are new battles to be fought, new causes to support, new ways to make the world a better place. It's all right to change paths. You'll find something right for you."

And then she buried her face in my shoulder and cried—happy tears. As though she was relieved.

It was a good moment. We had helped accomplish something that relieved a lot of suffering and helped put away some bad guys, or at least cut off their revenue streams. You must savor your victories when you have them. Most of the time in the struggle against the evils of the world, you lose.

When we went back to the hospital, Michiel contacted her mentor and advisor, Professor Tsuneo Akaha, and let him know that she would be changing her focus. She was happy about it, and I was happy for her.

I kept delivering her gluten-free snacks from the U.S. I refused a lot of due diligence work, as I had some money saved up. I put my house in order, and redecorated it. I went to museums. I slept a lot. And I visited Mimi whenever she could see me. I was going back and forth to the States often. I wanted to spend time with Beni and Ray, in case I didn't have as long as I once imagined I'd have.

In the fall of 2011, I walked with Beni through the local mall, and we stopped at her favorite trinket store, Claire's, where she bought headbands and earrings, and all the things that an eleven-year-old loves to have and share with her friends.

I spotted a strange little necklace for $9.99 with a Yin and Yang dangling off it—the symbol of peace and balance in the Far East, and especially in Taoism. The white side (Yin) had a "B" in black, and the black side had "FF" in white. You could pull the necklace apart and put it back again, because the two halves were magnetic. I didn't know what BFF meant, because I was square and three decades away from being eleven. I asked Beni to translate for me. She gave me that look.

"Dad," she said, "BFF means Best Friends Forever. You take one half, and you give the other half to your BFF. That's how it works."

"Do you have a BFF?"

"Maybe Leila, but I'm not sure. I might have two."

"Two?"

"Technically speaking, you can have more than one, Dad."

"Oh, technically speaking," I replied. She didn't catch my hint of sarcasm.

"That means 'in a way.' You probably should have only one BFF, but some people have two. You're lucky to have even one."

I was a lucky man. I bought the necklace for Michiel. It was a cheesy gift, but I hoped she'd like it. We were both fans of Eastern philosophy, and she'd been reading quite a bit of it over the years. According to some schools of Taoism: "Yin and Yang are dependent opposing forces that flow in a natural cycle, always seeking balance. Though they are opposing, they are not in opposition to one another. As part of the Tao, they are merely two aspects of a single reality. Each contains the seed of the other, which is why we see a black spot of Yin in the white Yang and vice versa."

When I came to visit her at the hospital, I took out the box and showed her the necklace, and told her that I'd been shopping with Beni when I'd found it. I then tried to explain to her what it was. She stopped me, laughing. "Jake, I was an eleven-year-old-girl once. I know what a BFF is! You're so silly."

I pulled the necklace apart, and put her half around her neck and tried to put on my half, but my fingers were a little numb. She did it for me. And then we leaned in and joined our halves a couple of times to make sure the magnet was working right. It made a pleasant click. I felt happier than I had in months. It was the best $9.99 I'd ever spent.

We were very different people, and yet we were very similar. Maybe we had grown to be that way. She was the Yin (the female/principle of light) and I was the Yang (the male/principle of darkness). But really, I think she was much stronger than me, and she had a dark sense of humor.

In early October, as we walked around the hospital grounds, Mimi took me aside to have "a serious talk." I remember that it was just beginning to get cold, and we were in that strange, wondrous part of dusk known as *tasogare*.

Tasogare refers to that moment as we edge from day into night when you can make out the shapes of the people walking toward you, but you can't see their faces. The word comes from old Japanese, meaning, "Who goes there?"

For months, I'd sometimes been interrupting our walks to go off for a short smoke. I didn't do this today. I had stopped smoking on October 1, the day Japan's exclusionary ordinances directed at organized crime went into effect nationwide. Michiel had helped me prepare the article on it for *The Atlantic Wire*.

I understood what a big deal that was. It was going to make all of Japan a lot less yakuza-friendly; it was the start of the Big Chill. The laws varied in the details, but they all criminalized sharing profits with the yakuza or paying them off.

In other words, if you paid protection money to the yakuza, or used them to facilitate your business affairs, you would be treated as a criminal. You might be warned once, but if you persisted in doing business with them, you would have your name released to the public, and be fined, imprisoned, or all of the above.

It was the beginning of the end of the yakuza; they were on their way out. I could feel it. Just like fighting human trafficking in Japan was fighting a war that was almost over, crusading against the yakuza was only going to speed up what was now inevitable.

Who goes there? The yakuza. But not for long.

Autumn would be one long *tasogare*: Yakuza *tasogare*. Human trafficking *tasogare*. Seasonal *tasogare*. Summer was leaving, fall was coming, and winter was not far away.

I'd spent the whole night working on the article, woken up the morning of October 1, and immediately lit up a clove. I couldn't taste anything, and thought the pack was stale. I lit up another one. Same problem. Then I opened a fresh pack. Nothing.

At this point, I realized my face was numb. I ran to a clinic open in the mornings, explained my symptoms, and the doctor immediately had me swallow some aspirin. He suggested I'd just had an ischemic stroke, which happens when a blood vessel gets blocked, depriving part of the brain of oxygen. It was sometimes seen in heavy smokers. I took the hint. I stopped smoking.

As we were walking, Michiel asked me if I wanted to smoke. I told her that I'd quit and explained why. She was delighted.

"Oh my God, Jake. I thought you'd never quit."

"Mimi, I thought you'd never be able not to tell me to quit, and you never did. You never said anything about it."

"Would you have listened?"

"Probably not."

"Well, listen to me now." Michiel took my hand and said, "Jake, remember I said I wanted to have a serious talk."

"Yes, I'm avoiding it."

She didn't laugh.

"Jake, you're getting a lot better. You need to get back to work. You can't spend all your time here with me. The hospital is for sick people, and you're well now."

I protested. She nodded, but was firm.

"I love it, too. But you're a writer. That's who you are. Time to start writing again. I'll be your back-up. Just like the old days."

And so I reconciled myself to the fact that I wasn't going to die anytime soon, and I went back to work. There was plenty to do.

I still spent a lot of time with Mimi at the hospital. We were getting very close. In addition to watching movies and doing yoga on her bed, we discussed books we read, and went for walks. Yoga wasn't easy for me. Michiel joked that I was the stiffest human being on the face of the Earth.

I brought her lots of magazines to read. *Cosmopolitan*. *Women's Health*. *Bitch*—which isn't what you're thinking it's about. *Elle*. Of course, *The New Yorker*. I developed a fondness for *Cosmo*. We'd take the quizzes together now and then.

At times, we escaped the hospital grounds, for a few hours at least. That was dependent on how she was being medically treated at the time. I would work on due diligence reports on the ride up to the hospital, and we would review them in her room.

And then, in November, something magical happened.

They say that when you reach *satori*—the great enlightenment—it hits you like a bolt of lightning, without warning. Until I get there, I won't really know. I do know that my closest experience to it happened on the night of November 8, 2011, when I was sitting on the edge of Mimi's hospital bed with her head on mine, and we were watching *The Adjustment Bureau* together. The movie had been on her wish list for a long time. I wanted to see it, too, and with her. Philip K. Dick, who wrote the original, is one of my favorite writers.

As we watched the film, there was a moment when I felt as if I was seeing her for the first time. After so many years. I had been seeing her as I remembered her, not as the amazing woman she had become.

The chemotherapy had turned her long hair prematurely gray, but her smile and the sparkle in her eyes hadn't changed at all. She wasn't Mimi-chan. She wasn't an over-enthusiastic, idealistic college kid with big cheeks and a big smile. She wasn't Little Orphan Annie.

She was more alive than ever, despite her fourth relapse of leukemia. She was a woman who had suffered, endured, survived, and blossomed. She was a beautiful woman. Her smile was ethereal and mystical. She glowed. However, that may have been caused by the sunlight coming through the window—what photographers call the golden hour.

"Mimi," I nudged her gently, "what did you think of the film? Did you fall asleep?"

She said sleepily, "No, I didn't fall asleep, Jake. I loved the movie."

"What did you love about the movie?"

"You promise not to laugh?"

"I promise not to laugh unless you tell me you love Matt Damon."

She giggled, and didn't say anything else.

"Come on. Don't keep me in suspense."

"I loved it because I believe in angels—*tenshi*. I really do. And I've seen them. Sometimes I write to them in my diary."

"*Tenshi?*" I asked her in Japanese. This is a habit you develop when you're bilingual and your friend is, too. After hearing the word in English, you repeat it in Japanese just to make sure you really heard it.

"Yes. *Tenshi na no yo.*"

I could not give a snappy reply, because she was very sincere. She had survived the disease three times. If anyone had seen an angel, it was her. After taking a deep breath, I pondered for a moment.

I took her hand. "I find that beautiful. It's wonderful. No, I am not laughing. I have never seen them, and I don't believe in them, but I am open to the possibility."

She squeezed my hand.

"What did you think of the movie, Jake? Did you like it, too?"

"It departed from K. Dick's original story."

"Definitely. But I was wondering if you liked it. Did you like it? Honestly. Tell me what you think."

I stumbled for the right words, gently touching the Yin necklace around her neck, and then let it go. "I think that this world of ours needs an adjustment."

She looked up at me and I looked back, and we both leaned forward. Our lips met. She smelled of sandalwood. This wasn't the sachet I'd made for her; it was just her. Honestly, I hadn't really thought about it, but I thought Michiel would taste like strawberries and cream. Her kiss was cinnamon-sugar, spice, chilli pepper, and salted caramel.

I'm ashamed to say as a writer that I didn't have any dazzling thing to say to her. I just muttered, "Holy fuck."

And she feigned shock.

"Such language, Jake!"

We kissed again. I mumbled, "We really shouldn't be doing this."

"But we are," she whispered back.

I didn't know where this would go, but I didn't want to think about it.

She put her arms around my back and pulled me close, and I followed her lead. And the world went silent. The last flash of sunlight lit up her face, and it reflected in her eyes like a sunburst.

"Mimi," I said, "let's sneak the hell out of here."

And we did. We closed the curtain on her bed, and out we went into the night.

We had a blast. I booked us the best room available in the closest love hotel. It was "The Ritz of Love Hotels," I assured her. We took a bubble bath in the lit-up jacuzzi. We ordered a pizza—even though it wasn't gluten-free. We speculated as to whether the lights in the bathtub actually lit up in any discernible pattern. We fiddled with the body sonic, a kind of built-in speaker in the bed that made it vibrate. We listened to every kind of music, including gamelan music from Indonesia, on one of the many channels of music available.

She told me that she had bought an album by Adele and that I'd really love it.

"Maybe we can find a channel playing her?"

No luck. There was no dedicated Adele channel.

I suggested we pull up one of her songs on my iPad. "I'll buy it from iTunes, and we can listen to it! What's the best song?"

"Oh, that would be 'Rolling in the Deep.'"

"Really? What a surprise."

"Why?"

"She doesn't even live in Japan, and she's writing songs about love hotels."

Michiel threw a pillow at me, and it landed solidly on the back of my head. It was a great song. We listened to that, too. And then we rolled in the deep. And we slept together, and we woke up and slept again. There was nothing awkward about it. It felt as natural as diving into a swimming pool on a summer's day.

While we were recuperating on the sofa—I was exhausted, but she'd been given so many steroids that she was full of limitless energy—I told her about the MEG case, in which a group of enterprising criminals had hidden cameras in love hotels, taken photos of couples having sex, and then sold the footage in a series of commercial videos.

"You're so romantic, Jake," she cooed sarcastically with her head on my chest and her chin on her hands, looking up at me.

"I'm just sharing with you my vast knowledge of love hotels."

She raised her thin, red eyebrows and gave me a faux-angry face.

"I'm sorry, I'm sorry. It's an occupational hazard."

She just smiled and tapped me on the chest with a finger.

"Well, Jake, if we are being filmed, don't you think we should be giving our best performance? C'mon, wake up. It's show-time, *ne*."

She fell asleep around 4.00 am, and I let her sleep. I'd have to sneak her back into the hospital by 6.00 am.

I remember watching her sleeping curled up in a ball, a smile on her face, with the gamelan music still playing, and waiting for a wave of guilt and regret to hit me. It didn't come.

Everything seemed right with the world. And as I stroked her reddish hair streaked with gray, she pulled me closer, and we both fell asleep.

In the end, I managed to get her back to the hospital on time. I think we framed it as an early-morning walk. We returned by 5.55. A nurse—let's call her Akimoto-san—told me as I walked Michiel back to her room, "It is way too early for visiting hours. However, I will let it slide this time."

I sent Michiel a quick note on my way back: "Thanks for the lovely very long afternoon. It was really good seeing you and watching the movie."

Rather than tip-toe around our new relationship, we foot-sied. People in Japan excel at living in gray zones. Neither of us discussed what the future held or what the status of our relationship was.

Were we now going to be boyfriend and girlfriend? Or were we just hooking up? Would we be friends with benefits? I wasn't sure, and didn't ask. There was nothing different about us, except that we were physically intimate. As best as I could, I had been there for her when she was suffering, empathizing with her and helping when I could, and she had done the same for me. I was happy for her when she was happy, and she felt the same way for me. There was nothing complicated about it.

Michiel had a mischievous side that many people were unaware of, and I liked that, too. She told me how, in high school, she and her friends went to Hawaii under the pretext that it was a school trip, and she made a fake brochure that explained it all. Perhaps she would have gotten away with it if she hadn't messed up by not answering her phone. Her parents called the school, which of course knew nothing about the fake trip. Her cover was blown. Her parents were horrified, and she was grounded for weeks.

I had always pictured her as a little Miss Goody Two-Shoes, but as she told me the story in sheepish tones, I started laughing out loud.

"Michiel, you're a little con artist. Or con woman!"

"Jake, I felt so bad. My parents were angry and disappointed. That was the last time I did anything like that."

I assured her that among the crimes of the world, it ranked very low, but I gave her an A for effort. We had about four days of bliss before I had to return to the real world and get back to work.

We talked like we had never talked before, and about things we wouldn't normally discuss. Despite her wanting children, the multiple bouts of leukemia had made it nearly impossible for her. I told her adoption was always an option. I almost said, "We could adopt children" during our conversation, but I refrained from saying it.

As the doctors tried to prepare Michiel for more chemotherapy, which was needed to keep the leukemia at bay, they had to put a port in her. However, the port became infected.

Her temperature rose to forty degrees on November 17. She shivered violently for the entire week. However, the fever subsided. She was allowed to go home for a few days on the 22nd. While she was at home, we slipped out for a few hours.

We didn't stay out very long. We came back, checked in, had Chinese food at the hospital restaurant. After dinner, while we were walking outside the hospital grounds, discreetly holding hands, she leaned into me and said, "*Ne, ne,* I have a question."

"Shoot."

And then, with a wicked smile on her face and pulling me close as though she was going to confide a great secret in me, she whispered, "Which do you think will die first: me, you, or our romantic relationship?"

It took me a second to compute this, but she was already throwing back her head, laughing so hard that she could barely breathe. I gently pulled her closer.

"Oh, definitely, our romantic relationship. I'm a terrible man-whore. Of course, I'll fuck this up."

"Yes, probably. So we live?"

"We live on, and I get to say, 'See I told you so.'"

"That would be really nice, Jake. Please tell me we will always be friends, with benefits or without benefits."

We sat on a bench, and I put my arms around her while she leaned back on me. I assured her that no matter what, we would always remain friends, in whatever way that worked.

"Michiel, you have been the most beneficial person in my life, even before we ever kissed, and if we never locked lips again, that wouldn't change. Every day with you is a benefit."

She drew a kanji on my hand with her finger, but I don't know what it was.

We sat there a little while longer in a comfortable silence— the silence of two people who know each other so well that they don't need to say a word.

Then we went back to the hospital and sat in the little canteen, trying to figure out why multi-strike convertible bonds were such a boon to enterprising financial fraudsters. She had a better grasp of this than I did.

On the stairwell, we kissed once more, and Michiel told me that it would be a while before we could meet in the flesh again.

"I may not be able to see you again until after the transplant. Because ... you know."

"I know," I told her. "It's part of the process. The clean room awaits. We can email!"

"We will!"

She playfully reached under my shirt and found the Yang half of our necklace, and pressed it into my chest with one finger and kissed me on the cheek.

"I'm still looking forward to our next night out at the Blue Note. Maybe some big band. More bang for your buck," she told me with a wink. "Save a date for me," she whispered, and she snuck out of the stairwell first and went back to her room.

I wasn't really worried. I believed in miracles.

In the summer of 2010, I had gotten a phone call from someone I had long believed was dead. She wasn't, and that was a gift. I heard her voice, and years fell off my shoulders. She was out somewhere leading a new life with a new job, a new name, and a new motorcycle.

Things work out sometimes.

I went home in May for Ray's eighth birthday, which was on May 19. I had planned to stay for a while. I couldn't visit Michiel anymore, and I wasn't able to concentrate on my jobs.

I arrived back in Japan two days before Mimi's transplant, on May 29. Saigo picked me up at the airport. I spent the day bumming around Shimokitazawa aimlessly, not knowing what to do or say. I wanted to be there for the surgery. Even if it was just waving across the room. But …

While I was looking around the area, on a whim, I dropped by Ragtag, a high-end used-clothing store, and was checking out the women's section when I found the perfect red dress—not strapless, but beautifully made and in Michiel's size. It was elegant and simple. It felt like silk. I don't know what it would have cost new, but it was $250 used. If the right woman wore it, she would turn heads. I knew Michiel would look absolutely stunning wearing it when we went out after her recovery. The Cotton Club was more likely to have big band jazz than the Blue Note, but either place would do for her.

That night, Saigo brought me a box of rosters and old yakuza fanzines he had collected for my organized crime database. I repaid him, and he made coffee while I entered the data.

It's always a little uncomfortable to think that you're being served coffee by a former yakuza boss, but if I made the coffee, he would be upset. He wanted things spelled out. He worked for me, not the other way around. I let him make the coffee.

As he put it down, he asked, "Are you going to the hospital tomorrow?

No, I told him. I wouldn't be able to do much more than wave at her from across the room, Michiel had told me.

"Jake-san," he said, "You know, it's not our culture to express ourselves directly, and although Michiel is Japanese and American, there's a lot of Japanese in her, and she's saying more than you're reading. So you need to think through some of these things. And you need to start thinking about the possibility that she may die this time. She knows it; you shouldn't deny it either."

Meanwhile, he made another pot of coffee and continued to talk.

"I lost my second wife to cancer. There are some things I wish I'd said to her while I still had the chance. You have a chance to say and do the right things."

He sat down, handed me a cup of coffee, three sticks of sugar, a pair of chopsticks to stir it, and began speaking. He told me the whole story. I had never known he'd had a second wife. After he was done talking, we were both silent.

"Jake-san," he said, "I give bad advice. I'm not the brightest of guys. I went from being in the top fifty executives of a

10,000-man organization and running an organization of 150 people to being your driver, on the run from debt collectors and the yakuza you pissed off—all in a few months."

"Hey," I said, "You say that like it's a bad thing."

We both laughed. He thought it was funnier than I did.

"What I'm saying is, I wish I had been more honest with my wife. I wish I had said that I loved her. I wish we had talked about dying. I wish I had been there more often, when I could have been there."

I nodded, "Yeah. Well, it's different."

He shook his head.

"No, it's not so different. I've known you for years. Whenever Mimi-chan has been sick, you've visited her in the hospital. Every year, she sends you a Christmas card and a New Year's card. And you do the same.

"I listen to you guys talk in the car. You laugh together; she finishes your sentences. You know so much about her, and she knows everything about you. She worries about you. I can hear it in her voice.

"You go up to the hospital almost every week, and you spend hours with her. You bring her books to read; movies to watch. Every time you go to the U.S., you come back with her favorite magazines and the cookies that her dietician will let her eat— those awful gluten-free things. I see how she looks at you and how you look at her, and I can tell you love each other. You just don't verbalize it. I don't know why."

He paused.

"And I can't figure out why you don't tell her how you really feel. Because most of the time—pardon me for saying this—you never know when to shut up."

I protested.

"She's my BFF."

"Isn't it a little bit more than that? Forgive me if I'm speaking out of place, but isn't it a lot more than that?"

I didn't want to talk about it. Because emotions are messy. Because it's theoretically a bad idea to fall in love with your best friend. Because I didn't want to think about a world where Michiel wasn't there anymore.

Saigo continued speaking, softly and slowly.

"I know you want to reassure her. Tell her it'll work out. And even if all you can do is wave at her, shouldn't you?"

I sat in my chair, not really sure what to say. He took the coffee cups off the table and washed them. He walked to the door and bowed. He had some final words of advice.

"Jake-san, whatever you think you might want to tell Mimi-chan, now is the time. If you can see her, you should. You may not have a better chance. If I were you, I'd seize the opportunity."

The bone-marrow transplant was postponed, and was finally scheduled for the morning of May 31, but I still didn't know what to do. I spoke to Mimi's father, Bob, who said that he was fine with me coming and that I posed no risk to her, even if I did. He and Hiroko (Michiel's mom) would also be in the room with her. One more person wouldn't make a difference, he told me.

But I didn't want to be a burden. I went to bed at midnight. I didn't sleep well.

Saigo showed up at my door at 9.00 am on the 31st, ringing the bell. He didn't call in advance like he usually did when he was going to pick me up. I went downstairs, and before I could say anything, he said to me, "Jake-san, we're behind schedule. I'm terribly sorry. I woke up late. Please get in the car. We're going, right?"

"I told you I wasn't going."

"Really? That's not how I remember hearing it. We'd better leave now. I think you said the operation starts at noon."

"I thought I told you I wasn't going."

"No, I think you said you were thinking about not going. That's not saying you're not going. And here I am."

He cocked one eyebrow, tilted his head, and motioned toward the Mercedes-Benz. I got in the car.

We arrived at the hospital before noon. I walked directly toward her room. The nurses just nodded at me and smiled. They knew my face. Nurse Akimoto guided me to where Michiel was going to be treated. She took my hand and gently pulled me. It was a sweet gesture.

Michiel was in the clean room. I disinfected my hands outside her door, and one of the nurses brought me a mask to wear.

I walked in.

Michiel was in bed, in her purple pajamas, I think. The bed was tilted up slightly; she had her head on the pillow, her long gray-and-red hair gently splayed across it, and she was facing slightly toward the door. She was paler than I'd ever seen her.

Her face lit up when she saw me. She smiled.

"Jake! How did you get in here?"

"Michiel, you underestimate my ninja-like stealth. Besides, the nurses like me. I practically have a free pass anywhere in this hospital."

She laughed, which turned into a slight cough.

"*Sasuga,* Jake-chan. I'm glad you're here."

Her father was there, and I wasn't supposed to stay long. I stayed a little longer, and Michiel and I talked. We talked even as the nurse began the IV drip that would feed the bone marrow into her blood.

I couldn't take off my mask. I didn't want to go, but I made myself say goodbye. As I was getting ready to leave, she reached out her hand, and I took it in mine.

Of course, we probably weren't supposed to touch. But my hands were clean, and when she held out her tiny hand, holding it in mine was as natural as breathing. And we stayed like that for a long time, our eyes met, and we didn't say a word.

She let go and waved goodbye. I hovered in the hall a bit more, but she was falling asleep. I waved at her, and she winked and then closed her eyes. Even after I left the room, I could still feel her hand in mine. Even now, sometimes, I can feel that warmth. I can feel her hand in mine, like we were still touching.

Once I got outside, I called Saigo. He came and picked me up near the emergency room ten minutes later.

"How was she?" he asked.

"Good. She was tired. All the chemotherapy up to the transplant has really been hard on her. They have to kill the cancer cells in her body before they transplant the bone marrow cells."

"Yes, of course. That makes sense."

Saigo knew a surprising amount of medical lore and terminology. Maybe it was because he had diabetes or because of what had happened to his second wife. Maybe it was because he had been treated with interferon to cure his Hepatitis C years before.

We drove for thirty minutes back to Tokyo, and I didn't say anything. I was afraid my voice would crack. Finally, I cleared my throat and said what I should have said.

"Thanks for taking me there today."

He waved his hand and shrugged his shoulders.

"No thanks, necessary. I was just following orders, boss. That's what I do."

Mimi had a heart attack a few days after the bone-marrow transplant, and was put into a medically induced coma. I was told that it might be a long time before she was taken out of the coma, so I went home to the United States. When I heard from her family that she was recovering, I booked my ticket back to Japan. I arrived on June 30.

There had been some good news. She was awake and alert and in good spirits, even though all of her hair had fallen out. The bone-marrow transplants and chemotherapy over the years had done strange things to her hair. It had given her curly hair, had gotten straight again, and had gone prematurely gray. Maybe she'd have green hair when it grew back this time.

I was so excited to be able to see her that I had knots in my stomach. I felt giddy—so happy that I could have gone to karaoke and sang. Even sang sober. And I know I'm a terrible singer.

On July 9, I was on the train platform of Shimokitazawa Station heading to her hospital when I got a Facebook notice. Maria, our mutual friend, posted that Michiel had died.

And that's how I found out. From a Facebook post.

I missed my train. It rushed past me. I recall being the only person on an empty platform, but that can't have been right. There must have been other people there. But that's not how I remember it. My memory is of me being left alone on the station with no one there at all.

I didn't want to believe it, but I knew it was true. I waited a few hours, and I called her mother to be sure.

I don't even remember how I got home.

A day later, I woke up and began helping with arrangements for her wake and memorial service in San Francisco, scheduled for July 18.

I had consulting work to do in the U.S., and I couldn't stick around in Japan for the funeral that her parents were planning. Michiel's funeral service was going to be held on July 12, starting at 1.00 pm, at the Asagao Church. I knew I couldn't make it.

She wasn't here anymore anyway. She wasn't coming back to life. You have to be practical about these things. I did want to pay my condolences. I arrived in San Francisco on July 16.

That evening, I treated myself to a full-body massage at a

neo-hippie New Age romiromi Swedish massage parlor place. At random, they give you some pithy advice with your massage, printed on faux washi.

I kept mine. It was a quote from a famous Vietnamese Buddhist teacher:

> The Zen Master Lin Chi said, "The miracle is not to walk on water but to walk on the Earth. We can enjoy every minute of our lives. In walking like this, we can inspire others to do the same."

It was from a book called *No Death, No Fear*. I read over the quote. Maybe it should have been inspirational. All I could do was think that, of course the dead don't have fear—they're dead. Someone should yell at the book editor for that title.

I had managed to get hold of Mimi's brother, her professor, her friends, and others who couldn't make it to the funeral in Japan. We had a lovely service on July 18.

At the memorial service, I met Emi Tojima. Emi was a friend from Mimi's American school in Japan, and she was a freckled half-Japanese hippie spiritualist and ex-hospice nurse, who I hit it off with instantly. We became friends. She offered me some hospice-quality pot, if I recall correctly, but I wasn't up for it. We all shared stories of Michiel and pictures. Cris was there, too. I hadn't seen her since that night at the club, when we were all dancing and Michiel felt sick. It made me think. I had been there trying to take care of Michiel when she first fell ill with leukemia, and I had been there almost to the end.

Professor Tsuneo Akaha had very kind words to say. He was already discussing a posthumous graduation for Michiel, and setting up a fund in her name. Talking to her friends was a revelation. There was so much about her that I didn't know, but then again, there were many things I never asked. You never really know anyone as well as you think you do, and sometimes you don't even know yourself.

After I got back to Japan, I went to visit her parents again to express my condolences. They lived close by, and it seemed like the right thing to do. We talked for a long time. I mentioned casually after Bob offered me a beer that I was trying not to drink anything. I told him that I was worried I might start drinking alone. "When you're drinking alone, Mr Brandt, you've got problems," I told him.

He asked me if I'd like to see her room. "It's as she left it. Top of the stairs, first door on the left. If there's anything you'd like, let me know."

When I went upstairs, on her dresser was the other half of the BFF necklace, the counterpart to the one I still had around my neck.

I picked her half up, and put it next to mine. When the two pieces magnetically clicked together, I fell apart. I felt a wave of heat flash through me that made my eyes moist, and everything got blurry. I could barely breathe. I took the necklace off my neck and carefully put it in my coat pocket.

I walked downstairs, and I showed the black-and-white Yin-Yang pendant necklace to her parents. I explained to them what it meant, and they were happy for me to have it. I said my goodbyes to Mr and Mrs Brandt, and stumbled toward the nearest train station. It struck me as I boarded the train that the name of the station, Eifukucho, translated literally as "Eternal Happiness Town."

It would be such an amazing place to be if it was real.

I rode the train back home shedding tears like a fat American shedding sweat in a Finnish sauna. It felt as though translucent fingernail polish had spilled into my eyes. When I got to my room, I put the necklace in an envelope, and I put it in a box where I kept Michiel's Christmas cards, her birthday cards to me, her New Year cards, her notes, and her letters over the years. The Christmas CD was in there, too.

I listened to it that day. The last song was a weepy ballad by Sia entitled "My Love." I'd always thought the CD ended with KT Tunstall's "The Universe and U," but that wasn't the case. Michiel hadn't written the song down on the list. I hadn't realized it. It felt like it had been snuck onto the CD while I wasn't looking. I listened to it over and over.

And now I am home.

Lyrics are always open to interpretation. But I felt like that was the last thing she wanted to say to me. Of course, that's wishful thinking. You don't hear things as they are; you hear them as you want them to be. I put the CD back in the box.

Years went by.

I eventually took the red dress back to the resale shop. There's someone who should go dancing in it, but I'll never take Michiel to the Blue Note in that dress. There is not a world in which that is going to happen.

Michiel graduated posthumously in 2010. Professor Akaha did set up a scholarship in Michiel's name. I contributed to it every year.

During the pandemic, he died as well.

In my own mind, I don't think of myself as being particularly emotional. I consider myself a Vulcan, although I have only one pointed ear, so I'm only a quarter Vulcan. I strive to be a rational and somewhat detached human being. I'm not stoic, but I understand that everything ends.

Still, I never thought I would miss someone so much for so long.

Every July, when the anniversary of her death comes, I deal with it. And I look at her photos, and I feel that radiant smile when I think about her. And I'm okay. And I repeat to myself a little mantra—not that it makes much sense, but it helps.

Michiel isn't really gone. She's just not here right now.

PART III

RECONSTRUCTION

CHAPTER SEVENTEEN

Murder is expensive

When Michiel died, I fell apart. I didn't allow myself much time to think about it, but I had lost my zeal for due diligence work and for many things. The job itself was fading away, as the yakuza started fading away themselves. I didn't want to do anything at all. But, unfortunately, the world decided not to accommodate my feelings or my mental health.

If there's one thing in this world that can help you focus on living, it's a reminder that someone would like to see you dead—especially someone who has a talent for killing people. And getting away with it.

There's a Japanese saying you should know. *Jigoku no sata mo kane shidai*. Even at the gates of hell, it all depends on how much money you have.

In Japan, money solves everything. Even cold-blooded murder. In mid-October 2012, Tadamasa Goto agreed to pay 110 million yen, or $1.1 million, to settle the lawsuit filed by the family of Kazuoki Nozaki, who had been assassinated by members of his organization in 2006.

Goto then fled the country and moved to Cambodia. I breathed a little easier.

The Tokyo Metropolitan Police spent five years working the case, but the prosecution was reluctant to go forward after a serious hitch occurred. Goto's former lieutenant, Takashi Kondo, the only gangster who allegedly had been given direct orders to make the hit, was gunned down in Thailand in April 2011.

A Tokyo police officer who worked on the case said, "We wanted to nail the bastard, but the prosecutors would never give a thumbs-up. They were afraid to try the case on the evidence alone."

Yes, Goto was never prosecuted for that murder. But even for him, having to pay $1.1 million must have stung, and settling with the family was probably humiliating.

They say the pen is mightier than the sword. Sometimes, that's true. It was in September 2012 that I heard the police were pushing the family of a murdered real estate agent to sue Goto in court. They were going to ask for $2 million.

I was determined to write an exposé to help make sure that he paid up—the whole amount, and not a single yen of it from the coffers of the Yamaguchi-gumi. The responsibility for that murder was with him and him alone. If the prosecutors in Japan had any balls, he would have been criminally prosecuted for murder.

But we can't always get what we want. Over twenty-five lawyers handled the lawsuit, and none of their names were ever published. When I asked one of the lawyers why there were so many of them on a fairly simple case, the deadpan response was, "He can't kill all of us, so he's less likely to kill any of us." That made sense to me.

The one lawyer I spoke with, who will remain unnamed, was very nervous when I showed up at his door. I hadn't made an appointment; I just went to his office. When I was asking him some details of the lawsuit, he interrupted me.

"Igari-sensei, he was your friend and your lawyer, right?"

"Yes, he was."

He didn't say anything for fifteen seconds. He seemed to be holding his breath. I broke the silence.

"I'm not putting your name in the article. It's like I was never here. There are twenty-five of you right?"

"Yes, twenty-five of us."

"Well, then, that's a lot of suspects. I'll just write up the article as if I spoke to none of you."

"I would, we would, immensely appreciate that."

I had pitched the article on the lawsuit to *The Atlantic Wire*, who wanted me to explain how it was that in Japan you could hold a yakuza boss civilly responsible for murder, but not criminally responsible.

There's not a single active Yamaguchi-gumi boss who will go on the record—except for the big boss, and he makes the rules. Some guys, like Satoru Takegaki, a former boss of the Takenaka-gumi, would speak on the record, but only after he'd retired. The rule is that an underboss can't speak to the press and have their name printed while in the organization. Ideally, as a journalist, when you quote someone, you want to use their real name, but when it comes to cops and criminals in Japan, that's very difficult to do. Cops can get fired and even prosecuted for "leaking secrets," due to provisions in the laws governing civil servants. Yakuza can get banished or killed for speaking out of turn.

For this article, I went directly to the Elder. He wanted a copy of what the lawyers had distributed to the press, but I couldn't do that. I read the relevant portions to him out loud over the phone. He was happy to give me a comment on background. He pointed out to me that it was unfair to ask his boss, the head of the Yamaguchi-gumi, to pay any part of the fine being sought. He explained why, and I promised that the article would at least reflect that position.

I knew that Goto would never give me a comment about

the lawsuit, but I had one underling close to him brief me on his reaction. The underling was planning to leave Tokyo and go back to take care of his elderly parents in northern Japan. Also, Goto had smashed him across the face with a walking stick on a particularly moody day, and he was done working for the bastard.

Goto had loudly complained about the lawsuit at a dinner party with several of his wealthy patrons, and so I was certain that my source wouldn't be burned for telling me. I put it in the article. I wondered what Shinobu Tsukasa, the head of the Yamaguchi-gumi, would think of that comment, but I didn't have time to run it past the Elder.

Finally, I put it all together. I wrote up the following article. But it was the real-world follow-up to the article that ensured the results.

It's Not Easy Being a Yakuza Boss

These days the price of a standard civilian hit-job can run as high as $2 million. That's not the price to get the job done—that's the price if one of your underlings gets caught. The whole inflationary spiral started with one dumb yakuza stiffing McDonald's on the price of a cheeseburger in Kyoto a few years ago.

The Yamaguchi-gumi, Japan's largest organized crime group with 39,000 members and their notorious former underboss Tadamasa Goto (at left, from a 2005 video of a Yamaguchi-gumi celebration) are expected to reach a settlement this month with the family of a civilian killed in 2006. The surviving family members, represented by a group of twenty-five lawyers, filed the lawsuit last month, asking for ¥187 million in damages, or $2.4 million.

However, it's the current "CEO" of the Yamaguchi-gumi, Shinobu Tsukasa, who has the most to lose. At the time of the murder he was in jail on gun possession charges, had no knowledge of the plan, did not approve it, and is not very happy to be cleaning up the mess. He doesn't want to pay for a crime he didn't commit or condone. Naturally. The whole thing is bad for business and terrible PR. It really damages the Yamaguchi-gumi corporate brand. And if the lawsuit actually goes to court, it could be a very bad legal precedent for "Yakuza Inc."

It is an unusual lawsuit. Police sources say it represents the first time Japanese yakuza bosses have been sued for crimes pre-dating the 2008 revisions to the Anti–Organized Crime Laws that made it possible to hold organized crime bosses responsible for the actions of their underlings in civil court, by essentially recognizing yakuza groups as corporations.

Former National Police Agency officer and lawyer Akihiko Shiba says that since it is very difficult to prove the criminal responsibility of the top yakuza bosses, lawsuits are one way of seeing justice partially served. "The Anti–Organized Crime Laws are administrative laws, not criminal laws. The 2008 revisions made it clear that designated organized crime groups function like a Japanese company, and therefore the people at the top have employer liability," Shiba explained. Since 2008, there have been at least three lawsuits against top yakuza bosses for damages by lower ranking members. All were settled out of court. "For the time being the use of civil lawsuits against top yakuza certainly has a deterrent effect on the management. The damages add up after a time," Shiba says.

Others would agree.

These days, being a yakuza boss isn't what it once was. In exchange for supreme status you get blamed for everything. In August of 2008, three months after the countermeasures laws went into effect, a Yamaguchi-gumi boss found himself dealing with one of his low-ranking underling's unpaid McDonald's tab. We all know that the modern yakuza in Japan are essentially corporations. The Yamaguchi-gumi itself is a listed corporation. And in Japan the CEO has to take responsibility for the screw-ups under his command. A 38-year-old Yamaguchi-gumi member had ordered a burger combo at a drive-through in Kyoto. He picked up his order, but then claimed since his meal had gotten wet in the rain, he owed nothing. He drove off clutching his burger and fries. (It's unclear whether it was a plain hamburger or a cheeseburger, accounts vary, but it was definitely not a happy meal.) Several days later, a bill arrived at the Yamaguchi-gumi headquarters in Kobe from a very angry McDonald's manager. The organization paid.

It was the most expensive cheeseburger in the world.

The cheeseburger compensation was just the start of a series of legal headaches for the Yamaguchi-gumi. Other yakuza groups felt the burn as well. Over time, and with additional revisions to the laws, and broader interpretations by the courts, yakuza bosses now find "employer liability" increasingly burdensome. A boss can be held liable for any damages his cohorts inflict in the course of their business activities, including extortion.

There are a number of things about the lawsuit concerning Nozaki's death that are different from anything preceding them. "If this case goes to court and the defendant loses, it could be a major setback for the yakuza," says a retired police investigator formerly with the Tokyo Metro Police, who had over 20 years' experience investigating organized crime.

The Nozaki murder is still officially unsolved and who is ultimately responsible, criminally or civilly, has not been settled. The Goto-gumi member who police suspect of receiving the orders for the hit, Takashi Kondo, was assassinated in Thailand last year after an international arrest warrant had been issued. Dead men can't be sued.

Tadamasa Goto, who is suspected but has never been charged with ordering the hits on Nozaki and Kondo, was kicked out of the Yamaguchi-gumi two years after the Nozaki murder on October 14, 2008, so his legal responsibility is unclear.

The Yamaguchi-gumi boss, Tsukasa, has never faced a criminal investigation for the murder. As noted above, law enforcement sources believe (and underworld sources agree) Tsukasa never gave the order for the killing, never approved it, and was in solitary confinement when the job was done. He did finally approve the banishment of Goto while he was still in jail, via his second in command.

A high-ranking member of the Yamaguchi-gumi, on background, feels that a lawsuit this time is decidedly unfair. This member explains, "Mr Tsukasa has never condoned the killing of a civilian. The Yamaguchi-gumi under Mr Tsukasa forbids dealing in drugs, theft, robbery, and violence against ordinary citizens—that's not acceptable. Extortion and blackmail, that's another issue. Anyway, one of the reasons the Yamaguchi-gumi finally kicked out Goto is because he continually violated even our lowest ethical standards. And now, six years after the fact, we have to clean up his mess again."

Goto may pay his share of the damages but he is balking about paying the bill for his former godfather (*oyabun*), Tsukasa. Goto has supposedly told his associates, "Who do you think put up the bail money for the old man in 2005? That was my ¥1 billion ($10 million) in cash! He kicked me out of the organization. And he still hasn't paid me back. He can pay his damages out of what he owes me."

In the meantime, Goto is not strapped for cash. His defiant autobiography, *Habakarinagara (Pardon Me But …)*, was a bestseller after it was published in 2010, and his new "business ventures" are reportedly highly successful.

Attempts to reach Goto for comment, including calls to his private cellphone, were unsuccessful. Sources close to Goto said he is hiding out in Cambodia until the lawsuit is settled.

While it's certainly hard to feel any sympathy for Tsukasa, you can see why it's a headache, at least, to keep homicidal sociopaths on the payroll. All you can do is fire them—if you can't get them buried somewhere. And $2 million may seem like a drop in the bucket for a Japanese gang lord, but keep in mind, with bail running around $10 to $15 million, it's getting much harder to make a dishonest living these days.

The article was a hit on the internet, for something that was rather esoteric. I was pleased. Someone summarized it for the top dogs at the Yamaguchi-gumi. I think it had been up for less than twenty-four hours when I got a call from one of the Elder's lieutenants.

"Greetings. He asked me to call you. He says it was a great article. Some of the jokes were a little … a little dark. Thank you for clarifying that the *oyabun* couldn't be responsible."

"Of course. It's the truth."

"He had a question."

I waited.

"He wanted to know if Goto really said that. About the Big Boss owing him money and that shit."

"I didn't hear it directly from him, as you can see in the article. I did hear it from a person who was in a position to know."

"Who would that be?"

"That would be telling. I can't say, or rather I won't say."

There was an awkward silence.

"The person who told me is a source. Sources are confidential. We have to protect them. That's the journalist code," I told him.

"You don't trust us?"

I expected that line of argument.

"I don't even trust myself. I trust you, but you have to report it to someone else. People talk. Somewhere along the way, the wrong person hears his name and he's dead. I don't need that on my head. And, professionally, that's the end for me."

More silence.

"For example, you and I are talking now. But we never talked. We never had this conversation."

"I get it. So Goto said what he said."

"Yes, he said what he said. You know the man. Isn't that exactly what he would say?"

He laughed.

"The boss has a request. He would like you to translate it into Japanese and put it up on your crappy website."

I wanted to protest the use of the word "crappy" as an adjective for the website, but I held my tongue.

"Sure," I said, "Give me twenty-four hours."

"You have twelve."

He hung up.

Yeah, sometimes, a request isn't really a request. I didn't know why he wanted a translation posted, but I could guess. I did it in four hours, and called up the lieutenant.

"Hey," I said, "It's done. It's up on the net. It's not 'live' yet, not for public viewing, but I'll send you the URL, and you can read it."

"Please do. Also, print out five copies. Preferably in color."

"Why? You don't have a printer?"

"I have a printer."

"Okay, then …?"

"Things vanish from the internet. They get posted; they get taken down. Paper lasts forever. So print out five copies."

I asked him where I should send them. He said he would

send someone to pick them up—at my house. I tried to give him the address, but he replied nonchalantly, "It's okay. We already know where you live."

He was there in an hour.

The lieutenant always seemed to be dressed in the same suit: a black, two-button jacket, and always with a cobalt blue necktie. I suspect that he'd bought several copies of the same suit and just kept changing them. Maybe black was his lucky color, but I never asked. He was tall for a Japanese man, and thin. He had an almost flat face, thin eyebrows, crew-cut gray hair, and almost always wore sunglasses. He may have had some sort of photosensitivity, because when he took the sunglasses off in bright light, his eyes watered.

He was kind enough to park their two cars at the coin parking lot down the road, because I told him my neighbors would get upset if several black Mercedes-Benz vehicles lined up in front of the house. That would sort of scream "yakuza visit."

He sat down in the living room, took the copies from me, called his boss, and read one of them over the phone to him. He had trouble reading some of the legal terminology in kanji, so I quietly rewrote some sections on a memo pad and slipped it to him while he was speaking. He gave me a thumbs-up thank you.

After the phone call, he told me, "The boss wishes to express his appreciation. Good work. We'll take care of this now. Expect a settlement very soon. You'll get a call."

And then he took the five copies, put them in a black folder, and put the folder in the briefcase he brought with him and got ready to leave. I walked him to the door, where he bowed twice, and then left. I waited a few minutes before double-locking the door. I didn't want to appear rude.

Goto settled. He paid out about $1.1 million. Who says there's no justice? It costs a lot of money to get away with murder when you're a yakuza bigshot.

As a side note, it also costs a considerable amount of money to stay alive when you're a yakuza boss. According to a letter from the office of Senator Chuck Grassley in 2008, Goto had paid $400,000 to UCLA in order to jump to the head of the line and get himself a liver in 2001. In addition to that, he made a $100,000 donation to the institute.

So, when you consider those figures, maybe $1.4 million seems high.

Admittedly, that's a little less than the 187 million yen of damages specified in the family's original suit. But they got something in return: according to those involved with the lawsuit, at one point in the negotiations, Goto and the Yamaguchi-gumi organization offered to pay the full amount requested in the lawsuit, but in the final negotiations only Goto ended up paying, with the provision that he expressed his condolences. In Japan, an apology is worth quite a lot.

Shinobu Tsukasa did not pay a single yen of what had been originally requested.

The lawyer representing the family members issued a press statement outlining the details of the agreement: first, Goto accepted responsibility, as the head of the organization at the time, for the actions of his soldiers in Nozaki's killing, and agreed to pay damages and express his condolences to the family. There was no admission from Goto, however, that he had commanded the killing.

The Elder called me directly eight hours after my follow-up to the first article was published. It was the lieutenant's number, but it was the Elder on the other end of the line. He said he had plenty of time to talk.

"I'll tell you," he said, "I think Goto whacked Kondo in Thailand. Had him killed. That's cold-blooded. For an *oyabun* to kill his *kobun* (child) to protect himself, that's low. That's as low as you can go. The only thing worse is the reverse."

I agreed.

"So," he said, "You still under police protection?"

"Yep," I added, "probably not for much longer. It's not everlasting."

"I read your book, *Tokyo Vice*. Well, read a translation of it. It was good—in fact, elucidating. And, yeah. You must really hate the bastard. You think he whacked your lawyer?"

I said I didn't know. "But," I added, "when you hire your lawyer to sue Goto, and ten days later he's dead, you have to wonder if that's a coincidence or just bad luck. I don't know. I still don't know."

There was a silence. And then he spoke very slowly, in his deep, raspy voice.

"Goto," he said, "*Yatchau ka?*"

I felt like my whole body started to freeze when he said that—from my hand gripping the phone, to the hairs on my arm, all the way up to my neck.

In Japanese, "*Yatchau*" is a colloquial way of saying "*Yatte Shimau*," which means "to do something completely."

It can also have a very different meaning: *Do you want me to do him in?*

For a split second, I wanted to say chipperly, "Yes. *Yatchau!*"

Have you ever watched an action movie in which, all the way through, the hero is killing people right and left, but when he finally gets his chance to take out the supervillain, he doesn't? It almost always goes like this: "I'm going to leave this to the law." Or, "I'm not going to drop to your level. Boys, cuff him and take him away."

I'm in the audience watching, and I think to myself, *Hey, dude, you've been going vigilante on every other henchman in the whole damn film, and now you're suddenly about law and order?* But that's the movies.

And I took a deep breath, and I said, "No."

And immediately, to my surprise, the Elder apologized.

"I am at fault. I shouldn't have asked you. I should have just done it. I'm sorry."

"It's totally okay," I reassured him.

"I'll tell you what, I'll have a talk with him. I've been meaning to have another talk with him. I'll make it clear to him that if anything happens to you—or anyone who is very close to you—that it will come back on him."

"Meaning?"

"If you slip in the bathtub and die, or get hit by a car and die, something unpleasant will happen to him. If one of the ladies you're fucking suddenly vanishes … You get it, right?"

"I don't really need to know any more about the terms. Yes, if that was communicated to him, that would be nice."

"It's a done deal. As long as I'm alive and you're alive, he's going to wake up every day hoping you're not dead."

"Well, thank you."

"Don't mention it."

"Leave it in my hands. Sleep well tonight. *Shitsurei shimasu.*"

That worked out much better than I expected. My nemesis was gone from Japan. An outside force had imposed a mutual self-assured destruction clause in our "relationship," and I felt certain that he wanted to live.

I had much less to fear now and many reasons to live. And I decided that if I was prudent, I could take on some dangerous work. Gold-medal-level dangerous.

CHAPTER EIGHTEEN

The yakuza Olympics: publish or perish

A picture is worth a thousand words, but it can also get both of your knees broken with a baseball bat. A certain picture, which had never been published, of the vice-chairman of the Japanese Olympic Committee (JOC) sitting next to the head of the Yamaguchi-gumi, had already gotten a reporter beaten to a pulp. I didn't want to be the second.

There were several pictures, in fact, but the one that I knew was going to grab the attention of everyone was a photograph from around 2005 depicting Hidetoshi Tanaka (the vice-chairman of the JOC) alongside Shinobu Tsukasa (the head of the Yamaguchi-gumi). They were looking pretty chummy at a hostess bar in Nagoya. If you looked closely at his left hand, you would have noticed something missing.

I was in a hurry. I needed an article I'd written about all this, which would be accompanied by the incendiary photograph, to go up as quickly as possible, and my editor at *Vice News* was running late on it.

"Ky, it's publish or perish. For God's sake, get the damn thing online as soon as possible. That was our deal, dude."

"Jake, I totally get it. I'm working on it. Have no fear!"

That was easy for him to say. He was safe in Los Angeles. I was in Tokyo, and I'd already set fire to a story possibly connecting the JOC to organized crime. And I only broke this story because a reporter from *Keiten Shimbun,* a right-wing scandal sheet, had had their legs broken when they tried to report it.

When you're poking around on a potentially dangerous story, speed is important. You have to prepare the article in advance, confirm your facts, and then hit all the people involved at once—within a twenty-four-hour period. I don't know how it works in the U.S. or Europe, but in Japan you have to give the subject of an exposé the opportunity to defend themselves before publishing.

There's only one problem with that professional rule. When you approach the yakuza or powerful politicians while you're writing an exposé to give them the opportunity to defend themselves, they may go on the offensive and try to eliminate you. They may take steps to ensure your article is never published. That's a substantial risk.

Saigo said that when you give people time to ponder things, problems arise because "air gets in." I never quite understood what that meant, but I think the phrase means that if you give people time to mull things over, they may start to plot and scheme, and call upon allies. So I'd sent all my requests for comments early on the morning of the 17th, and told everyone they had twenty-four hours to respond. I didn't want to let any air in.

The photo had been sent anonymously to several media outlets. One magazine received a note with the photos that read:

I am an employee of Nihon University, where many are in conflict with chief director Tanaka. Six or eight years ago, when Tanaka was elected as the chief director of the board, he went to a club in Nagoya and celebrated his promotion with the head of the Yamaguchi-gumi and many other Yamaguchi-gumi … members. He has shown us these photos over the years to intimidate us into silence. Please investigate.

The 2020 Tokyo Olympics were predicted to cost at least $5 billion. That meant there was a lot of money to be made in construction. Yakuza are said to get 5 percent of all the revenue from construction in Japan, so it looked like the Yamaguchi-gumi had someone on the inside to help ensure that they got a juicy cut.

I had heard about the photo and the attack first from Kumagaya, the *kaishaya,* in October 2014. He had become a sort of *jōhōya* (information vendor), a dealer in incriminating and potentially career-destroying information. I went to his office in early October to have a chat and to trade rosters—I had lists of people he wanted, and he had lists of people I wanted to have on file.

I had a directory of a small bank, and he had a directory of a third-tier group in the Inagawa-kai, and one for the Sumiyoshi-kai as well. I brought coffee and whisky, the good stuff. You could still buy mini bottles of Suntory's Hibiki for a few hundred yen back then.

He filled me in while carefully drinking his coffee. He was wearing, as always, a white suit. It was a miracle to me how he kept them white. If I had a white suit, it would be covered with coffee stains, ink from my pen, and spots of gyoza sauce within a day. Maybe within hours. I'd have to carry a Tide to Go Instant Stain Remover Pen* along with my other pens, and maybe a

---

*   Thank you Tide to Go Instant Stain Remover Pen for your sponsorship and product placement in this work of narrative nonfiction. Tide to Go is the choice of all former yakuza and underworld denizens in Japan who wear white suits. Or black suits. It helps remove even the toughest of grease stains, blood splatter, and gunshot residue while on the go! With a combination of a powerful cleaning solution that breaks bloodstains or gunshot residue down, and a microfiber pad that lifts and absorbs them, Tide to Go is the number-one choice for someone fleeing a crime scene. Go! Go! Go! (Just kidding. Sadly, Tide to Go is unavailable in Japan.)

cheap bottle of white-out just in case.

He didn't have a copy of the photos, but he had seen them. He wouldn't say who had showed them to him. Let me tell you what I heard.

"Last month, every major magazine got the photos. Some with a note, others without. So this reporter from *Keiten Shimbun* attempted to seek clarification from Nihon University and Tanaka regarding when the photograph was taken and what Tanaka's relationship, if any, is to the Yamaguchi-gumi now. While walking back to the newspaper office on September 30—I'm sure that's the date—he was ambushed by two men with metal baseball bats who pulverised his knees. And they hit him repeatedly somewhere else, too."

There was no doubt in my mind that confirmation of this could be easily obtained from a second source. I told him I wanted the photos and would pay for them—not much, but something.

As we talked, I started thinking back about what had already happened. Let's rewind a bit. This wasn't going to be the first time writing about Tanaka's shady connections to powerful yakuza. I wasn't surprised that these photos had surfaced. I'd already written an article for *The Daily Beast* in February 2014 about Tanaka and his past connections to the Sumiyoshi-kai. The Sumiyoshi-kai were the second-largest yakuza group in Japan. They had offices in Ginza, and while the leaders spouted the usual rhetoric about "helping the weak and fighting the strong," they were knee-deep in the drug business.

The Sumiyoshi-kai were in the news frequently in 2014 because they had been supplying drugs to a Japanese rock star, Aska. Aska had been part of a music duo that had a mega-hit with the love ballad "Say Yes." Apparently, Aska had a habit of saying "Yes!" to almost every illegal drug he could find. Aska had been arrested early in the year, and the cops used his cellphone and his testimony to go after the organization supplying him.

Sumiyoshi-kai's third-tier group, the Daisho-kai, was also known as the "Pharmacy of Shinjuku." It was a huge, illegal drug-trafficking operation. Two of its executives were arrested for selling MDMA to Aska, and six of its traffickers were arrested for violating the Methamphetamine Control Act. Tokyo Organized Crime Control Division Five (Drugs and Guns) led the investigation. As a crime reporter, I used to cover that section, and now, almost ten years later, I still had contact with police working that section.

There was no doubt that Tanaka was a shady figure. That was not a secret.

In January 2014, a scandal-sheet editor set me up with a Sumiyoshi-kai-backed real estate developer. The developer was very polite, very well dressed, and got right to the point. He handed me the photos of Tanaka with a Sumiyoshi-kai boss in a vinyl folder, and explained to me where they came from, how I could verify they were real, and the significance of them. With a laugh, he added that Goto was still alive and still hated me.

I asked him, "How do you know Goto?"

"The underworld is small," he replied. "It's just a junior high school. After a while, everyone knows everyone."

He was very clear about why he was giving me the photos. Tanaka was once a patron of the Sumiyoshi-kai, but a few years before he had switched allegiances to the Yamaguchi-gumi. The Yamaguchi-gumi was receiving all the juicy construction projects from Nihon University that were supposed to go through Sumiyoshi-kai. Revenues were down.

Yet even then, I wondered why he would show me photos of his boss, the chairman of the Sumiyoshi-kai, buddy-buddy with Tanaka. Wouldn't that attract unwanted attention, I asked him.

He just smiled, and said nothing. I didn't really need to know all his reasons.

My last question was: Why me?

"Well, that's because you're brave or stupid enough to write it. You have earned that reputation. No magazine here wants to be the first to break the story." He gestured at the editor who had scheduled the meeting. The editor shrugged his shoulders and laughed.

I didn't want to get my ass kicked, and I didn't want trouble with the Sumiyoshi-kai. Once I had some outside confirmation, I submitted the photos and my story to *Weekly Bunshun*, the biggest news weekly in Japan and well known for handling taboo topics. The editors agreed that we could publish the story without attribution. I told them I would follow up on *The Daily Beast*.

Bunshun has had a large readership and an army of reporters and researchers. The reporters were too numerous for retaliation to be a good idea or practical, and any act of violence toward them would have a massive social impact. By writing it for them first, I could give myself a shield.

I did exactly that. I wrote it for them, and the night the magazines started showing up in bookstores and 7-Elevens, I chased my own story for *The Daily Beast*. I'd dubbed the 2020 games "the Yakuza Olympics" for that article, and for good reasons. Even a year before the photos of Tanaka and the head of the Yamaguchi-gumi emerged, I'd heard he was well connected to the Yamaguchi-gumi, and had included that detail in the *Daily Beast* article. Of course, I had to get his comment before writing it up.

We do have to give the devil his due. Tanaka was a distinguished figure in Japan's sports world. He was a former amateur sumo champion, president of the International Sumo Federation, and the chairman of the board of Nihon University, well known for its strong sumo club. He was also a problematic person for the sumo world, which was rocked by a scandal involving sumo wrestlers engaging in an illegal gambling ring run by Yamaguchi-gumi members in 2010. The Sumo Association pledged to end yakuza ties the same year.

There is a terrible irony in JOC members having possible yakuza ties that people in Japan understand better than most.

The JOC had been running a "Zero Violence in Sports" campaign since 2013, designed to discourage the brutality common in Japanese sports. Sumo, in particular, has had problems with violence, and a sumo stable master was arrested for the fatal hazing of a young sumo wrestler in 2008.

If you are trying to rid the sports world of violence, you don't want the yakuza around.

In 2012, 4,933 yakuza were arrested for violent crimes such as assault and battery, inflicting bodily injury, and murder. Non-violence isn't their thing. You know by now that even though the yakuza claim to be humanitarian groups promoting traditional Japanese values such as reciprocity and loyalty, in practice many of them are nothing more than violent thugs and a far cry from icons of good sportsmanship.

When not apparently hobnobbing with shady figures, Tanaka had been a strong advocate of making Japan's national sport, sumo, an Olympic event, and lobbied hard for it. He reportedly asked for help from some strange quarters—including Kyo Eichu, a consigliere in the Yamaguchi-gumi.

Without boring you with too much history, Kyo Eichu, a Korean Japanese national, was a major player in the Japanese underworld in his day—a fixer, a conman, and a criminal. He was not a savory character.

In March 1996, Tanaka visited Kyo Eichu's home, and the two discussed getting funds to build a sumo stadium in Osaka. Kyo pledged to use all his power and political connections to help make sure sumo was an Olympic event by 2008.

Unfortunately, Kyo, who was on bail for charges of special breach of trust and corporate tax violations, jumped bail in 1997, only to be later arrested in 1999—and didn't make good on his promises.

The JOC not only had Tanaka on board, but the JOC sister organization, The Tokyo Organizing Committee of the Olympic and Paralympic Games, was headed by former prime minister Yoshiro Mori, who is also well known for his past social yakuza ties, according to Japanese law enforcement sources.

Mori's alleged organized crime ties are noted in the book, *The Yakuza: Japan's Criminal Underworld*. Mori attended the wedding of an organized crime boss's son, and was close with a yakuza-backed right-wing group leader. In December 2000, pictures of the then prime minister Mori appeared in the weekly magazine *Shukan Gendai* showing him drinking in an Osaka bar with a high-ranking yakuza. The scandal hastened the end of his term as prime minister. Mori sued the publisher of the magazine for defamation, but dropped the lawsuit in November 2011.

In fact, the reporting on Mori's unsavory ties spurred the Liberal Democratic Party to pass the odious Personal Information Protection Laws, which did little to protect anyone other than LDP politicians. It should have been called the Politicians' Privacy Protection Laws. It also made determining who was a yakuza much more difficult. A group of lawyers even issued a handbook to get around the Personal Information Protection Laws when trying to determine if a client, customer, business, or business partner was connected to the yakuza.

The Japanese government has an Orwellian knack for creating laws that do the opposite of what they are supposed to do if you take the name at face value. The Peace Preservation Act, ramrodded into law despite massive protests, enabled Japan's

Self Defense Forces to wage war overseas. So much for preserving the peace.

Tanaka's alleged ties to the yakuza aren't news to the alternative media. They have been written up in FACTA, the investigative journalism magazine that broke the story of the $1.7 billion accounting fraud at Olympus.

As I dug deeper, it turned out that even Nihon University was aware of Tanaka's unsavory underworld connections many years before. Nihon University, apparently concerned over Tanaka's alleged connections to anti-social forces, had a special investigation called by the chairman of the board (at the time) in 2005.

According to a former Nihon University board member, it was staffed by six of Japan's finest lawyers, including a former head of the Public Security Bureau, Japan's version of the CIA.

I hunted down the people on that committee, and I hunted them down one by one until I finally got a copy of the August 17, 2005 report produced in connection with the investigation. It took a lot of pounding the pavement, but it was worth it.

One section stood out. Titled "Relations with Organized Crime Associates," it noted that Tanaka met with Kyo Eichu even after he skipped bail and was in hiding. It also asserted that Tanaka was present at a party for a construction company where members of organized crime groups were also in attendance. The report noted: "It is problematic for a board member of our distinguished university to be attending private events with organized crime figures and members of the construction industry … Tanaka denied all association with the yakuza to the committee, but it does not bear upon our findings."

One of the committee members told me on background, "The committee did not have the power of the police, and couldn't reach definite conclusions. We couldn't search and seize evidence. However, right-wing groups threatened the board directors who opposed Tanaka around the period the investigation took place. It's likely not a coincidence."

The police and law enforcement entities that actually gave a fuck feared that Tanaka and Mr Mori could be conduits for organized crime influence in the Games. There was certainly a lot of money at stake. The National Construction Industry Association of Japan estimated 2020 Olympic construction costs to be as much as $3.8 billion in 2014.

I had to get a comment from Tanaka directly for the *Daily Beast* article (and later would have to try and do it again), but that was impossible to do. Nihon University's public affairs department, speaking on behalf of Mr Tanaka, said, "The photo was taken a long time ago, and he has no memory of the event. He attended many parties in the past. Mr Tanaka has met Kyo Eichu, but they had no special relationship."

The office of Mr Mori responded at the time, "He is currently at the Sochi Olympics and can't be reached for comment."

It was possible that Tanaka and Mori no longer had tight associations with the yakuza and that they were as clean as the snow in Sochi. There was a time in Japan, decades before, when socializing with the yakuza was acceptable. Now, it was more or less against the law. Tokyo had vowed to make the 2020 Olympics safe and "drug free," but the Tokyo Olympic Committee and the JOC didn't seem to have an interest in keeping them "yakuza free."

I'd put all of this information into my article for *The Daily Beast* on February 7, 2014. Now it was October. I was writing a follow-up to that *Daily Beast* article I'd never thought I would be writing, and this time, instead of writing it for the *Beast*, I was writing it for *Vice News*.

The hits kept coming. Literally and metaphorically.

CHAPTER NINETEEN

The yakuza Olympics redux: paying respects

So there I was talking to Kumagaya, and I knew that I couldn't let this story go. The JOC was promoting its "Zero Violence in Sports" campaign, but it became clear to me that violence had already come to the Olympics. The beating of the reporter had been severe. Kumagaya gave me the business card of a magazine editor who had been sent the photos. I thanked him, left an envelope with a small amount of cash on his desk, and continued to work on the story.

The reports of the assailants hitting the reporter repeatedly on the same spot intrigued me. Where? A cop buddy told me they couldn't specify the location of the injury "because it's something only the assailant would know, and we wish to weed out possible false confessions."

I also learned that the day after the assault, almost every major media organization in Japan had received threatening phone calls telling them not to publish the photo. One magazine editor, who spoke to me, said the threat was, "We attacked *Keiten Shimbun*. If you get uppity and publish that photo of those two, you'll meet the same fate."

More than a month after the attacks, the photo of the

Yamaguchi-gumi big boss and Big Tanaka remained unpublished. However, *Keiten Shimbun* did publish another photo of Tanaka toward the end of October. In that photo, from some time in 2004, Tanaka is pictured with another senior member of the Yamaguchi-gumi named Iwao Yamamoto, who was once close to Tsukasa. Yamamoto shot himself in front of the grave of his godfather in December 2010.

There may have been another reason that *Keiten Shimbun* didn't publish the more sensational photo. Allegedly, the special advisor to the company that ran the newspaper was Goro Hanabusa, head of the Yamaguchi-gumi Hanabusa-gumi. Dead men don't have mouths, so Yamamoto couldn't have complained, but Hanabusa as special advisor—a senior Yamaguchi-gumi boss—would have had reservations. He probably advised the newspaper not to publish a picture of his *oyabun* (Shinobu Tsukasa). There was at least one thing about that photo that Tsukasa really didn't like. But it wasn't what you might think.

Knowing these things didn't help me much. My problem was that I still didn't have a photo of Tanaka and the Boss together. It would be a hell of a story if I could get the photos. I thought of one person who might have them, but for good reasons hesitated to go ask him. That would be Fumio Akiyama.

He was the shady yakuza-connected real estate broker, with a serious drug problem, who had once kicked me in the head. I hadn't really seen that much of him over the years, although there were no hard feelings between us. I ran into him at the wake of a Tosei-kai (Korean yakuza) boss, but we didn't really talk.

He'd cleaned up his act, gotten off meth, and was now making a living as a *jōhōya*. He probably still dabbled in real estate. He ran a website full of scandalous information, and was raking in huge amounts from companies and individuals who paid him *not* to write about their scandals. If I was someone who wanted to spread scandalous photos of Tanaka and a yakuza boss, I'd send it to him. He'd print or post anything.

His office was in a bookstore in Jimbocho, not the place where you'd expect a yellow journalist to set up shop, but I figured it was just a tax dodge. Even yakuza pay taxes in Japan. And ex-yakuza as well. Of course, they want to pay as little tax as possible. I didn't bother to set up an appointment; I just went to his place. Just to be on the safe side, I had a knife-proof vest on and an unbreakable umbrella with me. The umbrella had been made in Poland, and designed so that, if you stood on it, it wouldn't break; you could also crush someone's chest with it, and it wouldn't break.

Jimbocho is full of old bookstores. His bookstore was large, and filled with tall, thick wooden cabinets. The shelves must have been fresh, because the faint scent of Japanese cedar still emanated from them. Near the entrance, there were posters advertising mystery novels, including the latest in the Shinjuku Shark series, which was about a vice detective in Kabukicho and his adventures while solving complex crimes.

The place was remarkably clean, except for a cart over-flowing with books that needed to be shelved. There were no magazines in sight; it was nothing but books. There was a bright sign in each aisle indicating the genre: I could see there were a lot of books about law, crime, gardening, and a surprisingly large children's section.

There were a few small tables with wooden chairs where you could sit down and thumb through the books that inte-rested you. However, most customers seemed reluctant to sit down, and they were engaging in one of Japan's old and favorite pastimes, *tachi-yomi*, standing and reading. In the old days, I often went into convenience stores, and would stand for half an hour reading magazines, looking for something interesting. Nowadays, many convenience stores seal the magazines in plastic, so there's no way to look through them or skim them. I think it discourages people from buying them, but the asswipes who run these franchises probably don't want people standing in the aisles reading magazines all day.

The place was pleasantly quiet. There was some jazz, which sounded like Coltrane, playing over the Bose loudspeakers. You could hear the sound of people turning pages. The clerk at the front was talking to a customer when I came in. I waited for the customer to finish his purchase, and said that I was looking for Akiyama. The clerk pointed to the staircase, and off I went. I had a nervous feeling going up the stairs that I can only describe as something like going to have what is meant to be a friendly cup of coffee with an ex-girlfriend whom you had parted from on very bad terms.

The door to his office was wooden within an opaque glass window embedded in the door. The doorknob was made out of bronze. I opened it with some trepidation, and found him inside, his feet up on the desk, a laptop computer in his lap, and a cup of coffee on the table. He looked remarkably healthy and he wasn't wearing glasses. He was still skinny but had put on some muscle, and he was wearing a dark green polo shirt instead of a suit.

"Jake-san," he said, "what a delightful surprise. You should've told me you were coming."

I didn't really know how to read that. Was he being sarcastic? Did he mean: *You should've told me you're coming so I could load my gun?* He seemed genuinely happy to see me. He asked me to sit down, and I did. He had an espresso maker on top of a short wooden shelf close to his desk. He made us both coffee, and we returned to our seats.

"It's quite a bookstore you've got here," I began. "It's beautiful, and I like that you let people peruse the books at their leisure."

"I always like to look at books without being rushed, and so my bookstore follows the same policy. Actually, the place is making money, which wasn't my intention."

Yes, I had guessed right—it was supposed to be a tax dodge.

I wanted to get right to the point, but he was in the mood for small talk, and so I thought I would go along with that.

"You seem surprisingly happy to see me, considering all that happened."

"You were the kick in the ass that I needed. I managed to dry out while I was in the hospital, and I haven't touched that crap since. I was out of my mind. So I owe you a thanks."

"You're welcome. I'd heard that you'd started a new business. I know a lot of reporters read your website religiously."

"I gather you're one of them," he said with a half-smile. "I heard you'd left the journalism business, but now you're back."

"For a few years, I was sort of a private detective, doing due diligence and other investigations. Now I'm primarily back to journalism—that's my calling."

"It's wonderful to have a job you love. Who would've thought that you and I would ever be in the same business?"

I knew that I probably shouldn't contradict him, but I couldn't help myself.

"It's not quite the same. I make a living writing the stories that people don't want written, and you make a living not writing the stories that people don't want written, if they pay you enough. If they don't pay you enough, then you publish the story."

And then, to my surprise, Akiyama began to sing. He sang very well, while pointing a finger at me and raising his eyebrows:

You say tomato and I say tomato
You say potato and I say potato
tomato, tomato, potato, potato

"Let's call the whole thing off," I interjected, to which he cackled for a few seconds with a wheezing sound.

"You know," he said, "I often publish things that don't make me any money because I think that the public has a right to know, and because I can't stand the scum of the world getting away with some of the things they do. Of course, sometimes I do get paid for discontinuing an avenue of reporting, but one has to earn a living to support their investigative journalism habit."

Jesus F. Christ. Maybe we were closer than I thought. I figured now was the time to get to the point.

"There are some pictures circulating of the vice-chairman of the Olympic Committee being chummy with the head of the Yamaguchi-gumi. Someone sent those pictures to every scandal sheet, every newsweekly, and probably every major newspaper. I'd like to have them, if you have them. I want to write it up."

He nodded, and pushed his finger up the side of his nose. I think he'd forgotten that he wasn't wearing glasses anymore. That was the gesture of someone who'd been wearing glasses for a long time.

"Jake-san, you do know what happened to the last reporter who tried to publish those photos?"

"Yes, I am aware of what happened. But if everyone has those photos, someone's gonna write it up, and I want to be the one. I'm surprised you haven't published them."

"Jake-san," he said, speaking very precisely and slowly now. "I only have one good knee left. So I decided to pass on that story."

Ouch. That was quite a zinger, and I wasn't sure what to say. Should I apologize again? I didn't know, so I just nodded my head.

"Well, I said, "if you're not going to do anything with the photos, can I please have them? I would be very grateful."

"Sure," he said with no hesitation. He took an envelope out

of a lower desk drawer addressed to him, and handed it to me.

I stood up, took it with both hands, and bowed profusely.

"Do you think it's real?"

"Oh, I know it's real. That's why I'm not going to publish it. I do not need to have the *oyabun* angry with me. You can leave the organization, but you're never really out. You're going to make some enemies by publishing that. You may also make some friends, but you have to decide whether that balances out."

He filled me in on the details of when the photo was taken and why. It was on background, and of course I would've never published his name.

It turned into a very friendly meeting. We talked for a little bit more.

"Are you still seeing that stripper?" he asked. "The one at the club, Karma Sutra, or something like that?"

"You mean Tantra."

"Yes, that's the one. Great club. I haven't been in years."

"She's not a stripper. She's a pole dancer. Actually, more of a pole dance fitness instructor these days."

"Is that a thing?"

"It's a thing."

"She's like half-Chinese, right? But good for you. Glad you're still with her. I liked her."

"Well, not really with her. It's an on-and-off thing. I'm sort of a between-boyfriends-guy as far as she goes."

"How does that work?"

I tried to think of a Japanese equivalent of the word "booty call," but failed. So I explained.

"When she's single and she's in the mood, she calls me or texts me that she'd really love a café au lait. And I go over to her place, or we meet somewhere."

"What if you're not single when she calls?"

"Then I instantly become single. You've seen the girl."

He laughed.

"You haven't changed."

"No, actually I've changed a little. If I really am in a mono-gamous relationship and she calls, I tell her I'm out of coffee."

"Has that ever happened?"

"At least twice now. I'm a changed man. I can refuse a cup of coffee."

And almost on cue, he said, "Have another," and turned on the espresso machine.

I drank the coffee.

He had a bit of parting advice.

"You need to give the organization a heads-up. You need to tell someone high up in the Yamaguchi-gumi that you wrote this article and that it's going to come out, whether they like it or not, before it comes out. That's courtesy. *Jingi o kiru.*

Jingi o kiru is an old phrase that in the world of the yakuza, especially the street merchants, originally meant to make proper greetings when first meeting another person in your field. Those greetings were expected to be conducted in a loud and clear voice, smoothly, and with some panache while introducing your-self. Over time, the expression had come to mean explaining the situation to those involved before things got troublesome. In other words, it had come to mean giving someone a heads-up before doing something that would affect them. *Jingi*, the word itself, refers to Confucian ideals of humanity and justice. It's also come to mean the code of honor in a gang. The Japanese version of the saying "There is honor among thieves" uses the word *jingi*.

He was right. I knew who I needed to speak with, but before I did that there were other things I had to do.

I needed to triangulate the data and write the article. Akiyama loaded me up with a few books before I left, walking me over to the non-fiction crime section, barely limping but still dragging his leg just a little. He pulled down a copy of a book next to Goto's *Habakarinagara*. It was titled *Chinkon (Farewell to the Yamaguchi-gumi I Loved)* by Kenji Seiriki, a former powerful underboss in the Yamaguchi-gumi. He was expelled in 2009 from the organization and given a 50,000,000-yen pension (around $450,000). That's one of the secrets of the success of the Yamaguchi-gumi; if you work hard and are lucky, you can leave the organization and get a severance fee or a pension. The book was his autobiography and exposé; it had come out in 2013.

"There's some interesting material in there, but mostly bragging bullshit, like Goto's book. I'll tell you something, Jake-san. Years ago, when you asked to interview me for your book, that was a scary thing. People who talked about the secrets of the organization got whacked. Nowadays, everyone who leaves writes a fucking tell-all book. They have no shame."

"Well, maybe it's time to join the club, before the market gets saturated."

"It's tempting, but you and I and the smart people know that a few years ago, Japan changed the statute of limitations on a lot of crimes. Attempted murder—twenty-five years. And a successful murder —there's not statute of limitations on those."

I held up my open hand, palm forward.

"Say no more. I got it. You could always consider posthumous publication."

"Hah! What fun would that be, and who would even do that?"

"I know one person who did. The ex-prosecutor Toshiro Igari."

"Oh yeah. Right. That was an amazing book. No living prosecutor would admit to that stuff."

He got on a stepladder and pulled down another book, a little dusty. It was Igari's *Gekitotsu*. He handed it to me.

"Both books are on the house. Take them. And good luck."

I was in good spirits. I had a solid lead on a good story. I knew that my *Vice* editor, Ky Henderson, would go for it.

I'd learned from Akiyama that when things go wrong, they can really go wrong. I took the picture and started talking to some cops. I knew, as usual, that no active police officer would go on the record. This is one thing that sucks about crime reporting in Japan. Because the civil servants' law technically forbids police from telling you about a continuing investigation, they can never be named as sources. Thus, most newspaper articles on criminal investigations now lead with "According to an announcement by the police," and then follow up with the details and juicy information by writing, "In subsequent interviews with those related to the investigation ..." Well, who the hell is that supposed to be? It can only be the cops, or the prosecutors. But that one line gives the reporters cover, and the police plausible deniability.

That's the game. I started knocking on doors. There was a lot of preparation needed for this article.

"Whether or not he [Tanaka] still has associations with Yamaguchi-gumi members is something under review," said an official at the National Police Agency. "Under the Tokyo Organized Crime Control Exclusionary Ordinances, such ties would be illegal."

Fukuda, the chairman of the Sumiyoshi-kai, and Tsukasa, the head of the Yamaguchi-gumi, were both well known to U.S. law enforcement. The U.S. treasury department, starting in 2012, had declared both individuals to be leaders of transcontinental organized crime groups, and had sanctioned them. The U.S. froze their assets in the United States, and forbade any U.S. company or individual from doing business with them.

The fact that Tanaka seemed to have been friends with both of them did not go over well.

An investigator for Homeland Security Investigations (HSI) gave me a comment: "In 2012, the United States put in place economic sanctions against these two yakuza groups and forbade U.S. citizens to associate with the groups or their leaders. These photos raise concerns about Japan's seriousness in the fight against transcontinental crime."

Th JOC, however, did not appear to share those concerns. They were as amoral as the International Olympic Committee (IOC). They were also said to be privy to information about construction taking place for the games—information that would be very valuable in winning lucrative construction contracts. The JOC did not respond to questions submitted to them. The IOC didn't give a fuck either.

I wasn't sure how Tanaka and Tsukasa had gotten to know each other, but the cops thought it might have been through Tanaka's sumo connections. Sumo was plagued by a scandal in 2009 when it was revealed that many wrestlers had been placing bets on baseball games with Yamaguchi-gumi bookies—yakuza members connected to the Yamaguchi-gumi Kodo-kai. The Kodo-kai was Tsukasa's faction. I thought that maybe Tanaka had been placing bets as well, but there was no evidence of this.

Questions remained about who attacked the journalists and threatened harm to other magazines if the pictures were published. The police were operating on the theory that the Sumiyoshi-kai may have released the photos and staged the attacks to make people believe the Yamaguchi-gumi was responsible. This might have initiated a crackdown on all Yamaguchi-gumi front companies in the construction industry, forcing them out of the lucrative Olympic racket. The remaining pie could then be divided among other yakuza.

The least likely suspects for the assault and threats were the Yamaguchi-gumi, who generally wouldn't resort to tactics such as that against a reporter, thanks to Tsukasa's influence.

After leaving prison in 2011, having served time for weapons charges, the longtime yakuza strictly enforced the old code of the Yamaguchi-gumi: *Don't assault civilians, don't engage in petty theft or robbery, don't sell or use drugs*. That said, not everyone in the organization shared Tsukasa's beliefs in traditional yakuza family values.

Questions also remained about where the photos had come from and why they had suddenly surfaced. According to the monthly news magazine *Facta*, the Tokyo Regional Taxation Bureau had begun an investigation of Nihon University on suspicion of tax evasion, and there was a possibility that the photos had surfaced during this process. The note attached to the photos might have been authentic—perhaps a frustrated board member leaking photos that were used to intimidate Tanaka's political opponents in the university. The police were still attempting to date the photos precisely, but viewed them as authentic.

When you write an article like this, you try to think one step ahead. What happens when the piece goes live? The more I thought about it, the more doubtful I was that the revelation of past or present connections between Tanaka and the yakuza would result in any attempt to clean up the committee or the Olympics.

Prime Minister Shinzo Abe's grandfather Kishi Nobusuke—a former prime minister himself, whom Abe was known to admire— had friendly ties with the Yamaguchi-gumi; in 1971, Nobusuke had even helped put up the bail money for a Yamaguchi-gumi member accused of murder. In 2012, a photo surfaced of Abe and Yamaguchi-gumi member Ichuu Nagamoto—along with U.S. politician Mike Huckabee—taken in 2008.

Abe insisted that he didn't know Nagamoto, and claimed he'd been photo-bombed. I doubt that. When Abe was running for the position of top dog of the Liberal Democratic Party

(LDP) in 2007, which he won, making him the de facto prime minister, Nagamoto campaigned on his behalf. Nagamoto approached the Inagawa-kai, specifically Kanazawa, the head of the Inagawa-kai Yokosuka-ikka, and asked them to lean on local LDP branches to vote for Abe in the elections. That's how the prime minister is usually determined in Japan. The LDP has elections to select a president; the lawmakers get votes; and the local branches of the LDP get votes. The yakuza have a history of making or breaking who gets to be prime minister, or remain as prime minister, in many different ways.

I didn't know what Abe's deal was, but since he had taken power, the push to get rid of the yakuza had taken a nosedive. He wasn't interested.

And so it was possible that the yakuza involvement in the Olympics wasn't going to be a problem, because the Abe administration didn't see it as a problem—just as they didn't appear to see yakuza involvement in the nuclear industry, and the construction industry, as problems. The Tokyo district court had ruled in January 2013 that one of the major construction companies handling Olympic projects had hired yakuza to intimidate someone during negotiations. That had no effect on the company's ability to land Olympic construction work.

I had everything I needed to write the article, but I knew that asking Tanaka for a comment would set off alarm bells. And that the people who'd whacked the previous reporters were likely to come looking for me.

I had one more thing I had to do before I ran the article. That was *jingi o kiru*. I considered consulting with Precision Man, but he wasn't the right guy. I needed to give the Elder a heads-up. He could tell Tsukasa, and then I'd have to let the chips fall where they might. But reaching him on short notice wasn't ever easy.

Now I was going to light the fuse to a time bomb. I called Nihon University very early in the morning of November 17. The countdown had begun. A spokesperson at Nihon University said, "The University received these photos with a written threat in early September and have filed a report with the police on charges of intimidation. Mr Tanaka has no memory of ever meeting these individuals, and we consider the photos to be fakes."

Nihon University had not submitted the photos to an outside institution for forensic analysis, and could not explain how the photos might have been faked. I was told it was not possible to speak to Tanaka.

I had my comment. I turned the article in to *Vice*.

And then I made my way to the offices of the Elder's lieutenant. I could have called, but that would have been weaselly. This required a face-to-face talk. And just like he knew where I lived, I knew where his front company in Nishi-Azabu was located.

When we sat down, I noticed that he was dressed a little differently. He had on a black three-button jacket—not a two-button jacket—and a cobalt blue necktie.

When I filled him in and showed him the pictures, he started to sweat a little. He took off his sunglasses. I don't think I'd ever seen him not wearing sunglasses. He had gray eyes. Maybe he was mixed race, or wore colored contact lenses? It wasn't the time to ask.

"I don't suppose we can talk you out of this," he said.

"No, you can't. The dice is cast. I've already submitted the article."

"I'm going to have to talk to the big boss about this. Can you stick around for a bit?"

He stepped into the back room of his office.

I was a little nervous. I was there on my own, and nobody knew I was there. He came back with a shiny new cellphone in his hand. I assumed it was a burner.

The Elder was waiting to talk to me on the line.

Before he could say anything, I went into my spiel.

"Look," I said, "everyone has this photo. Sooner or later, someone is going to write it up. And if someone is going to do it, wouldn't you rather have it be someone who is at least fair?"

There was a long pause at the end. He didn't say anything like, "After all I've done for you …" or protest. He just listened.

"You're going to do this, publish this sketchy photo?" It was an attempt to put some doubt into my mind about its authenticity, but I didn't bite.

"I'm not asking for confirmation or clarification. I'm not asking you for anything. I'm just telling you what I'm going to do as a professional courtesy. This is my job."

"I understand. We didn't do the kneecapping, you know."

"I believe you."

"Okay. Can I ask for one thing?"

"You can, but I may not be able to do it."

"Can you crop the photo so his missing pinkie isn't showing? He's sensitive about that."

I wanted to say yes, but I had to refuse.

"I can't touch the photo. I can't crop it, alter it, or touch it up. It has to go as is. What I can do is give your boss some credit for being a decent-enough type as yakuza go. I can do that."

"That would help. When does it go up?"

"In twenty-four hours."

Except that's not what happened. I left the office of the lieutenant nervous, a little queasy, and on full alert. Now the article had been delayed. I wasn't going to panic, but I was nervous.

It ran on the 19th, and it had a hell of an impact. The foreign media gobbled it up, but the Japanese media did their best to ignore it. The tabloids and the weeklies wrote that *Vice* had published an article about the photo, but they didn't put themselves on the hook by doing their own reporting. It was the classic escape formula: Vice *reported it, and this is what they reported, but we're just reporting what they reported, so don't break our knees.*

Only *Nikkan Gendai*, an evening tabloid, contacted me and asked for more details before they translated my article into Japanese. That article went viral.

And then to my delight, just when I thought the article had faded into oblivion, a Japanese lawmaker named Yoshio Maki (from the Japan Innovation Party) began looking into possible links between the yakuza and the Olympics. In parliament, during education committee meetings in April 2015, he held up several newspaper and magazine articles that included the photo of Tsukasa apparently with Tanaka, and demanded an explanation.

I was there for the meeting. Maki-sensei had snuck me into the parliamentary session. I was really enjoying the proceedings.

Maki asked Hakubun Shimomura, the education minister who was now also in charge of overseeing preparations for the Tokyo Games, why the government had yet to investigate the Olympic committee's possible ties to organized crime.

When Maki said "Yamaguchi-gumi," Shimomura grimaced like he'd eaten a rotten Japanese plum. Shimomura had his own alleged ties with the group to worry about.

Shimomura pledged to investigate the claims personally, and, given his alleged connections, he might have been the right man for the job. After all, some of his patrons were very close to the Yamaguchi-gumi Kodo-kai, the faction that was directly under Tsukasa, the Yamaguchi-gumi's supreme leader.

He said he would press the JOC and Nihon University to look into it.

"Shimomura's reply is just a formality," Maki later told me. "Asking the JOC and Nihon University to investigate on their own will only produce an answer that is expected."

I wrote up Maki's parliamentary stand for *Vice News* as a follow-up. The Japanese media ignored my article, as expected.

What was unexpected was that Maki's grilling of Shimomura made the cowardly Japanese press finally take up the issue of Tanaka and his shady connections. Some of them actually mentioned my *Vice* article. Tanaka quietly resigned from the JOC.

Shimomura never gave a public answer after his alleged yakuza connections and other scandals forced him to step down. Nobody noticed, and nothing was done. The Olympics marched on. Later, when it was revealed that Japan had won the Olympic bid by bribing ex-IOC officials through a front company in Singapore, I wasn't surprised either.

The billions of dollars in cost overruns weren't shocking. I'm pretty sure the yakuza got their cut after all, but nobody in the Japanese government wanted to look into that.

The lesson from all this was that if you were going to award the governments of East Asia medals based on their level of corruption, Japan would have won the gold for sure.

It was great to have a scoop, and I felt like I had my mojo back as a reporter. And some other people noticed. This opened doors that I had never expected to open. They say that everyone loves a winner—and it wasn't long after the *Vice* scoop that *The Los Angeles Times* asked me to be their special correspondent. I was thrilled. This was the big time—at least in my mind.

CHAPTER TWENTY

A new life in a ghost town

If 2011 was the year my life melted down, 2017 was the year that I began to rebuild it and myself. I'd never lost a job before. I hadn't been fired from *The Los Angeles Times*, but I had been made redundant, restructured, phased out—whatever the word is for letting someone go. No one at Tronc, the monolith running the company, gave a damn about it, but I did. Business looked bleak. Everywhere I looked, people were getting laid off. My editor at *Vice*, Ky Henderson, was "let go" as *Vice News* was downsized. More foreign bureaus in Tokyo were closed down. Japan was losing its importance as a place to cover; the Rising Sun was setting rapidly in the shadows of China.

Tokyo had begun to feel like a ghost town to me; I wandered around in a semi-corporeal existence: sometimes a friendly spirit like Casper, sometimes a poltergeist. It was probably a sign I'd been here too long—but when I checked, my feet were still on the ground, so I really hadn't made the transition to being a *yurei* yet. Japanese ghosts tend to lack feet.

When you spend too much time looking back, you're bound to trip going forward, but there I was. I was in the midst of a strange depression and reflecting on everything that had come so far. I'd arrived in Japan in 1988, moved into a Zen temple three months after arrival, and started working in 1993. By

2017, I'd been a reporter there for about twenty-five years. I felt like I was having what young Americans call a quarter-life crisis. Except it wasn't my life that was in crisis, it was my career. And for a workaholic, life and career were indistinguishable.

In early 2017, I was thinking, *This year I'll be forty-eight*. If I rounded it up, I'd practically be fifty. My due diligence work had gone from a steady river of revenue to a trickle of income that only appeared sporadically. Everything seemed to be a repeat of what had gone before. Saigo and I had parted ways, semi-amicably, but not on the best of terms. I kept doing stupid things. The years of taking Halcion to get to sleep had started to take their toll.

When I looked back at 2016, I could barely remember what I had done that year, other than write for *The Los Angeles Times* and *The Daily Beast*. The highlight of the year had been waking up one morning naked with a bottle of tequila, next to a blonde model who was also naked and telling me to keep quiet, because "my husband is on the phone." That was the start of a relationship that went about as well as Halcion and alcohol can. She had her charms, and in another world, maybe it would have worked out. But here I was, still in Tokyo. Still doing the same things. Just older.

There's a word in Buddhism for the endless rat race of life. *Samsara*. It's a Sanskrit word for the endless cycle of birth, death, and rebirth. We're all trapped in it, chasing desires, facing our karmic debts, and trying to make sense of the mysteries of life.

It's like riding the Yamanote line, which circles the city over and over again. The stations never change. Only the passengers do.

I was knee-deep in Tokyo *Samsara*.

Sometimes I thought I'd leave, yet I stayed like someone destined to haunt this megapolis until the end of time—or until the United States had public health care. Donald Trump had been elected president of the United States, and was intent on dismantling the slipshod public health care we had in place and replacing it with … nothing. Which meant I'd probably never really leave Japan. After I'd survived liver cancer, no insurance company in the United States would have me on their books, pre-existing conditions being what they are. I'd come to a point where I felt like I was stagnating as a journalist, a writer, and a human being.

I had finished and published only one book in English. Thank God, I was appreciated in France. Vive la France!

Tokyo Vice had been published all over the world by now. It was a memoir of my first twenty-one years in Japan, including twelve years as a police reporter and staff writer for the *Yomiuri Shimbun*—and a few years working on a project investigating human trafficking in Japan for the U.S. State Department. It was also a cautionary tale of what happens when you try to do the right thing the wrong way. It might have been the best thing I'd ever write—I was fine with that. Everything I had ever learned worth knowing is in that book somewhere.

It had also been seven years since yakuza gang boss Goto Tadamasa, my personal Voldemort, had published his book, and almost ten years since he'd been banished from the Yamaguchi-gumi. He was still alive and well, ruling over his new fiefdom in Cambodia, going in and out of Japan sometimes as well.

In Shizuoka, the prefecture he came from, he was trying to revive a cultural tradition: dog fighting. It was Goto as we know and love him. He loved dog fighting, pitting sentient creatures against each other, and betting on the outcome. It's possible there is a visceral sadistic pleasure in watching the dog you're betting on wreak havoc on the loser. It's a bloody sport for bullies, and that's Goto and his ilk.

Back in 2002, I interviewed Andrew Vachss, the hard-boiled author and social justice crusader, about bullying in Japan. What he said always stuck with me, even after his death.

"If you look at bullying logically, then you can see it's the root of all evil. Not money, but bullying. That's all it takes: the imposition of your will, your desires, your wishes, on another human being by force or intimidation. You can see it in Rwanda, just as easily as you can see it in the schoolyard. Different canvas, different color paint, but it's exactly the same thing: 'I can make you do what I want you to do, because I'm stronger than you. It's not a question that I'm smarter, or I'm more ethical, or I'm more entitled. I'm simply stronger.'"

It was the best explanation of the rationale of most of the yakuza, Liberal Democatic Party politicians, and thugs I'd met. In fact, "the act of bullying" described Goto's life perfectly.

I'd heard he had gotten a new liver to replace his $500,000 one—but couldn't be sure.

In December 2015, the U.S. Treasury Department put him on a blacklist. The department stated in a December 9, 2015, press release:

> Goto headed the Goto-gumi until October 2008, when he was expelled and forced into retirement from the Yamaguchi-gumi and relocated to Cambodia. Despite his retirement from mob life, Yakuza figure Tadamasa Goto reportedly still associates with numerous gang-tainted companies that he utilizes to facilitate his legitimate and illicit business activities. He continues to support the Yamaguchi-gumi and remnants of his semi-defunct Goto-gumi by laundering their funds between Japan and Cambodia. Additionally, Goto has reportedly established links with the notoriously violent Namikawa Mutsumi-kai group, formerly known as the Kyushu Seido-kai, which is recognized by Japan as a Yakuza group.

Tadamasa Goto's assets held in the United States or controlled by U.S. citizens were frozen, and U.S. citizens are prohibited from engaging in business with him. I received a letter from a U.S. journalist in Cambodia who wanted to write about how Japanese businesses in the capital were paying protection money to the yakuza, and probably to Goto. He knew a couple of businesses that had had to close their shops down. He wanted to know if there was a safe way to do the reporting. I told him that I couldn't think of a way to do it safely and also to do the story justice.

A lot had happened since the publication of Goto's book and mine. Well, at least I had managed to stay in Tokyo. The city doesn't remain the same for long. And sometimes what I notice the most is what isn't there anymore. I don't reference the future when giving directions: I reference the past.

Let's say I met someone at the outer edges of Kabukicho, at the Mister Donut, and they asked me, "Hey, pal, how do I get to the statue of Godzilla?"—I don't think my directions would be useful. I'd tell them:

"Well, just take a right where Meisei 48 burned down in September 2001 and 40 people died—you know the building where there was the mahjong parlor and the medical-themed erotic parlor, the Sexual Harassment Clinic? Go straight past where all the local yakuza used to meet at the coffee shop in the bottom of *Furinkaikan*. It's next to Black Swan—the transsexual cabaret. That's still there.

"If you find yourself at the Lion's Mansion where 'The Buddha' aka Inoue Takahiko, Buddhist priest and yakuza boss, allegedly fell from the fifth floor to his death, you've gone too far.

"Go past the love hotel where all the Disney costumes used to be displayed in the lighted windows, and keep going until you find the row of coin lockers, next to the capsule hotel.

"It's 200 yards from where there used to be ABCX, maybe the only sexual massage parlor that would allow in foreigners. You can't miss it."

That would be the place.

There's a song by Laurie Anderson, "Big Science," that plays in my head when I visit my old haunts. These lyrics from the song go through my head when I'm in Kabukicho:

Here's a man who lives a life of danger. Everywhere he goes he
Stays—
a stranger.
Howdy stranger.
Mind if I smoke?

In the old days, I wouldn't have minded if a stranger lit up in front of me. Nowadays the smoke of other people makes me cough.

Do I mind if you smoke? Yes, I sure as hell do.

Although being in Kabukicho makes me crave a cigarette, especially when I'm walking past the host clubs. Kabukicho is part of Police District 4, where I spent much of 1999 and 2000 covering the area's assorted crimes, calamities, and criminals. I can remember getting my big scoop about the first police raid on a host club, which had been ripping off their female customers and employing under-aged hosts. Takeshi Aida, the creator of Club Ai, the first host club in Japan, then invited me to work at his establishment for a night so that I would see that not all host clubs were rip-off bars. I was a terrible host. I can't dance and can't light cigarettes well. I spent a lot of my shift fumbling with the lighter. I'm not exactly handsome either, although my Japanese was good enough to crack some jokes.

I used to smoke clove cigarettes, Gudan Garam, in a red-and-gold pack. There was only one little tobacco shop that sold them three blocks from the Shinjuku Police Station. They had a sign in English that read "Sin-Juku Smokes." The "Sin" romanization always made me chuckle a little. That's no longer there.

There's a 7-Eleven. They don't sell clove cigarettes. You can't even smoke in Kabukicho on the streets anymore.

These days, everyone wants to go to Kabukicho. I can't see the point. It's turning into another Times Square—between the tourists, the city, and the cops, the place has become a shadow of its shady self. I suppose that's a good thing.

I really do feel like a stranger there now.

In 2011, when Michiel was still thinking of going into social work and combatting human trafficking, Japan had already significantly tackled the problem. The thugs that made money from sexual enslavement had almost completely turned toward domestic trafficking, but the scale of the crime was nothing like it was in 2007 or 2008. The yakuza themselves have been reeling from body blows due to changes in the law and the relentless enforcement of these new laws by the police.

The yakuza are still entrenched in the entertainment and nuclear industry, which remains one of their largest cash cows.

In a way, I feel like the Tokyo I used to know is another realm, another lifetime away.

The days when yakuza strutted the streets in their badges and menaced ordinary citizens with impunity are fading away. When they have a meeting, badges are handed out at the start and returned at the end, much the way my gym, Tipness, might give you a locker key and a towel when you check in. Known yakuza now aren't allowed to have bank accounts, rent apartments, get insurance (like me in the U.S.), check into hotels, or even play golf. The complex series of contract law changes, ordinances, and revisions of the Anti–Organized Crime Laws had reduced their numbers from 80,000 to less than 10,000 nationwide.

If Toshiro Igari was still alive, he would have been pleased to see just how effective the measures had been. But he wasn't alive. I pass by his office sometimes. I would like to go light some incense there, but I don't think there are many people left at the office who remember him, and I'm not sure I would be welcome. The office may have moved.

I've moved many times in the more than thirty years I've lived in Japan. I rarely go back to the places where I lived, except for one, the Buddhist temple where I spent much of my college life.

That was lucky. We'll get to that story later.

When I was moving in 2016, I found buried at the bottom of a drawer a pair of neatly folded socks and a Christmas card from Michiel. I think of her now and then, as I do Detective Sekiguchi—my mentor in Saitama. He died of cancer as well. He smoked a lot. I still see his kids sometimes. They have kids of their own now.

I don't go past where Club Yellow used to be. I'm over fifty, and dancing until the first train arrives doesn't seem like much fun. If you really wanted to see the remains of the place, it's not so far from where the fake-gambling-themed club One-Eyed Jack used to be. The Lehman Brothers crowd would go blow their money on the girls there and blow their noses with cocaine, back in the days before the financial collapse. They sold harder stuff in a bar in the area close to where the Hamburger Inn used to be. Drugs are a big deal in Japan. Like guns.

People overdosing on cocaine laced with heroin—especially prominent *gaijin*—that was news. In 2004, there was a series of drug overdose deaths in Roppongi—primarily because a little Iranian fellow was selling the local investment-banker types cocaine laced with huge amounts of heroin. One of those who got the bad batch was a top executive at Pfizer Japan. I worked with the Tokyo Metropolitan Police Department on that story, giving them the name of the de facto bar owner and relevant data. Our working relationship was good; they had the dealer marked, but they wouldn't publicize the deaths. No matter what happens, when you have a big scoop, you often get banned from the squad room, and sometimes even from the press conferences. I had this terrible feeling that by not writing about it, other people would overdose and die.

I had an agreement with the Drugs and Guns Violations Enforcement Division chief, Tanaka-san, that I'd keep a lid on the story, and in exchange he'd give me the scoop when they made the arrest. But I realized that while I was waiting for that to happen, more people might dip into their rainy-day stash and die.

So before I wrote the story, I gave a heads-up to chief Tanaka about what I was going to do. *Jingi o kiru.* I was at least polite about it.

When it came out, on the front page of the newspaper, the article upset people, and my reward was being banned from walking into the drug enforcement section for months. I had to sneak around to meet the detectives for the rest of my term on the beat. But that was almost twenty years ago. I'd like to think that I've graduated from covering crime, yakuza, murder, mayhem, and tragedy. I have definitely expanded my fields of interest.

But every now and then, like on October 31, 2017, I'd get a compelling call at a weird hour, from an old friend.

"Jeiku! You'll want to cover this one."

"Uh … well, not unless it has some sort of international angle.

"Nine heads with no bodies in nine coolers. One apartment."

Magic words. Of course, I went.

It felt like déjà vu. It was how I'd started my year.

On January 1, 2017—at 4.00 am—I caught the train (they used to run all night from the last night of the year into the first day of the new year) to a crime scene on Takeshita-dōri, where a disgruntled twenty-one-year-old had run over eight people in his car going in reverse. It was a brutal way to start the new year. The incident had occurred ten minutes after the temple bells rang out 108 times to signify the end of the year and a farewell to the sins of 2016. I didn't get the call to check it out until 3.30 am. Normally, I don't stay up late.

Late nights in Kabukicho are no longer part of my job.

While Kabukicho has turned into a pale imitation of Times Square, Roppongi just seems to be rotting from the inside.

Juliana's—once the largest disco in Asia—was in Roppongi. It was a grand symbol of Japan's economic bubble in the late 1980s and 1990s, when it looked like Japan would rule the world. The founder of the disco would later go on to make a fortune running a labor-dispatch company, Goodwill Corporation, taking advantage of changes in Japan's labor laws that benefited a few greedy assholes. The changes in those laws made guys like Masahira Origuchi aka "Disco Man" wealthy, but they ended up reducing the number of people with "lifetime employment" from 80 percent of the workforce to about 55 percent. Japan is just a gig economy nation now. We owe that to the Liberal Democratic Party, economic hyenas like Heizo Takenaka, chairman of a labor-dispatch company now, and the Disco Man. Fuck you all. Very much.

Disco Man's company was later shut down after labor-law violations, but not before it bought up a reputed yakuza front company called Crystal, a deal in which $100 million of the company's funds magically disappeared.

Yes, sometimes it's amazing how money just goes missing in Japan.

Roppongi Hills, Japan's answer to Beverly Hills, is still standing. That's where Lehman Brothers Japan used to have their offices. In 2008, they were swindled out of $350 million by a small company called Asclepius. The money vanished before Lehman did. I have a good idea where it went, but it's not like I can stake a claim on it.

Roppongi is another ghost town in progress. Between the luxurious and over-priced Roppongi Hills and the glitz of Tokyo Midtown (which is home to the Ritz Carlton) is a seedy area of clubs and restaurants and touts that is slowly being bought out by developers and torn down. Once a month, you will see the area around Midtown fill up with Mercedes-Benz and increasingly high-end Japanese cars—all black—with no-necked thugs in cheap suits with short haircuts standing outside the cars, while old men in expensive black suits file in and out of one building in the area. The Inagawa-kai still has its office there, but it's empty most of the time.

I can take you to the building where there was a popular club called Flower. It's the club where nine thugs clubbed a man to death with a baseball bat. Three strikes to the head of a customer with a baseball bat, and you're out—out of business.

I can't think of any good clubs left in the area. Years of police raids on clubs where dancing after midnight was taking place pretty much killed the nightlife there.

The sign that used to hang over the area, "Roppongi High-Touch Town"—gone as well.

We could never figure out what "high-touch" meant. Roppongi Low-Ball Town. That would have worked.

Aoyama Book Center, the bookstore next to the Azabu Police Station—that's gone, too.

The club where Lucie Blackman, rest in peace, used to work—long since out of business.

There was a wonderful sukiyaki place not far from Nishi-Azabu. The tender beef was all flown in from the Miyazaki prefecture. The place was practically hidden away, not too far from Gonpachi. I am not sure I remember how to get there. A charming, bodacious, and beautiful woman named Helena once took me on a joyride through Tokyo on the back of her motorcycle—and that was the starting point. I don't think I've ever ridden on a motorcycle with anyone else. I think she may be riding that motorcycle somewhere else now. I hope she's happy.

Sometimes, I wonder if Tantra, near what was the ROA Building, is still in business. I spent more time than I'd like to admit in that strip club with the mystical name, erotic Hindu sculpture, and bevy of lovely dancers. Most of the dancers and staff I knew have moved on—some married, some went home, some have kids, some now teach pole dancing as a fitness class. The scent of cigars, sweat, musk, metal, and cognac must still linger in the air if the club is still there at all. I'd go look, but I might go in, and nothing good would come of that.

And so there I was. I was still a reporter, but I was thinking about doing something else. I was thinking of becoming a Zen Buddhist priest. You know what they say about that job: as long as people are dying, you can make a living. It's not where I saw myself winding up.

A Zen master allegedly once said that every night we die and every day we are reincarnated. You're considered very lucky to be born in this world, because it's only in this world where you can finally escape from the cycle of birth and death.

Buddhism in Japan posits six realms of existence:

1. Hell
2. Hungry Ghosts
3. Animals
4. Warring Demigods
5. Humans
6. The Blessed

I can think of areas of Tokyo that could match each realm. Hell is any stop on the Tozai line during rush hour.

It's only in the human realm that we have a chance of redemption and escape from the wheel of suffering. Although I wouldn't mind languishing in the realm of the blessed for a few years. It's not often in this mortal life we get a chance to do things over.

In many ways, since April 1993, death and trouble have been my work—and work and death in Japan are closely related—there's even word for it. It was doing a story on one tragic death that led to a rebirth in this life.

CHAPTER TWENTY-ONE

Shukumei and the meaning of March 28

In February 2017, a woman wrote to me about her colleague, a baker, who had died suddenly in his sleep. They had both been working for a famous bakery chain in Japan—with offices in the U.S. and France—that had terrible working conditions. The bakery is so famous in France that if I wrote the name here, you'd recognize it immediately. I followed up her tip, and I went to the wake of the baker, a Zen Buddhist wake, to see if I could talk to his colleagues about the working conditions and what had happened.

A wake in Japan is called *tsuya*, which literally means "through the night." It's usually a short service followed by those in attendance lighting a stick of incense at an altar and paying their respects to the dead. The body is often still there, and sometimes the ceremonies really do last all night. There's rarely a guest list, so I didn't think I would have any trouble sneaking in. I didn't feel out of place at the service either, since I did indeed know one of the deceased's friends. I took the opportunity to interview those who knew him, to see if his passing would fall into the category of "death by overwork"—known as *karoshi* in Japan.

It was a tremendous turnout. He had many friends. They spoke to me. He was well liked. He looked a little like Anpanman—the animated hero who is also an anthropomorphic pastry stuffed with bean paste. Just like the anime hero, he was always giving of himself.

His case met most of the classic criteria of *karoshi*—he was young and had no health problems but had been working days on end without enough sleep or even a decent lunch break. The company had even sent out a work memo ordering employees to "always run in the kitchen." He had to wake up early every day to bake the bread, usually at 5.00 am. He'd lived alone, but his grandmother would always call him on his cellphone to wake him up. He would work twelve-hour days or longer. He was chronically sleep-deprived.

Hiroshi Kawahito, one of Japan's leading experts on *karoshi*, and the lawyer who has represented death from overwork victims against advertising monolith Dentsu twice, says that fatigue and sleep deprivation is the common background to victims' fatal heart attacks, cerebral hemorrhages, and suicide.

The wake wasn't all hobnobbing and conversation. It included a memorial service for the departed. The ceremony was performed by a Soto Zen Buddhist priest—it was weirdly nostalgic for me. I had spent most of my college life living in a small four-tatami mat room above a Zen Buddhist temple, under the care of my landlord and later Zen master, Ryōgen.

The smell of the sandalwood was Proustian. In a strange way, the scents, the chiming of the bells, the chanting, and the entire the ritual itself made me feel as if I had gone home. It had been decades since I'd lived in the temple, but I continued to sit in *zazen* (zen meditation). Sometimes, even now, I would recall the five moral precepts that a lay Buddhist is supposed to uphold.

While sitting among the bereaved, listening to the words of *The Heart Sutra*, I felt my mind drifting back into the past.

The priest who ran the temple, Ryōgen, and I met randomly, and hit it off. He could see I was serious about my studies, and the temple had an empty room; it was supposed to be for a monk in training. However, in 1988, no one wanted to be a Buddhist monk—Japan was in the middle of the bubble economy. He offered me the room for free.

He let me stay under three simple conditions:

1. Keep your hair cut short
2. Be polite, and show up for *zazen* practice every Sunday at 6.45 am
3. No girls in your room after 8.00 pm

It was a great experience. I learned the basics of *zazen*, Zen Buddhism, funeral etiquette, and how to shave my head with clippers, and Ryōgen was also very socially conscious and active, doing charity work and in the peace movement. I was apolitical, but I did admire his zeal. And without even trying, I memorized at least one Buddhist sutra that I could chant without looking at notes. It was also a wonderful place to learn obscure Japanese sayings and characters, and especially to acquire the self-discipline that I sorely needed.

I had forgotten how much I enjoyed the semi-monastic life. The whole funeral and the talks with the friends of the deceased left me feeling remarkably depressed and nostalgic at the same time. It made me recall a former co-worker and friend who had suddenly died by suicide. I believe job stress was part of it—a different shade of *karoshi*.

A supervisor of the deceased baker agreed to meet me the following Monday, in Saitama. However, the day before we were supposed to meet, the supervisor changed the time and place to Ikebukuro, two train stops away from my former temple home.

I hadn't been to see Ryōgen in over a year. I knew that from the station it was just a short ride to his place and it seemed to me that I should make the most of the proximity.

And in the tightly knit world of Soto Zen Buddhism, I had a feeling he could introduce me to the priest who had performed the memorial service. And perhaps that priest could introduce me to the parents of the deceased.

I called up Ryōgen, and asked if I could drop by and say hello. I had been meaning to give him a bottle of wine from Israel that I'd bought as a souvenir. He said I was more than welcome to come by,

And so, after the interview with the supervisor, I made my way to the temple, and we had a cup of dark green tea and caught up. I told him about the funeral, and he nodded. "These things happen far too often. People should work to live, not live to work, and certainly not work themselves to death."

He asked, "How was the wake? Did it help the family?"

I said that I didn't know.

"Was there ever a service for your friend, Michiel?"

There had been a service of sorts, years later. And her ashes were buried. She had a grave. And as we spoke, he casually said, "Aren't you going to be forty-eight this year?"

Before I could respond, he continued, "Maybe it's forty-nine? You're getting old. You look old, too. You've also got fat. Old, fat."

He's an incredibly honest guy. Not much of a diplomat.

"Yes, Ryōgen-san, I'll be forty-eight," I acknowledged.

And in his own slightly indirect way, he asked me if I'd ever considered giving up my life of being a muck-raking reporter and maybe get back on the noble eightfold path. The eightfold path is the Buddhist roadmap to inner peace and a better reincarnation in the next life. He poured us both a cup of tea.

"I have great respect for your work, Jake-san, but you could be living your life a little better. Didn't you once consider the priesthood?"

Indeed, I had.

"Perhaps, perhaps ... just maybe, it might be time to rethink your life as a daredevil man-whore."

I acknowledged that I had been rethinking my life. But I had doubts. I had doubts about whether reincarnation, karma, and cosmic justice existed. I didn't have doubts about the mental and physical benefits of Zen meditation, nor about the ethical code, but ...

"I'm not sure I could keep the vows."

"Oh, you could. You don't have to be celibate—you just have to be less slutty and more honest."

Thank you, Buddha, I thought to myself. Because giving up sex would be a no-go for this man. But that wasn't the only vow I wasn't sure I could keep. There are ten vows that a Soto Zen Buddhist priest must take. They're not easy.

Dōgen Zenji, the founder, called them the Ten Grave Precepts. Here's a liberal translation of what they mean.

The Ten Grave Precepts

I vow not to kill, but to cherish all life.

I vow not to steal, but to respect that which belongs to others.

I vow not to misuse sexual energy, but to be honest and respectful.

I vow not to lie, but to speak the truth.

I vow not to misuse drugs or alcohol, but to keep my mind clear.

I vow not to gossip about others' faults, but to be understanding and sympathetic.

I vow not to praise myself by criticizing others, but to overcome my own shortcomings.

I vow not to withhold spiritual or material aid, but to give freely and generously when needed.

I vow not to unleash anger, but to seek its source.

I vow not to speak ill of truth and ideals, but to cherish and uphold them.

I told him that I wasn't sure I could be both an investigative journalist and a Zen Buddhist priest. Difficulties abounded. If you can't lie, can you bluff? If you ask a yakuza an honest question, you won't get an honest answer. And not criticizing others? That's a great deal of what journalism is about. He wasn't stumped by my questions.

"It's not criticism if you're just telling the truth. This, of course, means you must learn to separate facts from opinions. Many people mistake opinion for truth. They are not the same."

He paused to think of an illustration.

"You may think the Southern All-Stars are a great rock band, but that is subjective. It is not an objective truth. That is an opinion. If someone stole 10 million yen and you wrote that they stole 10 million yen, that is a fact. When your girlfriend asks you if she looks good in her kimono, that is asking for an opinion, not the truth."

I was beginning to see why he'd never married. Speaking the bare-bones truth wasn't a great way to win a woman's heart, or a man's heart. Of course, refusing to voice opinions might not be so bad. I was still on the fence. He asked me point-blank, "When is your birthday? We would need time to prepare."

"My birthday is March 28."

He did a stoic double-take, raising an eyebrow.

"Really? That is the day I took my Buddhist priest vows. When I was fifteen."

His father had been a Buddhist priest as well, but he had found his own master, and decided early in life that he wanted to enter the priesthood. His parents had made him wait a year, he said. It seemed like an amazing coincidence.

"Are you sure? March 28?"

"Of course, I'm sure. It is an important day for me. I'll bring you the photo album."

He got up gracefully and went out of the room, gliding across the tatami, and came back down five minutes later with a black-and-white photo album. I checked the date. It was indeed March 28. And then I checked the year, which was written according to the imperial Japanese calendar: Showa 44.

In the western calendar, year 44 of the Showa era was 1969.

"That's amazing," I pointed at the date. "You became a Buddhist priest on the day I was born."

"No, no, no" he corrected me. It was a matter of emphasis. "You were born on the day I became a Buddhist priest. This is karma. Clearly."

He threw back his head and laughed deeply—a rolling laugh, a bellows-breath laugh. He closed his eyes and continued to laugh.

I agreed to take the vows.

I had to hit the books and prepare for my vow-taking ceremony.

I did one more important thing. I threw away all my Halcion and my Nerubon tablets. I dumped all my sleeping pills in the toilet. It took me weeks to learn to sleep on my own again. The withdrawal was terrible, but that was what I had to do to keep vow number five: "I vow not to misuse drugs or alcohol, but to keep my mind clear."

My mind was clear. I could even clearly remember, to some extent, what I had done the day before.

It was a small ceremony, held as planned, on March 28, 2017. It took less than an hour. I had a photo of my parents and sisters stand in as a proxy. It was all of us in front of a fireplace in the 1970s. At least I didn't have a turtleneck on in the picture.

Ryōgen had two helpers come to perform the rites, and I invited two close friends to attend. There was my partner and best friend, Mari Yamamoto, and Emi Tojima, the lovely, spiritual hippie nurse and astrologer I'd met at Michiel's wake in July 2012. It turned out that Mari and Emi also had the same birthday.

Synchronicity, dude.

I found this out after the ceremony ended. It went rather smoothly—I nearly tripped on the ceremonial kimono only once. My ability to remain composed was helped by knowing that Mari would cackle uncontrollably if I fell.

We all ate a lot of tempura afterward, and some of our neighbors joined us. After it was all over, I thanked Ryōgen and went back to work.

The training continues. A few weeks after taking the vows, I attended a retreat at Eiheiji, the head temple in the Fukui prefecture. The experience was spartan, and *zazen* started at 3.00 am. I grew to like the vegetarian meals.

What does becoming a priest mean? It means that I'll strive to be a better person, and eventually may run a small temple somewhere and conduct funeral services—possibly weddings.

I hear that Buddhist weddings are making a comeback. "Buddhism—it's not just for the dead anymore." That would be my Buddhist wedding-promotion slogan.

How am I doing so far in keeping the ten precepts? It's quite a list. I got through a few days without breaking them. Zen Buddhism doesn't really ask you to believe in anything. It's what you do that matters.

You can see that they are actually very nice guidelines for behaving well. I have my robes and my Buddhist name. It is really hard to pronounce: Wa-Shuu-Ryou-Jo. Ryōjo for short. Just don't call me "Joe."

Wa means "harmony," and the character also represents "Japan." *Shu* means "shoal" or "cay." *Ryō,* from the name of my teacher, means "good," "suitable," and "virtuous," and *Jo* means "grow" and also "gentle," "gradual," and "slow."

Thus Ryōjo, my daily Buddhist name, translates loosely as "chill out" or "do good gradually."

You may remember that a certain yakuza boss turned his Buddhist robes into a bullet-proof vest by becoming a Tendai Buddhist priest. Yet he's still out there doing evil, and has never seemed to repent for the suffering he's caused.

I wish I believed more in the metaphysics of karma. Because if there really is cosmic justice, he will eventually get what he deserves. And that won't be pleasant. But that's not my problem anymore. I'll leave it to the universe.

There's a lot of mysticism about Zen Buddhism, and mumbo jumbo that focuses on the esoteric aspects of the religion. "Zen" means to meditate, and, combined with Buddhism, it is basically a type of Buddhism that places great importance on the act of meditation, rather than on prayer, or on gaining salvation from some god-like Buddha, or from grueling esoteric practices. The word "Zen" itself has been reduced to a hip term used to explain "a mystical and/or mysterious way of doing something."

Thus you have books like *Presentation Zen*, which give you advice on the best way to engage your audiences without PowerPoint. Or mind-boggling things like *Osho Zen Tarot: The Transcendental Game of Zen (79-Card Deck and 192-Page Book)*. I don't think Zen Master Dōgen ever picked up a deck of cards in his life.

You may then be curious about what Zen Buddhism is all about. Historically, you could say it's a blend of Taoism and a movement to return Buddhism to its original roots. There are different schools of Zen. Soto Zen Buddhism places a lot of importance on the act of meditating. Rinzai Zen Buddhism places a lot of importance on achieving enlightenment by solving metaphysical or religious riddles (koans).

The classic koan: What is the sound of one hand clapping?

The top-secret answer is this: a slap in the face.

It's the best Zen joke ever.

Buddhists have a great sense of humor—a much better sense of humor than your average yakuza. It's not really that mystical.

Despite the many volumes written about Soto Zen Buddhism and the books by Dōgen Zenji himself, it's not so complicated. Master Dōgen summarized it in a passage:

> Do no harmful actions. Do not become attached to the cycle of death and rebirth.
> Be kind, respect the old, and show compassion for the young.
> Do not have a heart that rejects or a heart that covets and have no worry or sadness in your heart. This is what is called enlightenment.
> Do not seek it elsewhere.

If enlightenment is something located in your heart, I guess you can find it in Tokyo, then. By the way, the yakuza often see themselves as creatures in one of the six realms of existence posited in Japanese Buddhism. They are outside of being human. They see themselves as *shura* (*ashura*) the warring spirits, eternally locked in battle. The *shura* are motivated by anger and jealousy and love of battle. They are fierce and powerful, and love to fight. They are like humans, in that they are capable of both good and evil. Personally, I see the yakuza as being more like *gaki*—the hungry ghosts, the spirits of those who are caught between death and life, trapped by their own insatiable greed and attachments. Typically, these hungry ghosts are depicted with huge stomachs and tiny throats, doomed to live in agony, never able to satiate their desire. That's the yakuza. Maybe that's most people, unfortunately.

I tried to use my taking of Buddhist priest vows as a chance to stop reporting on the yakuza. I told a few sources still in the game, "I've turned over a new leaf now. I've 'washed my feet' and moved on."

That declaration had the opposite effect on one gang boss I spoke with. "That's great! It's so hard to find a Buddhist priest who will do a yakuza funeral these days, with the anti–organized crime ordinances and all that shit. Can we call you?"

I told him I'd need a few years to learn the intricacies of doing a wake or a funeral service.

I am still stalling.

Note: For months after, I attempted to finish the article about the French bakery that worked its employees to death. The family wouldn't speak to me, so I wrote to the bakery and to their head office in France. They assured me they'd look into it, but they never replied to my follow-up inquiries. I dropped a dime on the firm with the labor inspectors division of The Ministry of Health, Labor, and Welfare—and was told that the firm had been severely reprimanded. Maybe this made them change their ways and the tragedy won't be repeated. I hope that the spirit of the chubby baker has found peace and that he's made his transition to the next life.

Epilogue

I look back on the years between *Tokyo Vice* and now, and I feel lucky. The kids are both in college and doing well, knock on wood. Ray is on his way to becoming a biomedical engineer. Maybe he can grow me a new liver.

Tokyo Vice was turned into a successful TV series, and the second season should bring it to a satisfying conclusion. If only real life could be scripted that way.

In 2022–2023, I did something new—I finished a podcast about missing people in Japan, *The Evaporated: Gone with the Gods*. With the help of Shoko and Amy Plambeck and Josh Dean at Campside Media, the show was a well received and voted best podcast in Asia. And, to my delight, my daughter, Beni, even played a part in making it.

And I've been given a shot at reincarnation in this lifetime. Jake Adelstein, Private Eye, slowly gives way to Ryōjo, a Zen Buddhist priest and sometimes paladin.

I met a woman, Jessy Nakamura, who I love like crazy—on Bumble, of all places—and, so far, I haven't screwed it up. And I don't think I will.

I'm moving very slowly in learning all the ropes from my Zen master. I still must learn how to do funerals and weddings, and there are koans to solve. There's only one ritual I have come to know well. That's exorcizing hungry ghosts—banishing them from this world and helping them move on to the next world.

Interestingly enough, one of my first duties as an assistant priest was to hold a service for these hungry spirits, and to offer them food and prayers, in the hope that they would move on to a better incarnation. The ceremony is called *o-segaki*.

I've done it six times now. Lately, many people have been asking me if I can clear spirits from haunted homes. I'm willing to give it a try. I know the right sutras. I don't know if I believe in Buddhism's metaphysics.

Honestly, I don't know if there are really haunted places, or if there are spirits of people who died under bad circumstances and won't let go of this world. I understand why those who lose the people they loved can't let go. I imagine it's so much harder when you're a hungry ghost with no corporeal form and no idea of an exit strategy.

Even when you're alive, it's hard to move on.

I'm not sure how you can truly balance living out the vows of a Zen Buddhist priest and working as a journalist. I'm not sure how much you can really do to help another person find happiness and wisdom in this world.

What I do know is this: sometimes it's possible to do the right thing. Sometimes it's possible to exorcize the ghosts that are haunting other people.

The problem is that, no matter where you go, you can never quite get rid of your own ghosts. Not for me, and not in this city.

Acknowledgements

It doesn't take a village to write a book, but it sure does help.

First and foremost, this English edition would never have been published in such fine shape without the painstaking editing of Henry Rosenbloom at Scribe. Thank you for going above and beyond the call of duty.

I would also like to thank Shoko and Amy Plambeck, who both had a hand in editing this manuscript. Shoko did the first pass, and her sister, Amy, did the second pass, suggesting better wording and offering glib commentary here and there that helped tighten up the book. I had the pleasure of working with both of them from 2022 to 2023 on our award-winning podcast about those who go missing in Japan, *The Evaporated: Gone with the Gods*.

Jessy Nakamura, my sweetheart, who kept me company during most of the pandemic, was the dedicated reader—going over the book chapter by chapter, with great enjoyment and enthusiasm—and sometimes offering excellent advice. She's the best.

In addition, Lauren Hardie, formerly my copy editor at *The Daily Beast* and also a lifelong friend, lent a hand here and there. Julianne Yuki Chiaet, who was the amazing editor behind *The Last Yakuza*, also offered useful advice. As did Ben Dooley, journalist, fellow Jew, and a mensch. Kaori Shoji, the best writer I know in any language, also helped me get past a writer's block that could have derailed the whole book. William Clark, my debonair and Tibetan Buddhist saint of a literary agent, made sure this book would show up on your bookshelf and in the non-French-speaking world as well.

During my time as a private eye, Action and Zippy always had my back on everything I did, and were the best partners in security you could ever ask for. Action is like the older brother I wish I had. He's writing his own book—it will be amazing. I also would like to thank Mr Oldman, who's real name I can't put in the book: he was a joy to work for, and a man of tremendous moral integrity and courage.

I want to express my condolences and thanks to some people who are no longer here. Toshiro Igari, you were the best lawyer I ever had, and a wonderful mentor. I hope you come back as a well-taken-care-of bulldog in the next life. I wish that Christopher Dickey, of *The Daily Beast*, was still here to read this book. He was an amazing journalist, a superb editor, and, wow, do I miss him.

Nico Hines and Noor Ibrahim are doing a fine job of carrying on his tradition, as is Katie Baker. Noah jumped ship for *Rolling Stone*, but who could blame him? It's a great gig, and he's doing it well. Andrew Salmon, my editor at *Asia Times*, has also been a delight to work with.

A deep and humble thank you to my brutally honest and often very funny Zen master, Ryōgen. I swear I'll solve that koan and master folding my robes in this incarnation. Thank you also, to Pico Iyer for your Dalai Lama–like sense of humor and friendship. Larry Futa, everyone's favorite former special agent—I wish you were still in Tokyo, dude. Jim Stern, thanks for always having my back. Ken, don't go back to the agency. We civilians need you.

Thanks to Mari Yamamoto, my best friend, and co-writer at *The Daily Beast* since 2015. I cannot tell you how happy I am to see you succeeding in your other career, as an actor—although I miss doing the audition readings with you. Thanks to your occasional, "Could you try not to breathe?" admonitions during those tapings, I've developed better lung power. I may be amphibious someday. Jokes aside, you and Wolf are the best. I'm in debt to JT Rogers, playwright, wonderful friend, high-school pal, and the showrunner of *Tokyo Vice* (HBO Max). Because he and Alan Poul (and the magnificent Mari Yamamoto behind the scenes) did all the heavy lifting, I was able to concentrate on this book, the sequel to *Tokyo Vice*, rather than on the TV show.

A special thanks to Jessica Walker Roberts, Mimi's best friend, for her support and understanding.

I want to say I'm also very grateful to everyone on the crew of the *The Evaporated: Gone with the Gods* podcast, mentioned above, which was made during the writing of this book. Josh Dean, our fearless and ever-patient leader (Campside Media), Taka Yasuzawa (sound engineer supreme), Thisanka Siripala (our lovable producer and Japan's first Sri Lankan Private Eye), and, of course, the Plambeck Sisters (Shoko and Amy). Kudos to Himari Semans, intern and journalist, and the childhood friend of Beni Adelstein, who also worked on the show.

I'm also grateful for my son, Ray Adelstein, for working so hard to get a scholarship, enabling me to pay rent this last year as well.

My deepest and most profound thanks go to Cyril Gay, Clemence Billiaut, and Guillaume Guilpart, the founders of Marchialy. *Tokyo Vice* was the first book they ever published, and this is the fourth book that I've written with them. Like many authors, I can be stubborn and a little difficult, but they have always managed to work with me to make the final product something worthy of being a Marchialy title: creative, meaningful, and eye-opening narrative nonfiction. They're not my publishers—they're my second family. And the latest addition to the family, Doug Headline, did a superlative job in becoming my voice in French. I am very grateful for his translation and transmutation of the book from English to French.

Finally, thanks to you who are reading this now and have perhaps read my other works. A writer doesn't exist without a reader, and hopefully by the time you've finished this, you've not only been entertained, but you'll leave the book feeling a little more enlightened about the world. What wisdom I've learned in my fifty-five years of life is written down here for you.

Be well.